Credit Portfolio
Management

John Wiley & Sons

Founded in 1807, John Wiley & Sons is the oldest independent publishing company in the United States. With offices in North America, Europe, Australia, and Asia, Wiley is globally committed to developing and marketing print and electronic products and services for our customers' professional knowledge and understanding.

The Wiley Finance series contains books written specifically for finance and investment professionals as well as sophisticated individual investors and their financial advisors. Book topics range from portfolio management to e-commerce, risk management, financial engineering, valuation, and financial instrument analysis, as well as much more.

For a list of available titles, please visit our web site at www.Wiley Finance.com.

Credit Portfolio
Management

CHARLES SMITHSON

WILEY

John Wiley & Sons, Inc.

Published by John Wiley & Sons, Inc., Hoboken, New Jersey.
Published simultaneously in Canada.

CreditPro™ is a registered trademark of The McGraw-Hill Companies, Inc. ZETA® is the registered servicemark of Zeta Services, Inc., 615 Sherwood Parkway, Mountainside, NJ 07092. KMV® and Credit Monitor® are registered trademarks of KMV LLC. Expected Default Frequency™ and EDF™ are trademarks of KMV LLC. Portfolio Manager™ is a trademark of KMV LLC. RiskMetrics® is a registered service mark of J.P. Morgan Chase & Co. and is used by RiskMetrics Group, Inc., under license. CreditManager™ is a trademark owned by or licensed to RiskMetrics Group, Inc. in the United States and other countries.

For general information on our other products and services, or technical support, please contact our Customer Care Department within the United States at 800-762-2974, outside the United States at 317-572-3993 or fax 317-572-4002.

Wiley also publishes its books in a variety of electronic formats. Some content that appears in print may not be available in electronic books.

For more information about Wiley products, visit our web site at www.wiley.com.

Library of Congress Cataloging-in-Publication Data:

Smithson, Charles.
    Credit portfolio management / Charles Smithson.
        p. cm.
    ISBN 0-471-32415-9 (CLOTH : alk. paper)
    1. Bank loans—Management.   2. Bank loans—United States—Management.
  3. Consumer credit—Management.   4. Portfolio management.   I. Title.
    HG1641 .S583   2003
    332.1'753'068—dc21   2002151335

Printed in the United States of America.

10 9 8 7 6 5 4 3 2 1

To Nathan and Matthew

Preface

Like its sister book, *Managing Financial Risk* (which deals with market risk), this book evolved from a set of lecture notes. (My colleagues at Rutter Associates and I have been teaching classes on credit portfolio management to bankers and regulators for almost four years now.) When lecture notes get mature enough that they start curling up on the edges, the instructor is faced with a choice—either throw them out or turn them into a book. I chose the latter.

The good news about writing a book on credit portfolio management is that it is topical—credit risk is the area that has attracted the most attention recently. The bad news is that the book will get out of date quickly. In the credit market, tools, techniques, and practices are changing rapidly and will continue to change for several years to come. We will try our best to keep the book current by providing updates on our website. Go to www.rutterassociates.com and click on the *Credit Portfolio Management* book icon.

A number of people have contributed to this book. In particular, I want to acknowledge my colleagues at Rutter Associates—Paul Song and Mattia Filiaci. Without them, this book would never have been completed.

This book benefited greatly from my involvement with the newly formed International Association of Credit Portfolio Managers (IACPM). I learned a lot from conversations with the founding board members of that organization: Stuart Brannan (Bank of Montreal); John Coffey (JP Morgan Chase); Gene Guill (Deutsche Bank); Hetty Harlan (Bank of America); Loretta Hennessey (CIBC); Charles Hyle (Barclays Capital); Paige Kurtz (Bank One); Ed Kyritz (UBS); Robin Lenna (at Citibank at the time, now at FleetBoston Financial); and Allan Yarish (at Royal Bank of Canada at the time, now at Société Genérale).

For their contributions to and support for the 2002 Survey of Credit Portfolio Management Practices, I want to thank Stuart Brannan (IACPM and Bank of Montreal), David Mengle (ISDA), and Mark Zmiewski (RMA).

Colleagues who contributed knowledge and material to this book include:

Michel Araten, JP Morgan Chase

Marcia Banks, Bank One

Brooks Brady, Stuart Braman, Michael Dreher, Craig Friedman, Gail
    Hessol, David Keisman, Steven Miller, Corinne Neale, Standard &
    Poor's Risk Solutions

Susan Eansor and Michael Lavin, Loan Pricing Corporation

Chris Finger, RiskMetrics Group

Robert Haldeman, Zeta Services

David Kelson and Mark McCambley, Fitch Risk Management

Susan Lewis, Credit Sights

Robert Rudy, Moody's–KMV

Rich Tannenbaum, SavvySoft

A special thank-you is due to Beverly Foster, the editor of the *RMA Journal*, who convinced me to write a series of articles for her journal. That series formed the first draft of many of the chapters in this book and was the nudge that overcame my inertia about putting pen to paper.

Finally, as always, my biggest debt is to my wife, Cindy.

CHARLES SMITHSON
Rutter Associates

New York, New York
November 2002

Contents

CHAPTER 1

The Revolution in Credit— Capital Is the Key

THE CREDIT FUNCTION IS CHANGING

The credit function is undergoing critical review at all financial institutions, and many institutions are in the process of changing the way in which the portfolio of credit assets is managed. Visible evidence of the change is found in the rapid growth in secondary loan trading, credit derivatives, and loan securitization (and we discuss these in Chapters 5, 6, and 7). Less obvious—but far more important—is the fact that banks are abandoning the traditional transaction-by-transaction "originate-and-hold" approach, in favor of the "portfolio approach" of an investor.

Banks Are Facing Higher Risks

The portfolios of loans and other credit assets held by banks have become increasingly more concentrated in less creditworthy obligors. Two forces have combined to lead to this concentration. First, the disintermediation of the banks that began in the 1970s and continues today has meant that investment grade firms are much less likely to borrow from banks. Second, as we see in an upcoming section of this chapter, the regulatory rules incent banks to extend credit to lower-credit-quality obligors.

The first years of the twenty-first century highlighted the risk—2001 and 2002 saw defaults reaching levels not experienced since the early 1990s. Standard & Poor's reported that, in the first quarter of 2002, a record 95 companies defaulted on $38.4 billion of rated debt; and this record-setting pace continued in the second quarter of 2002 with 60 companies defaulting on $52.6 billion of rated debt. Indeed, in the one-year period between the start of the third quarter of 2001 and the end of the second quarter of 2002, 10.7% of speculative-grade issuers defaulted, the highest percentage of defaults since the second quarter of 1992, when the default rate reached 12.5%.

2000 SURVEY
OF CREDIT PORTFOLIO MANAGEMENT ATTITUDES AND PRACTICES

At the end of 2000, Rutter Associates, in cooperation with *Credit* magazine surveyed loan originators and credit portfolio managers at financial institutions. (Also surveyed were the providers of data, software, and services.) We distributed a questionnaire to 35 firms that originate loans and a different questionnaire to 39 firms that invest in loans. Note that some of the originator and investor firms were the same (i.e., we sent some banks both types of questionnaires). However, in such cases, the questionnaires were directed to different parts of the bank. That is, we sent an originator questionnaire to a specific individual in the origination area and the investor/portfolio manager questionnaire to a specific individual in the loan portfolio area. The following table summarizes the responses.

	Firms Receiving at Least One Questionnaire	Firms from Which at Least One Questionnaire Was Received
Originators		
U.S.	13	4
Europe	22	10
Total	35	14
Investors/Loan Portfolio Managers		
U.S.	24	9
Europe	15	8
Banks	11	11
Hedge Funds & Prime Rate Funds	18	4
Insurance Companies	8	1
Total	39	17

Banks Are Earning Lower Returns

Banks have found it to be increasingly difficult to earn an economic return on credit extensions, particularly those to investment grade obligors. In the 2000 Survey of Credit Portfolio Management Attitudes and Practices, we asked the originators of loans: "What is the bank's perception regarding large corporate and middle market loans?"

- Thirty-three percent responded that "Loans do not add shareholder value by themselves; they are used as a way of establishing or maintaining a relationship with the client; but the loan product must be priced to produce a positive NPV."
- Twenty-nine percent responded that "Loans do not add shareholder value by themselves; they are used as a way of establishing or maintaining a relationship with the client; and the loan product can be priced as a 'loss leader.' "
- Only twenty-four percent responded that "Loans generate sufficient profit that they add shareholder value."

Digging a little deeper, in the 2000 Survey, we also asked the originators of loans about the average ROE for term loans to middle market growth companies and for revolving and backup facilities.

- For originators headquartered in North America, the ROE for term loans to middle market growth companies averaged to 12% and that for revolving and backup facilities averaged to 7.5%.
- For originators headquartered in Europe or Asia, the ROE for term loans to middle market growth companies averaged to 16.5% and that for revolving and backup facilities averaged to 9.4%.

Banks Are Adopting a Portfolio Approach

At the beginning of this section, we asserted that banks are abandoning the traditional, transaction-by-transaction originate-and-hold approach in favor of the portfolio approach of an investor.

Exhibit 1.1 provides some of the implications of a change from a traditional credit function to a portfolio-based approach.

EXHIBIT 1.1 Changes in the Approach to Credit

	Traditional Credit Function	Portfolio-Based Approach
Investment strategy	*Originate and Hold*	*Underwrite and Distribute*
Ownership of the credit asset (decision rights)	Business Unit	Portfolio Mgmt. or Business Unit/Portfolio Mgmt.
Basis for compensation for loan origination	Volume	Risk-Adjusted Performance
Pricing	Grid	Risk Contribution

The firms that responded to the 2000 Survey of Credit Portfolio Management Attitudes and Practices indicated overwhelmingly that they were in the process of moving toward a portfolio approach to the management of their loans.

- Ninety percent of the respondents (originators of loans and investors in loans) indicated that they currently or plan to mark loans to market (or model).
- Ninety-five percent of the investors indicated that they have a credit portfolio management function in their organization.

And the respondents to the 2000 survey also indicated that they were moving away from "originating and holding" toward "underwriting and distributing": We asked the loan originators about the bank's hold levels for noninvestment grade loans that the bank originates. The respondents to this survey indicated that the maximum hold level was less than 10% and the target hold level was less than 7%.

Drilling down, we were interested in the goals of the credit portfolio management activities. As summarized in the following table, both banks and institutional investors in loans ranked increasing shareholder value as the most important goal. However, the rankings of other goals differed between banks and institutional investors.

What are the goals of the Credit Portfolio activities in your firm? Rank the following measures by importance to your institution. (Use 1 to denote the most important and 5 to denote the least important.)

	Reducing Regulatory Capital	Reducing Economic Capital	Reducing Size of Balance Sheet	Diversification	Economic or Shareholder Value Added
Banks	3.4	2.3	4.1	2.9	2.0
Institutional investors	4.5	3.5	4.0	1.8	1.3

When asked to characterize the style of the management of their loan portfolio, 79% of the respondents indicated that they were "defensive" managers, rather than "offensive" managers.

We also asked respondents to characterize the style of the management of their loan portfolios in the 2002 Survey. In 2002, 76% of the respondents still characterized themselves as "defensive" managers.

2002 SURVEY OF CREDIT PORTFOLIO MANAGEMENT PRACTICES

In March 2002, Rutter Associates, in cooperation with the International Association of Credit Portfolio Managers (IACPM), the International Swaps and Derivatives Association (ISDA), and the Risk Management Association (RMA), surveyed the state of credit portfolio management practices. We distributed questionnaires to the credit portfolio management area of 71 financial institutions. We received responses from 41— a response rate of 58%. The following provides an overview of the type of institutions that responded to the survey.

2002 Survey Response Summary

	Commercial Banks	Investment Banks
North America	18	3
Europe	15	1
Asia/Australia	4	
Total	37	4

However, the 2000 Survey suggests that the respondents may not be as far along in their evolution to a portfolio-based approach as their answers to the questions about marking to market (model) about the credit portfolio management group implied. In Exhibit 1.1, we note that, in a portfolio-based approach, the economics of the loans would be owned by the credit portfolio management group or by a partnership between the credit portfolio management group and the business units. The 2000 Survey indicates not only that the line business units still exclusively own the economics of the loans in a significant percentage of the responding firms but also that there is likely some debate or misunderstanding of roles in individual banks.

	Portfolio Managers Exclusively	Portfolio Management/ Line Units Partnership	Line Units Exclusively
Responses from the originators of loans	25%	25%	44%
Responses from the investors in loans (including loan portfolio managers)	24%	48%	19%

CAPITAL IS THE KEY

Why Capital?

Ask a supervisor "Why capital?" and the answers might include:

- Since it is a measure of the owner's funds at risk, it gives incentive for good management.
- I want to make sure there is enough capital to protect uninsured depositors.
- I want there to be sufficient capital to protect the deposit insurance fund.

And the traditional view from a supervisor would be that more capital is better than less capital.

Ask the managers of a financial institution "Why capital?" and the answers are similar to those above but significantly different:

- Capital is the owner's stake in a firm and is a source of financing—albeit a relatively costly source of financing.
- Capital provides the buffer needed to absorb unanticipated losses and allow the firm to continue (i.e., it provides a safety margin).
- Capital is the scarce resource. When a financial institution maximizes profit (or maximizes shareholder value), it does so subject to a constraint. And capital is that constraint.

Relevant Measures of Capital

Broadly defined, capital is simply the residual claim on the firm's cash flows. For banks and other financial institutions, capital's role is to absorb volatility in earnings and enable the firm to conduct business with credit sensitive customers and lenders. Bankers deal with several different definitions of capital—equity (or book or cash) capital, regulatory capital, and economic capital. Let's use the stylized balance sheet in Exhibit 1.2 to think about various measures of capital.

Equity capital turns out to be remarkably hard to define in practice, because the line between pure shareholder investment and various other forms of liabilities is blurred. For our purposes a precise definition is not necessary. By equity capital we simply mean the (relatively) permanent invested funds that represent the residual claim on the bank's cash flows. In Exhibit 1.2, we have restricted equity capital to shareholder's equity and retained earnings.

Regulatory capital refers to the risk-based capital requirement under

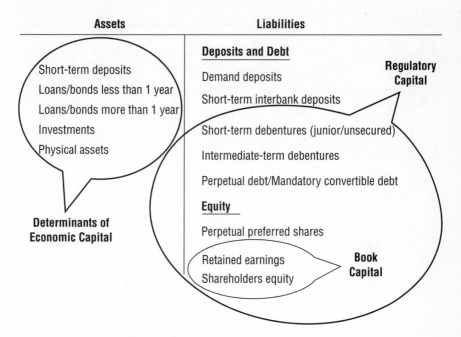

EXHIBIT 1.2 Relevant Measures of Capital

the Capital Accord (which is discussed later in this chapter). The purpose of regulatory capital is to ensure adequate resources are available to absorb bank-wide unexpected losses. Although the regulatory requirement is calculated based on the risk of the assets, it was never intended to produce accurate capital allocations at the transaction level. The liabilities that can be used to meet the regulatory capital requirement are more broadly defined than an accounting definition of equity, and include some forms of long-term debt, as shown in Exhibit 1.2. The characteristic of a liability that permits it to be used as regulatory capital is its permanence—to qualify as regulatory capital, it needs to be something that's going to stay for a while.

Economic capital is defined in terms of the risk of the assets (both on balance sheet and off balance sheet). That is, in terms of Exhibit 1.2, we do not look at the capital we have on the liability side of the balance sheet; rather, we look at the assets to determine how much capital is needed. Economic capital is a statistical measure of the resources required to meet unexpected losses over a given period (e.g., one year), with a given level of certainty (e.g., 99.9%). One minus the certainty level is sometimes called the *insolvency rate*, or equivalently, the implied credit rating. Since economic capital is determined by the riskiness of the assets, it is possible for a bank to require more economic capital than it actually has—a situation that is not sustainable in the long run. At the business unit level, however, certain businesses like trading require relatively little book capital, whereas their economic capital is quite large. Since the bank must hold the larger economic capital, it is essential that the unit be correctly charged for its risk capital and not just its book capital.

ECONOMIC CAPITAL

Economic Capital Relative to Expected Loss and Unexpected Loss

To understand economic capital, it is necessary to relate it to two notions—*expected loss* and *unexpected loss*. Exhibit 1.3 provides a loss distribution for a portfolio of credit assets. (It is likely that this loss distribution was obtained from one of the portfolio models we discuss in Chapter 4.)

Expected Loss   Expected loss is the mean of the loss distribution. Note that, in contrast to a normal distribution, the mean is not at the center of the distribution but rather is to the right of the peak. That occurs because the loss distribution is asymmetric—it has a long, right-hand tail.

Expected loss is not a *risk*; it is a *cost* of doing business. The price of a transaction must cover expected loss. When a bank makes a number of loans, it *expects* some percentage of them to default, resulting in an expected loss due to default. So when pricing loans of a particular type, the

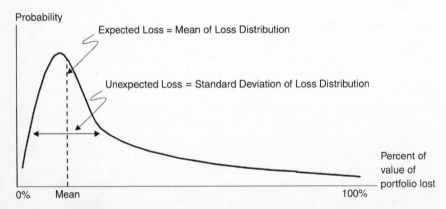

EXHIBIT 1.3   Loss Distribution for a Portfolio of Credit Assets

---

MEANS, MEDIANS, AND MODES

In a statistics class we would usually talk about two other *m* words, when we talked about means. Those other words are *median* and *mode*. The peak is the mode. The median is the point that divides the distribution in half (i.e., half the area of the distribution lies to the right of the median and half lies to the left of it). For a symmetric distribution, the mean, the median, and the mode would all be stacked on top of one another at the peak. As the distribution starts getting a tail to the right, the median moves to the right of the mode, and the mean moves to the right of the median.

---

bank will need to think about them as a pool and include in the price the amount it expects to lose on them.

Expected losses are normally covered by reserves. Would reserves be equal to expected losses? Usually not. A bank will want to maintain reserves in excess of expected losses; but it's fair to say that the reserve level is determined by expected loss. (Note that when we speak of reserves, we are not including those that are associated with impaired assets. Those are no longer really reserves; they have already been used. When we speak of reserves, we are talking about general reserves.)

Unexpected Loss The term "unexpected loss" is most likely attributable to the Office of the Comptroller of the Currency (OCC). As the OCC put it, "Capital is required as a cushion for a bank's overall risk of unexpected loss."

While an expected value is something that is familiar from statistics, an unexpected value is not. The OCC provided some insight into what they meant by the term unexpected loss: "The risk against which economic capital is allocated is defined as the volatility of earnings and value—the degree of fluctuation away from an expected level." That is, the OCC was referring to the dispersion of the loss distribution about its mean—what would be referred to as *variance* or *standard deviation* in statistics.

In contrast to expected loss, unexpected loss is a *risk* associated with being in the business, rather than a *cost* of doing business. We noted that the price of the transaction should be large enough to cover expected losses. Should the price of the transaction be sufficient to cover unexpected losses as well? No. Unexpected loss is not a cost of doing business; it's a risk. However, since capital provides the cushion for that risk, this transaction is going to attract some economic capital for the risk involved. And the transaction price should be sufficient to cover the rental price of the capital it attracts.

From Unexpected Loss to Capital   As we noted early on, economic capital is not a question of how much we have but rather how much we need (i.e., how much capital is needed to support a particular portfolio of assets). The more risky the assets, the more capital will be required to support them.

The question is: *How Much Is Enough?* After all, if we attribute more economic capital to one transaction or business, we have less to use to support another transaction or business. To answer the question, it is necessary to know the *target insolvency rate* for the financial institution.

The question of the target insolvency rate is one that must be answered by the board of directors of the institution. It turns out that many large commercial banks are using 0.03%—3 basis points—as the target insolvency rate. It appears that the way they came to this number was asking themselves the question: "What is important?" The answer to that question turned out to be their credit rating—in the case of these large commercial banks, AA. Looking at historical, one-year default rates, the probability of default for an entity rated AA is 3 basis points.

Once the board of directors has specified the target insolvency rate, it is necessary to turn that into a capital number.

It would be so much easier if everything in the world was normally distributed. Let's suppose that the loss distribution is normally distributed.

- If the target insolvency rate is 1%, the amount of economic capital needed to support the portfolio is the mean loss (the expected loss) plus 2.33 standard deviations. Where did we get the number 2.33? We got it out of the book you used in the statistics class you took as an undergraduate. In the back of that book was a Z table; and we looked up in that Z table how many standard deviations we would need to move away from the mean in order to isolate 1% of the area in the upper tail.
- If the target insolvency rate is $\frac{1}{10}$ of 1% (i.e., if the confidence level is 99.9%), the amount of economic capital needed to support the portfolio would be the expected loss plus 3.09 standard deviations.

If the loss distribution was normally distributed, it would be simple to figure out the amount of economic capital necessary to support the portfolio. Starting with the target insolvency rate, we could look up in the Z table how many standard deviations we needed, multiply that number by the size of one standard deviation for the loss distribution, and add that number to the expected loss.

However, as illustrated in Exhibit 1.3, the loss distributions that we are dealing with have that long, right-hand tail. (This is what is meant when someone says that the loss distributions for credit assets are "fat tailed." If a distribution has a fat tail, there will be more area in the tail of the distribution than would exist in a normal distribution.) With such a fat-tailed distribution, if the target insolvency rate is 1%, the amount of economic capital needed to support the portfolio will be much larger than would have been the case if the loss distribution was normal. The question is: How much larger?

A few firms have tried to use a rule of thumb and bump up the number that would have been generated if the loss distribution was normal, to approximate the right number for this long-right-hand-tail distribution. We have heard of financial institutions using multipliers of six to eight to bump up the number of standard deviations required.

However, given that most of the portfolio models that are discussed in Chapter 4 generate their loss distributions via Monte Carlo simulation, it makes more sense simply to plot out the loss distribution (or create a table). Instead of relying on the standard deviation and some ad hoc multiplier, we observe the loss distribution (either in table or graphic form) and find the loss that would isolate the target insolvency rate in the right-hand tail (see Exhibit 1.4).

REGULATORY CAPITAL

The trend in banking regulation over the past decade-and-a-half has pressured and is increasingly pressuring banks for changes in their loan portfolio management practices. Exhibit 1.5 traces the evolution of these changes.

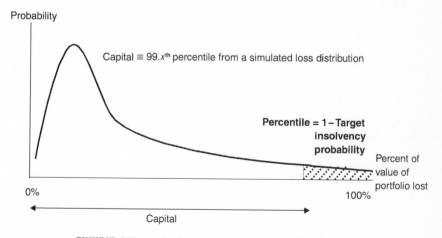

EXHIBIT 1.4   Calculating Capital from a Simulated Loss

EXHIBIT 1.5 Evolution of the Regulatory Environment

1988	Basle Capital Accord
1996	Market Risk Capital Amendment
1996–1998	Ad hoc rules for Credit Derivatives
Jun. 1999	Consultative Document from Basle Committee
Jan. 2001	Basle Committee proposes New Capital Accord

1988 Capital Accord

The 1988 Capital Accord represented the first step toward risk-based capital adequacy requirements. However, the blunt-instrument nature of the 1988 Accord gave banks an incentive to engage in "regulatory arbitrage," that is, using credit derivatives and loan securitization to decrease the percentage of the credit extended to high-credit-quality obligors (which attract too much regulatory capital).

The 1988 Accord was an agreement by the members of the Basle Committee on Banking Supervision with respect to minimum regulatory capital for the credit risk. Under these rules, the minimum regulatory capital associated with loans or other cash assets, guarantees, or derivative contract is calculated as

$$\text{Capital} = \text{Risk Weight} \times \text{Exposure} \times 8\%$$

The risk weight for a transaction is determined by characteristics of the obligor (except for loans fully secured by mortgages and derivatives). Exhibit 1.6 provides illustrative risk weights.

The exposure is determined by the type of instrument. For fully funded loans or bonds, the exposure is the face amount. For unfunded commitments, the exposure is 50% of the commitment for undrawn commitments with maturity over one year and 0% of the commitment for undrawn com-

EXHIBIT 1.6 Illustrative Risk Weights from the 1988 Basle Accord

OECD central governments	0%
Domestic public sector entities	0%, 10%, 20% or 50%
(excluding central governments)	Percentage set by domestic regulator
OECD banks and regulated securities firms	20%
Loans fully secured by residential mortgages	50%
Counterparties in derivatives transactions	50%
Public sector corporations; non-OECD banks	100%

mitments with maturity less than one year. For credit products (e.g., guarantees), the exposure is 100% of the notional value of the contract. For derivatives, the exposure is determined by the equation

$$\text{Replacement Cost} + (\text{Add-On Percentage} \times \text{Notional Principal})$$

where the add-on percentages are provided in Exhibit 1.7.

The 1988 Accord was criticized on three grounds: (1) it provided inconsistent treatment of credit risks. This can be seen in Exhibit 1.5 by comparing the risk weights for OECD banks to those for corporations (i.e., the 1988 Accord requires less regulatory capital for a relatively risky bank in an OECD country than for a relatively less risky corporation); (2) the 1988 Accord does not measure risk on a portfolio basis. It does not take account of diversification or concentration and there is no provision for short positions; (3) the 1988 Accord provides for no regulatory relief as models/management improve.

These flaws in the 1988 Accord led to some predictable distortions. The inconsistent treatment of credit risk tended to induce banks to lower the credit quality of their portfolios. That is, it discouraged lending to higher-quality corporate borrowers and encouraged banks to lend to lower-quality obligors. The preferential treatment of undrawn commitments (20% versus 100% for drawn loans) coupled with competitive forces have led to underpricing of commercial paper backstop facilities.

The 1996 Market Risk Amendment to the Capital Accord

In 1996 the Basle Committee on Banking Supervision amended the 1988 Accord to specify minimum regulatory capital for market risk.

While banks could elect for the supervisor to apply a Standardized

EXHIBIT 1.7 Add-On Percentages for Derivative Contracts under the 1988 Basle Accord

	Interest Rate	Exchange Rate and Gold	Equity	Precious Metals Except Gold	Other Commodities
One year or less	0.0%	1.0%	6.0%	7.0%	10.0%
More than one year to five years	0.5%	5.0%	8.0%	7.0%	12.0%
More than five years	1.5%	7.5%	10.0%	8.0%	15.0%

BASLE COMMITTEE ON BANKING SUPERVISION

The Basle Committee on Banking Supervision is made up of the bank supervisors from Belgium, Canada, France, Germany, Italy, Japan, Luxembourg, the Netherlands, Spain, Sweden, Switzerland, United Kingdom, and the United States. (This group is called the G-10 countries, even though there are 13 of them.)

The Basle Committee was established by the Governors of the Central Banks of the G-10 (in 1974) to improve collaboration between bank supervisors. While the secretariat for the Basle Committee is provided by the Bank for International Settlements (BIS), the Basle Committee is not part of the BIS.

The Committee does not possess any formal supranational supervisory authority, and its conclusions do not, and were never intended to, have legal force. Rather, it formulates broad supervisory standards and guidelines and recommends statements of best practices in the expectation that individual authorities will take steps to implement them through detailed arrangements—statutory or otherwise—which are best suited to their own national systems. In this way, the Committee encourages convergence toward common approaches and common standards without attempting detailed harmonization of member countries' supervisory techniques.

The Basle Committee is a forum for discussion on the handling of specific supervisory problems. It coordinates the sharing of supervisory responsibilities among national authorities with the aim of ensuring effective supervision of banks' activities worldwide.

The Committee also seeks to enhance standards of supervision, notably in relation to solvency, to help strengthen the soundness and stability of international banking.

Method to calculate minimum regulatory capital for market risk, the dramatic change embodied by the 1996 Market Risk Amendment was the Internal Models Approach. Under this approach, which is used by the vast majority of internationally active banks, the minimum regulatory capital for market risk is calculated *using the bank's own internal market risk measurement model*. Before this can happen, the bank must have its internal model approved by its national regulator, who specifies how the model is used (e.g., which parameters to use).

Attempts to Fit Credit Derivatives into the 1988 Accord

Credit derivatives did not exist when the 1988 Accord was agreed to. However, once they did appear, supervisors tried to force them into the structure of the Accord. In the context of the 1988 Accord, credit derivatives would have to be treated either as credit instruments or derivative instruments. As summarized in Exhibit 1.8, these two different treatments have very different implications for the amount of regulatory capital the transaction would attract.

To see how this happens, let's consider two ways that the bank could take a "long" position in a corporate credit:

- Cash market—The bank could make a $10 million loan to the corporate (or it could buy the corporate bond).
- Derivative market—The bank could sell a credit default swap referencing the same $10 million loan to the corporate.

While both of these transactions result in the bank's having the same exposure, the 1988 Accord could have them attract very different levels of regulatory capital.

If the bank makes the loan or buys the bond, minimum regulatory capital will be $800,000.

$$\text{Capital} = \text{Principal} \times \text{Risk Weight of Issuer} \times 8\%$$
$$= \$10 \text{ million} \times 100\% \times 8\%$$
$$= \$800,000$$

If the exposure is established via a credit derivative and if credit derivatives are treated like credit instruments, minimum regulatory capital will again be $800,000.

EXHIBIT 1.8 Credit Derivatives Could Be Credit Products or Derivative Products

Credit Derivatives	
Credit Products (Guarantee) Approach	**Derivative Products Approach**
Credit exposure determined by (notional value × 100%) Maximum risk weight = 100%	Credit exposure determined by (replacement cost + add-on) Maximum risk weight = 50%

Capital = Credit Equivalent Amount × Risk Weight of Issuer × 8%
=($10 million × 100%) × 100% × 8%
= $800,000

However, if credit derivatives are treated like derivative instruments, minimum regulatory capital would be only $24,000.

Capital = Credit Equivalent Amount × Risk Weight of Issuer × 8%
= ($0 + $10 million × 6%) × 50% × 8%
= $24,000

Exhibit 1.9 illustrates the long process of finding a way to fit credit derivatives into the 1988 Accord. The compromise solution was to calculate the minimum regulatory capital for a credit derivative using the credit product approach if the credit derivative is in the Banking Book and using the derivative product approach if the credit derivative is in the Trading Book.

The 1999 Consultative Document

Recognizing the inherent flaws in the 1988 Accord, the Basle Committee on Banking Supervision opened a discussion about revising the Accord with a Consultative Document issued in June 1999.

EXHIBIT 1.9   Regulatory Releases on Credit Derivatives

August 1996	Federal Reserve (SR 96–17), FDIC, OCC Banking book guidance
November 1996	Bank of England Discussion paper on credit derivatives
June 1997	Bank of England Trading book and banking book guidance
	Federal Reserve (SR 97–18) Trading book guidance
	Commission Bancaire (France) Consultative paper
Fall 1997	OSFI (Canada)
April 1998	Commission Bancaire (France) Interim capital rules
July 1998	Financial Services Authority (England) Updated interim trading and banking book capital rules

The 1988 Accord had focused only on minimum regulatory capital requirements. The consultative document broadens the focus, by describing the supervisory process as supported by "three pillars."

■ Pillar 1 is the minimum regulatory capital requirement. The central recommendation of the Consultative Document is to modify the risk weights of the 1988 Accord to correspond to public credit ratings; and, it holds out the possibility of using internal ratings. The Consultative Document also proposes risk weights higher than 100% for some low-quality exposures, the abolition of the maximum 50% risk weight for derivative transactions, a larger exposure for short-term commitments, and a possible charge for operational risk.
■ Pillar 2 is a supervisory review of capital adequacy. The Consultative Document notes that national supervisors must ensure that banks develop an internal capital assessment process and set capital targets consistent with their risk profiles.
■ Pillar 3 is market discipline and disclosure.

Proposed New Accord

In January 2001 the Basle Committee on Banking Supervision released its proposal for a new Accord. For Pillar 1—minimum regulatory capital standards—the Basle Committee proposed capital requirements associated with three categories of risk:

1. Market risk—The minimum capital calculations as defined in the 1996 Amendment would remain largely unchanged.
2. Operational risk—An explicit capital requirement for operational risk.
3. Credit risk—Three approaches to calculation of minimum regulatory capital for credit risk—a revised standardized approach and two internal ratings-based (IRB) approaches. The revised standardized approach provides improved risk sensitivity compared to the 1988 Accord. The two IRB approaches—foundation and advanced—which rely on banks' own internal risk ratings, are considerably more risk sensitive. The IRB approaches are accompanied by minimum standards and disclosure requirements, and, most importantly, allow for evolution over time.

Revised Standardized Approach   The revised standardized approach is similar to the 1988 Accord in that the risk weights are determined by the category of borrower (sovereign, bank, corporate). However, the risk weights would be based on external credit ratings, with unrated credits assigned to the 100% risk bucket.

Exhibit 1.10 provides the risk weights proposed by the Basle Committee. In this table, we use option 2 for banks (i.e., using option 2, the risk weighting is based on the external credit assessment of the bank itself, whereas using option 1, the risk weight for the bank would be set one category less favorable than that assigned to claims on the sovereign of incorporation.)

This revised standardized approach is clearly an improvement on the 1988 Accord, because it provides improved risk sensitivity. The revised standardized approach

- Eliminates the OECD club preference in the 1988 Accord.
- Provides greater differentiation for corporate credits.
- Introduces higher risk categories (150%).
- Contains the option to allow higher risk weights for equities.

Internal Ratings-Based Approach   The revised standardized approach was targeted at banks desiring a simplified capital framework. For the more sophisticated banks, the Basle Committee proposed the IRB approach.

Comparison of Foundation and Advanced IRB Approaches   As noted, the Basle Committee described two IRB approaches—foundation and advanced. As shown in Exhibit 1.11, the differences between the foundation and advanced approaches are subtle.

In the January 2001 consultative document, the Basle Committee proposed a modification to the equation used to calculate minimum regulatory capital for credit risk:

$$\text{Regulatory Capital} = [\text{Risk Weight} \times (\text{Exposure} + \text{Granularity Adjustment})] \times 8\%$$

EXHIBIT 1.10   Risk Weights in Standardized Approach of Proposed New Accord

	Risk Weights		
Rating of Entity	Sovereigns	Banks	Corporates
AAA to AA–	0%	20%	20%
A+ to A–	20%	50%	50%
BBB+ to BBB–	50%	50%	100%
BB+ to BB–	100%	100%	100%
B+ to B–	100%	100%	100%
below B–	150%	150%	150%
Unrated	100%	50%	100%

EXHIBIT 1.11 Comparison of Foundation and Advanced IRB Approaches

	Foundation	Advanced
Determinants of Risk Weights		
Probability of default (PD)	Bank determines	Bank determines
Loss in the event of default (LGD)	Supervisor determines	Bank determines
Exposure at default (EAD)	Supervisor determines	Bank determines
Maturity (M)		Maturity adjustment incorporated
Credit Risk Mitigation		
Collateral		
Credit derivatives		Greater flexibility permitted
Bank guarantees		
Calculation of Reg Capital		
Floor		90% of foundation approach for first two years

where the granularity adjustment was intended to reflect the banks' residual risk that inevitably remains within the bank since no bank holds an infinitely fine-grained portfolio. The granularity adjustment was subsequently removed from the proposed new accord.

Exposures   For on-balance-sheet exposures, the exposure number is simply the nominal outstanding.

For off-balance-sheet exposures, the calculation of the exposure number depends on the type of product. For committed but undrawn facilities

$$\text{Exposure} = (\text{Amount Committed but Undrawn}) \times \text{CCF}$$

where CCF is a credit conversion factor. For interest rate, FX, commodity, and equity derivatives, the Basle Committee proposed using the rules for Credit Equivalent Amount in the 1988 Accord.

Risk Weights   In the IRB approach the risk weights will be functions of the type of exposure (e.g., corporate vs. retail) and four variables:

- Probability of default (PD) of borrower over one-year time horizon
- Loss given default (LGD)
- Maturity (M)
- Exposure at default (EAD)

Before one can calculate the risk weight for the firm in question, it is first necessary to calculate the Benchmark Risk Weight (*BRW*) for that obligor. The benchmark risk weight for corporates is based on a three-year exposure and is calculated using the equation:

$$BRW(PD) = 976.5 \times N[1.118 \times G\{PD\} + 1.288] \times \left(1 + \frac{0.047 \times (1-PD)}{PD^{0.44}}\right)$$

where $N[\ldots]$ is the cumulative distribution for a standard normal variable and $G[\ldots]$ is the *inverse* cumulative distribution for a standard normal variable.

Interpreting the Benchmark Risk Weight Equation

At first blush, the benchmark risk weight equation seems arbitrary and mechanical. However, there are some important concepts embedded in this equation. Here is the benchmark risk weight equation once more, but, this time, we have divided it into three parts.

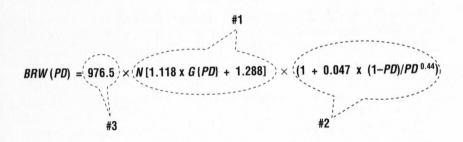

Part 1   The January 2001 Consultative Document describes this as the expected and unexpected losses obtained using a credit portfolio model to evaluate a hypothetical, infinitely granular portfolio of one-year loans.

There is a credit portfolio model embedded in the IRB risk weights. (If you want to read more on this, see the Appendix to this chapter.)

Part 2   The credit portfolio model in Part 1 is for a portfolio of maturity one year. This adjusts the BRW to reflect a portfolio of maturity three years.

Part 3   This calibrates the risk weight so that *BRW* is equal to 100% when the probability of default (*PD*) is equal to 70 bp. (Note that 70 bp corresponds to BB+/BBB– rating.)

In the foundation approach—no explicit maturity dimension—the Risk Weight (RW) for the corporate exposure is:

$$RW(PD) = Min \begin{cases} \left(\dfrac{LGD}{50}\right) \times BRW(PD) \\ 12.5 \times LGD \end{cases}$$

where

LGD is the loss in event of default

In the advanced approach, the Risk Weight (RW) for the corporate exposure is:

$$RW(PD) = Min \begin{cases} \left(\dfrac{LGD}{50}\right) \times BRW(PD) \times [1 + b(PD) \times (M-3)] \\ 12.5 \times LGD \end{cases}$$

where

LGD is the loss in event of default
$b(PD)$ is the sensitivity of the maturity adjustment to M[1]
M is the maturity of the transaction being considered

APPENDIX TO CHAPTER 1: A Credit Portfolio Model Inside the IRB Risk Weights

In Chapter 1, we asserted that the term

$$N[1.118 \times G\{PD\} + 1.288]$$

represents expected and unexpected losses obtained using a credit portfolio model to evaluate a hypothetical, infinitely granular portfolio of one-year loans. It turns out that, in order to see how this works, you have to look at the work of Oldrich Vasicek.

Vasicek provided an analytical solution for a Merton-model-based portfolio loss distribution in which the number of obligors tends to infinity. His solution results in a highly nonnormal distribution. The *cumulative* distribution function (Q) showing the probability of a loss less than or equal to x is given by

$$Q(x;PD,\rho) = N\left\{\frac{1}{\sqrt{\rho}}\left(\left(\sqrt{1-\rho}\right)G[x] - G[PD]\right)\right\}$$

where ρ = asset correlation between *all* obligors.

The *inverse* of this distribution gives the pth-percentile fractional loss L_{α} ($p = 100^*\alpha$):

$$L_{\alpha} = Q^{-1}(\alpha;PD,\rho) = Q(\alpha;1-PD,1-\rho)$$

$$= N\left[\frac{1}{\sqrt{1-\rho}}\left(\sqrt{\rho}G[\alpha] - G[1-PD]\right)\right]$$

Using the definition of the inverse standard normal cumulative function, $G(1-x) = -G(x)$, Vasicek's distribution is

$$L_{\alpha} = N\left[\frac{1}{\sqrt{1-\rho}}\left(\sqrt{\rho}G[\alpha] + G[PD]\right)\right]$$

After a little algebra, Vasicek's formulation can be expressed as

$$L_{\alpha} = N\left[\frac{G[PD]}{\sqrt{1-\rho}} + \frac{\sqrt{\rho}G[\alpha]}{\sqrt{1-\rho}}\right]$$

BRW is based on 99.5% coverage of losses (i.e., $\alpha = 0.995$) and asset correlation (ρ) of 0.2 among all obligors.

$$\frac{1}{\sqrt{1-\rho}} = \frac{1}{\sqrt{1-0.2}} = 1.118$$

$$\frac{\sqrt{\rho}G[\alpha]}{\sqrt{1-\rho}} = \frac{\sqrt{0.2}G[0.995]}{\sqrt{1-0.2}} = 1.288$$

So

$$L_{0.995} = N[1.118 \times G\{PD\} + 1.288]$$

NOTE

1. If the mark-to-market (MTM) model is used, then $b(PD)$ is given by:

$$b(PD) = \frac{.0235 \times (1 - PD)}{PD^{0.44} + .047 \times (1 - PD)}$$

If a default mode (DM) model is used, then it is given by:

$b(PD) = 7.6752 \times PD^2 - 1.9211 \times PD + 0.0774$, for $PD < 0.05$
$b(PD) = 0$, for $PD > 0.05$

The Credit Portfolio Management Process

CHAPTER 2

Modern Portfolio Theory and Elements of the Portfolio Modeling Process

The argument we made in Chapter 1 is that the credit function must transform into a loan portfolio management function. Behaving like an asset manager, the bank must maximize the risk-adjusted return to the loan portfolio by actively buying and selling credit exposures where possible, and otherwise managing new business and renewals of existing facilities. This leads immediately to the realization that the principles of modern portfolio theory (MPT)—which have proved so successful in the management of equity portfolios—must be applied to credit portfolios.

What is modern portfolio theory and what makes it so desirable? And how can we apply modern portfolio theory to portfolios of credit assets?

MODERN PORTFOLIO THEORY

What we call modern portfolio theory arises from the work of Harry Markowitz in the early 1950s. (With that date, I'm not sure how modern it is, but we are stuck with the name.)

As we will see, the payoff from applying modern portfolio theory is that, by combining assets in a portfolio, you can have *a higher expected return for a given level of risk;* or, alternatively, you can have *less risk for a given level of expected return.*

Modern portfolio theory was designed to deal with equities; so throughout all of this first part, we are thinking about equities. We switch to loans and other credit assets in the next part.

The Efficient Set Theorem and the Efficient Frontier

Modern portfolio theory is based on a deceptively simple theorem, called the Efficient Set Theorem:

An investor will choose her/his optimal portfolio from the set of portfolios that:

1. *Offer maximum expected return for varying levels of risk.*
2. *Offer minimum risk for varying levels of expected return.*

Exhibit 2.1 illustrates how this efficient set theorem leads to the *efficient frontier*. The dots in Exhibit 2.1 are the feasible portfolios. Note that the different portfolios have different combinations of return and risk. The efficient frontier is the collection of portfolios that simultaneously maximize expected return for a given level of risk and minimize risk for a given level of expected return.

The job of a portfolio manager is to move toward the efficient frontier.

Expected Return and Risk

In Exhibit 2.1 the axes are simply "expected return" and "risk." We need to provide some specificity about those terms.

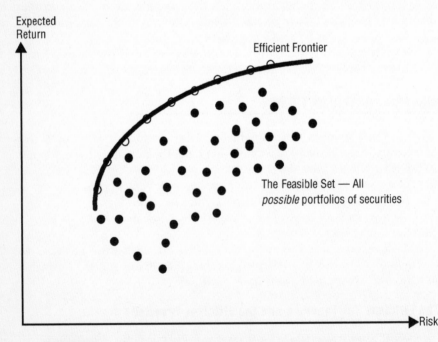

EXHIBIT 2.1   The Efficient Set Theorem Leads to the Efficient Frontier

In modern portfolio theory, when we talk about return, we are talking about expected returns. The expected return for equity i would be written as

$$E[R_i] = \mu_i$$

where μ_i is the mean of the return distribution for equity i.

In modern portfolio theory, risk is expressed as the standard deviation of the returns for the security. Remember that the standard deviation for equity i is the square root of its variance, which measures the dispersion of the return distribution as the expected value of squared deviations about the mean. The variance for equity i would be written as[1]

$$\sigma_i^2 = E[(E[R_i] - R_i)^2]$$

The Effect of Combining Assets in a Portfolio—Diversification

Suppose that we form a portfolio of two equities—equity 1 and equity 2. Suppose further that the percentage of the portfolio invested in equity 1 is w_1 and the percentage invested in equity 2 is w_2. The expected return for the portfolio is

$$E[R_p] = w_1 E[R_1] + w_2 E[R_2]$$

That is, the expected return for the portfolio is simply the weighted sum of the expected returns for the two equities.

The variance for our two-equity portfolio is where things begin to get interesting. The variance of the portfolio depends not only on the variances of the individual equities but also on the covariance between the returns for the two equities ($\sigma_{1,2}$):

$$\sigma_p^2 = w_1^2 \sigma_1^2 + w_2^2 \sigma_2^2 + 2 w_1 w_2 \sigma_{1,2}$$

Since covariance is a term about which most of us do not have a mental picture, we can alternatively write the variance for our two-equity portfolio in terms of the correlation between the returns for equities 1 and 2 ($\rho_{1,2}$):

$$\sigma_p^2 = w_1^2 \sigma_1^2 + w_2^2 \sigma_2^2 + 2 w_1 w_2 \rho_{1,2} \sigma_1 \sigma_2$$

This boring-looking equation turns out to be very powerful and has changed the way that investors hold equities. It says:

Unless the equities are perfectly positively correlated (i.e., unless $\rho_{1,2} = 1$) the riskiness of the portfolio will be smaller than the weighted sum of the riskiness of the two equities that were used to create the portfolio.

That is, in every case except the extreme case where the equities are perfectly positively correlated, combining the equities into a portfolio will result in a "diversification effect."

This is probably easiest to see via an example.

Example: The Impact of Correlation

Consider two equities—Bristol-Meyers Squibb and Ford Motor Company. Using historical data on the share prices, we found that the mean return for Bristol-Meyers Squibb was 15% yearly and the mean return for Ford was 21% yearly. Using the same data set, we calculated the standard deviation in Bristol-Myers Squibb's return as 18.6% yearly and that for Ford as 28.0% yearly.

$$E(R_{BMS}) = \mu_{BMS} = 15\% \qquad E(R_F) = \mu_F = 21\%$$
$$\sigma_{BMS} = 18.6\% \qquad \sigma_F = 28.0\%$$

The numbers make sense: Ford has a higher return, but it is also more risky.

Now let's use these equities to create a portfolio with 60% of the portfolio invested in Bristol-Myers Squibb and the remaining 40% in Ford Motor Company. The expected return for this portfolio is easy to calculate:

$$\text{Expected Portfolio Return} = (0.6)15 + (0.4)21 = 17.4\%$$

The variance of the portfolio depends on the correlation of the returns on Bristol-Meyers Squibb's equity with that of Ford ($\rho_{BMS, F}$):

$$\text{Variance of Portfolio Return} = (0.6)^2(18.6)^2 + (0.4)^2(28)^2$$
$$+(2)(0.6)(0.4)(\rho_{BMS, F})(18.6)(28.0)$$

The riskiness of the portfolio is measured by the standard deviation of the portfolio return—the square root of the variance.

The question we want to answer is whether the riskiness of the portfolio (the portfolio standard deviation) is *larger, equal to,* or *smaller than* the weighted sum of the risks (the standard deviations) of the two equities:

$$\text{Weighted Sum of Risks} = (0.6)18.6 + (0.4)28.0 = 22.4\%$$

To answer this question, let's look at three cases.

CASE 1: THE RETURNS ARE UNCORRELATED ($\rho_{BMS,F} = 0$):

$$\text{Variance of Portfolio Returns} = (0.6)^2(18.6)^2 + (0.4)^2(28)^2 + 0 = 250.0$$

In this case, the riskiness of portfolio is less than the weighted sum of the risks of the two equities:

$$\text{Standard Deviation of Portfolio} = 15.8\% \text{ yearly} < 22.4\%$$

If the returns are uncorrelated, combining the assets into a portfolio will generate a large diversification effect.

CASE 2: THE RETURNS ARE PERFECTLY POSITIVELY CORRELATED ($\rho_{BMS,F} = 1$):

$$\begin{aligned}\text{Variance of Portfolio Returns} &= (0.6)^2(18.6)^2 + (0.4)^2(28)^2 \\ &\quad + (2)(0.6)(0.4)(1)(18.6)(28.0) \\ &= 500.0\end{aligned}$$

In this extreme case, the riskiness of portfolio is equal to the weighted sum of the risks of the two equities:

$$\text{Standard Deviation of Portfolio} = 22.4\% \text{ yearly}$$

The only case in which there will be no diversification effect is when the returns are perfectly positively correlated.

CASE 3: THE RETURNS ARE PERFECTLY NEGATIVELY CORRELATED ($\rho_{BMS,F} = -1$):

$$\begin{aligned}\text{Variance of Portfolio Returns} &= (0.6)^2(18.6)^2 + (0.4)^2(28)^2 \\ &\quad + (2)(0.6)(0.4)(-1)(18.6)(28.0) \\ &= 124.6 + 125.4 - 250.0 = 0\end{aligned}$$

In this extreme case, not only is the riskiness of portfolio less than the weighted sum of the risks of the two equities, the portfolio is *riskless*:

$$\text{Standard Deviation of Portfolio} = 0\% \text{ yearly}$$

If the returns are perfectly negatively correlated, there will be a combination of the two assets that will result in a zero risk portfolio.

From Two Assets to *N* Assets

Previously we noted that, for a two-asset portfolio, the variance of the portfolio is

$$\sigma_p^2 = w_1^2\sigma_1^2 + w_2^2\sigma_2^2 + 2w_1w_2\rho_{1,2}\sigma_1\sigma_2$$

This two-asset portfolio variance is portrayed graphically in Exhibit 2.2.

The term in the upper-left cell shows the degree to which equity 1 varies with itself (the variance of the returns for equity 1); and the term in the lower-right cell shows the degree to which equity 2 varies with itself (the variance of the returns for equity 2). The term in the upper-right shows the degree to which the returns for equity 1 *covary* with those for equity 2, where the term $\rho_{1,2}\sigma_1\sigma_2$ is the covariance of the returns for equities 1 and 2. Likewise, the term in the upper-right shows the degree to which the returns for equity 2 *covary* with those for equity 1. (Note that $\rho_{1,2} = \rho_{2,1}$.)

Exhibit 2.3 portrays the portfolio variance for a portfolio of N equities. With our two-equity portfolio, the *variance–covariance* matrix contained $2 \times 2 = 4$ cells. An N-equity portfolio will have $N \times N = N^2$ cells in its *variance–covariance* matrix.

In Exhibit 2.3, the shaded boxes on the diagonal are the variance terms. The other boxes are the covariance terms. There are N variance terms and $N^2 - N$ covariance terms.

If we sum up all the cells (i.e., we sum the i rows and the j columns) we get the variance of the portfolio returns:

$$\sigma_p^2 = \sum_{i=1}^{N}\sum_{j=1}^{N} w_i w_j \sigma_{i,j}$$

The Limit of Diversification—Covariance

We have seen that, if we combine equities in a portfolio, the riskiness of the portfolio is less than the weighted sum of the riskiness of the individual equities (unless the equities are perfectly positively correlated). How far can we take this? What is the limit of diversification?

EXHIBIT 2.2 Graphical Representation of Variance for Two-Equity Portfolio

	Equity 1	Equity 2
Equity 1	$w_1^2\sigma_1^2$	$w_1w_2\rho_{1,2}\sigma_1\sigma_2$
Equity 2	$w_2w_1\rho_{2,1}\sigma_2\sigma_1$	$w_2^2\sigma_2^2$

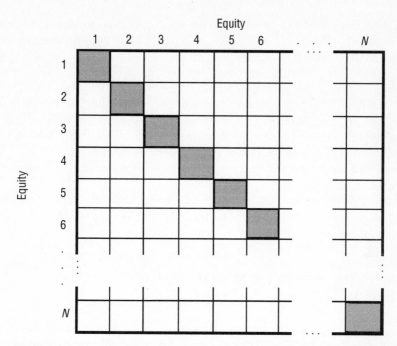

EXHIBIT 2.3 Graphical Representation of Variance for an N-Equity Portfolio

To answer this question, let's consider a portfolio of N equities where all the equities are equally weighted. That is, $w_i = 1/N$.

We can express the portfolio variance in terms of the average variances and average covariances. Remember that we have N variance terms and $N^2 - N$ covariance terms. Since the portfolio is equally weighted, each of the average variance terms will be weighted by $(1/N)^2$, and each of the average covariance terms will be weighted by $(1/N) \times (1/N) = (1/N)^2$:

$$\sigma_p^2 = N \times \left(\frac{1}{N}\right)^2 \times (\text{Average Variance})$$

$$+(N^2 - N) \times \left(\frac{1}{N}\right)^2 \times (\text{Average Covariance})$$

After doing a little algebra, we can simplify the preceding expression to:

$$\sigma_p^2 = \frac{1}{N} \times (\text{Average Variance}) + \left(1 - \frac{1}{N}\right) \times (\text{Average Covariance})$$

What happens to the variance of the portfolio returns as the number of equities in the portfolio increases? As N gets large, $1/N$ goes to zero and $(1-1/N)$ goes to one. So as the number of equities in the portfolio increases, the variance of the portfolio returns approaches average covariance. This relation is depicted graphically in Exhibit 2.4.

"Unique" risk (also called "diversifiable," "residual," or "unsystematic" risk) can be diversified away. However, "systematic" risk (also called "undiversifiable" or "market" risk) cannot be diversified away. And, as we saw previously, systematic risk is average covariance. That means that the bedrock of risk—the risk you can't diversify away—arises from the way that the equities covary.

For a portfolio of equities, you can achieve a "fully diversified" portfolio (i.e., one where total portfolio risk is approximately equal to average covariance) with about 30 equities.

CHALLENGES IN APPLYING MODERN PORTFOLIO THEORY TO PORTFOLIOS OF CREDIT ASSETS

In the preceding section, we saw that the application of modern portfolio theory results in *a higher expected return for a given level of risk* or, alternatively, *less risk for a given level of expected return.*

This is clearly an attractive proposition to investors in credit assets. However, there are some challenges that we face in applying modern portfolio theory—something that was developed for equities—to credit assets.

Credit Assets Do Not Have Normally Distributed Loss Distributions

Modern portfolio theory is based on two critical assumptions. The first assumption is that investors are "risk averse." Risk aversion just means that

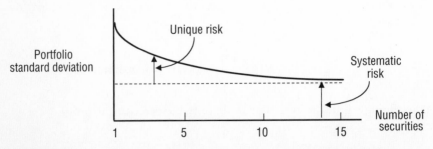

EXHIBIT 2.4   As the Number of Equities Increases, Portfolio Risk Approaches Average Covariance

if the investor is offered two baskets of assets—basket A and basket B—where both baskets have the same expected return but basket A had higher risk than basket B, the investor will pick basket B, the basket with the lower risk. And that assumption is not troublesome. It is likely that investors in credit assets are at least as risk averse as equity investors.

The second assumption—the troublesome one—is that security returns are *jointly normally distributed*. This means that the expected return and standard deviation completely describe the return distribution of each security. Moreover, this assumption means that if we combine securities into portfolios, the portfolio returns are normally distributed.

First, we have to do some mental switching of dimensions. For equities, we are interested in returns. For loans and other credit assets, we are interested in expected losses. So the question becomes: Can the loss distributions for loans and other credit assets be characterized as normal distributions? And, as long as we are here, we might as well look at the distribution of equity returns.

Exhibit 2.5 examines these questions. Panel A of Exhibit 2.5 contains a normal distribution and the histogram that results from actual daily price change data for IBM. It turns out that the daily price changes for IBM are not normally distributed: There is more probability at the mean than would be the case for a normal distribution; and there are more observations in the tails of the histogram than would be predicted by a normal distribution. (The actual distribution has "fat tails.") Indeed, if you look at equities, their returns are not, in general, normally distributed. The returns for most equities don't pass the test of being normally distributed.

But wait a minute. We said that a critical assumption behind modern portfolio theory is that returns are normally distributed; and now we have said that the returns to equities are not normally distributed. That seems to be a problem. But in the case of equity portfolios, we simply ignore the deviation from normality and go on. In just a moment, we examine why this is okay for equities (but not for credit assets).

Panel B of Exhibit 2.5 contains a stylized loss distribution for an "originate-and-hold" portfolio of loans. Clearly, the losses are not normally distributed.

Can we just ignore the deviation from normality as we do for equity portfolios? Unfortunately, we cannot and the reason is that credit portfolio managers are concerned with a different part of the distribution than are the equity managers.

Managers of equity portfolios are looking at areas around the mean. And it turns out that the errors you make by ignoring the deviations from normality are not very large. In contrast, managers of credit portfolios focus on areas in the tail of the distribution. And out in the tail, very small errors in the specification of the distribution will have a very large impact.

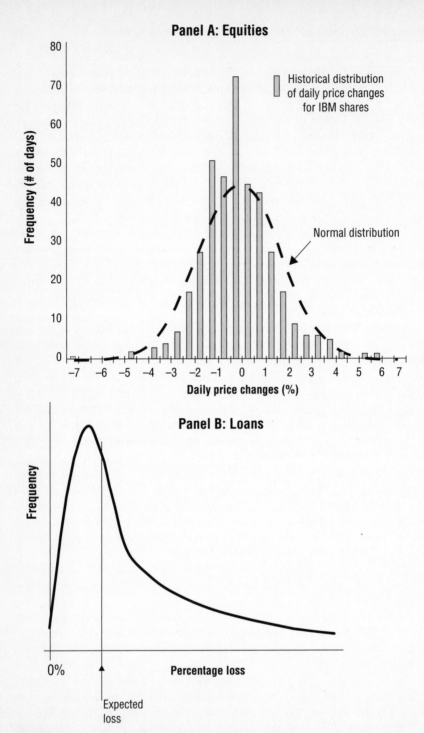

EXHIBIT 2.5 The Distribution of Equity Returns May Not Be Normal; but the Distribution of Losses for Loans Is Not Even Symmetric

---

WAYS THAT CREDIT MODELS INCORPORATE NONNORMALITY

In the discussion of Moody's–KMV Credit Monitor® in Chapter 3 we see that much of the technique is based on assuming a normal distribution. But we see that at the critical point where we need to go to a distribution to retrieve the probability of default, Credit Monitor does not use normal distribution. Instead, the probability of defaults is obtained from a proprietary distribution created from actual loss data; and this proprietary distribution is distinctly nonnormal.

In Chapter 4, we see that Credit Risk+™ is based on a Poisson distribution. Why? Because a Poisson distribution will have the long right-hand tail that characterizes loss distributions for credit assets.

In the other models we examine in Chapter 4, the loss distribution is simulated. By simulating the loss distribution, we can create distributions that make sense for portfolios of credit assets.

So what does this mean? The preceding tells us that the mean and standard deviation are not sufficient. When we work with portfolios of credit assets, we will have to collect some large data sets, or simulate the loss distributions, or specify distributions that have long tails.

Other Sources of Uncertainty

Working with portfolios of credit assets also leads to sources of uncertainty that don't occur in portfolios of equities.

We noted previously that, for credit portfolios, we work with the distribution of losses rather than returns. As is illustrated in Exhibit 2.6,

EXHIBIT 2.6   Additional Sources of Uncertainty

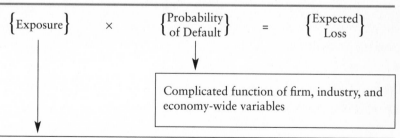

losses are themselves dependent on two other variables. Since probability of default is a complex function of firm-specific, industry-wide, and economy level variables, this input will be measured with error. In the case of the exposure at default, it depends on the amount outstanding at the time of default, the expected loss given default (or the inverse, recovery), and the volatility of loss given default.

Unlike equity portfolios, for portfolios of credit assets there is no direct way to estimate the covariance term—in this case, the covariance of defaults. Because the vast majority of the obligors of interest have not defaulted, we cannot simply collect data and calculate the correlation. Consequently, much more subtle techniques will be required.

Bad News and Good News about the Limit of Diversification—Covariance

We have some bad news for you. Look again at Exhibit 2.4. In the case of equity portfolios, we note that a "fully diversified" portfolio can be achieved with a limited number of equities. The number of assets needed to create a "fully diversified" portfolio of loans or other credit assets is much larger. It is certainly bigger than 100 assets and it may be larger than 1,000 assets.

But we have some good news for you as well. The diversification effect for portfolios of loans or other credit assets will be larger than the diversification effect for portfolios of equities. Remember that the bedrock risk—the risk that cannot be diversified away—is average covariance. As before, I find it easier to think about correlations than covariances, so, since both of them are telling me about the same thing, I switch and talk about correlation. The typical correlation of equity returns is 20%–70%. However, the typical correlation of defaults is much smaller—5% to 15%. So the risk that cannot be diversified away will be smaller.

The bad news is that it is going to take many more assets in the portfolio to achieve a "fully diversified" portfolio. The good news is once you have a "fully diversified" portfolio, you're going to get a much larger diversification effect.

ELEMENTS OF THE CREDIT PORTFOLIO MODELING PROCESS

The challenge has been to implement modern-portfolio-theory-based models for portfolios of credit assets.

Banks are currently the predominant users of credit portfolio modeling. The models are being used to accomplish a number of functions:

- Calculation of economic capital.
- Allocation of credit risk capital to business lines.
- Supporting "active" management of credit portfolios through loan sales, bond trading, credit derivatives, and securitization.
- Pricing transactions and defining hurdle rates.
- Evaluation of business units.
- Compensation of underwriters.

Insurance companies are using credit portfolio models to:

- Manage traditional sources of credit exposure.
- Guide the acquisition of new credit exposures—to date, mostly investment grade corporate credits—in order to provide diversification to the core insurance business. (Note: This has been accomplished primarily through credit derivatives subsidiaries.)

Monoline insurers use credit portfolio models to:

- Manage core credit exposure.
- Anticipate capital requirements imposed by ratings agencies.
- Price transactions and evaluate business units.

Investors use credit portfolio models for:

- Optimization of credit portfolios.
- Identification of mispriced credit assets.

Exhibit 2.7 provides a way of thinking about the credit portfolio modeling process. Data gets loaded into a credit portfolio model, which outputs expected loss, unexpected loss, capital, and the risk contributions for individual transactions.

In Chapter 3, we describe the sources for the data. We look at ways in which the probability of default for individual obligors and counterparties can be estimated. From the perspective of the facility, we look at sources for data on utilization and recovery in the event of default. And we examine the ways that the correlation of default is being dealt with.

To adapt the tenets of portfolio theory to loans, a variety of portfolio management models have come into existence. Four of the most

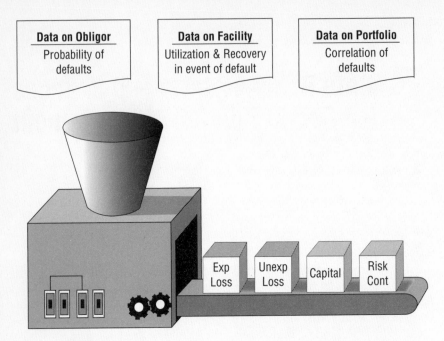

EXHIBIT 2.7   Elements of the Credit Portfolio Modeling Process

widely discussed models are Moody's–KMV Portfolio Manager™, the Risk-Metrics Group's CreditManager™, CSFB's Credit Risk+, and McKinsey's CreditPortfolioView™. In Chapter 4, we describe the various credit portfolio models.

NOTE

1. The Statistics Appendix contains more detailed explanations of these expressions.

CHAPTER 3

Data Requirements and Sources for Credit Portfolio Management

Exhibit 3.1 is repeated from Chapter 2, because it reminds us what data we need if we are going to do credit portfolio modeling and management. We are going to need data on the *probability of default* for the obligors. For the individual facilities, we are going to need data on *utilization* and *recovery in the event of default*. And we need data on the *correlation of defaults* or we need some way to incorporate this in the credit portfolio model. (As we describe briefly in the final section of this chapter and see in Chapter 4, correlation is handled within the credit portfolio models.)

PROBABILITIES OF DEFAULT

The measure of probability of default most widely used at most financial institutions and essentially at all banks is an *internal risk rating*. Based on public record data and their knowledge of the obligor, the financial institution will assign the obligor to a rating class. To offer some insight into what financial institutions are actually doing with respect to internal ratings, we provide some results from the 2002 Survey of Credit Portfolio Management Practices that we described in Chapter 1.

Where would a credit portfolio manager get external estimates of probabilities of defaults? Exhibit 3.2 lists the currently available sources of probability of default.

Probabilities of Default from Historical Data

If the obligor is publicly rated, the first place one might look is at historical probability of default data provided by the debt rating agencies or from an empirical analysis of defaults.

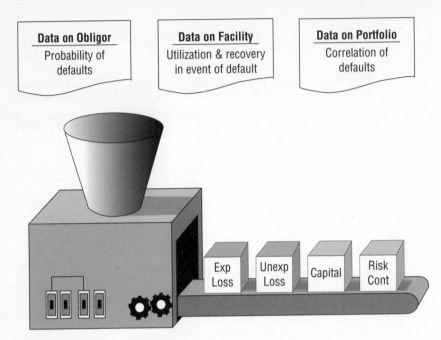

EXHIBIT 3.1 Data Requirements

EXHIBIT 3.2 Measures of Probability of Default

Historical data
- S&P—Using CreditPro™
- Moody's Credit Research Database
- Fitch Risk Management Loan Loss Database
- Altman's Mortality Study

Modeled using financial statement data
- Altman's Z-Score (later Zeta Services, Inc.)
- S&P's CreditModel™
- IQ Financial's Default Filter™
- Fitch Risk Management's CRS
- Moody's RiskCalc™ for private firms
- CreditSights' BondScore™
- KMV's Private Firm Model®

Implied from equity data
- KMV's Credit Monitor
- Moody's RiskCalc™ for public firms

Implied from credit spread curves
- Kamakura's KRM-cr
- Savvysoft's FreeCreditDerivatives.com

2002 SURVEY OF CREDIT PORTFOLIO MANAGEMENT PRACTICES

How many rating grades does your system contain?

		Large Corporates	Middle-Market Corporates	Banks	Other Financial
Non-defaulted entities	Average	13	12	13	13
	Range	5–22	5–22	5–22	5–22
Defaulted entities	Average	3	3	3	3
	Range	1–7	1–7	1–13	1–7

Do you employ facility ratings that are separate from the obligor rating?

No—One single rating reflects both obligor and obligation. 33%
Yes—We employ a separate facility rating.   65%

If you responded Yes:

Number of rating categories	Average	10
Do you explicitly link LGD estimates to specific facility ratings?	Range	2–25
	Yes	62%

Indicate the functional responsibility for assigning and reviewing the ratings.

	Assigns Ratings	Reviews Rating	Both
"Line" (unit with marketing/customer relationship responsibilities)	40%	13%	8%
Dedicated "credit" group other than Credit Portfolio Management	25%	30%	15%
Credit Portfolio Management	10%	25%	3%
Institution's Risk Management Group	10%	28%	15%
Internal Audit	0%	40%	0%
Other	17%	83%	0%

The survey respondents who indicated Other provided several alternative measures, including: Loan Review, Q/A, credit analysis unit, Loan Review Group, Credit Risk Review, Risk Review.

S&P Risk Solutions' CreditPro[1]   Through its Risk Solutions business, Standard & Poor's offers historical data from its long-term default study database (see www.risksolutions.standardandpoors.com). The data are delivered in a product called CreditPro, which permits the user to tailor the data to fit individual requirements. The user is able to create tables of default probabilities, transition matrices, and default correlation matrices, with sample selection by industry, by geography, and by time period. (The tables can be created with or without NRs and with or without pluses and minuses.) S&P Risk Solutions argues that rating migration rates and default rates may differ across time periods, geographic regions, and industries. They point to research showing that default and rating migration rates are correlated with macroeconomic, regulatory, and industry-specific conditions. [See Bangia, Diebold, and Schuermann (2002), Bahar and Nagpal, (1999), and Nickell, Perraudin, and Varotto (2000).]

Exhibit 3.3 provides two examples of historical default probability tables created in CreditPro. The user defines the time period over which defaults are tabulated. In Exhibit 3.3, we calculated one table on the basis of 1991–2000 data and another based on 1995–2000 data. Note the differences in the default probabilities.

Exhibit 3.4 illustrates a transition matrix created from historical Standard & Poor's data via CreditPro.

Moody's Investors Services and Moody's Risk Management Services

Moody's provides data from its Credit Research Database.

Moody's Credit Research Database*

Moody's Credit Research Database (CRD) is Moody's proprietary database of default and related information. It contains more than 110 years of data. (For example, the CRD indicates that the Harrisburg, Portsmouth, Mt. Joy, & Lancaster Railroad defaulted on its 6% mortgage due July 1, 1883) and it contains information from more than 80 countries.

The CRD covers corporate and commercial bonds and loans, private placements, and commercial paper.

The CRD is composed of three types of information.

1. Obligor-level data on defaulters and nondefaulters—Ratings, financial statements, equity market valuations, industry, and other data that can be used to predict default.
2. Obligation-level data—Cash flows to defaulted loans, defaulted bond prices that can be used to measure Loss Given Default.
3. Macropredictive variables—Interest rates, inflation, and economic growth.

*This description was obtained from the Moody's Risk Management Services website (www.moodysrms.com).

The sources of the CRD data include:

- Moody's default research team.
- Moody's internal financial library & Moody's analysts.
- Documents from regulatory authorities.
- Commercial information providers and research companies.
- Stock exchanges.
- Contributing financial institutions (the 7 largest banks in Australia, the 4 largest banks in Singapore, 2 major Japanese banks, the 4 largest banks in Canada, 1 large bank in Mexico, and 16 large banks, nonbank financial institutions, and corporations in the United States).
- European RiskCalc Sponsor Group. [As of November 2001, that group included Banco Bilbao Vizcaya Argentaria (Spain), Banco Espirito Santo (Portugal), Bank Austria (Austria), Barclays Bank (United Kingdom), Fortis Bank (Belgium), HypoVereinsBank (Germany), Lloyds TSB (United Kingdom), Royal Bank of Scotland (United Kingdom), and Santander Central Hispano(Spain).]

Fitch Risk Management   Within its Loan Loss Database product (discussed later in this chapter), Fitch Risk Management (FRM) measures commercial loan migration and default by tracking the performance of cohorts of borrowers over time. FRM defines a "cohort" as the sample of all borrowers with loans outstanding on January 1 of a given year. This includes all borrowers borrowing in the year prior to cohort formation plus all surviving borrowers (i.e., borrowers with loans that remain outstanding and have not defaulted) from previous years' cohorts. Each year, a new cohort is created. Once a cohort is established, it remains static (i.e., there are no additional borrowers added to it). Transition matrices are derived by grouping borrowers by their initial risk ratings at the time the cohort is formed and tracking all the borrowers in each risk rating group until they exit the lenders' portfolios. The performance of each cohort is tracked individually and is also aggregated with other cohorts to provide annual and multiyear averages. The system also allows customized transition matrices to be created by borrower variables, such as borrower size, borrower type, and industry of the borrower.

FRM argues that transition and default rates for borrowers in the commercial loan market differ from published rating agency statistics of transition and bond default rates. That is, FRM argues that borrowers with bank-assigned risk ratings tend to exhibit higher transition rates (especially in the noninvestment grade sector) than those institutions with publicly rated debt. FRM explains this difference by pointing out that a majority of banks tend to employ a "point in time" rating assessment as opposed to rating agencies that tend to encompass a "through the cycle" assessment of

EXHIBIT 3.3 Historical Default Probabilities from Standard & Poor's Risk Solutions' CreditPro

All Industries and Countries
Pool: ALL (1991–2000), N.R. Adjusted

	Y1	Y2	Y3	Y4	Y5	Y6	Y7	Y8	Y9	Y10
AAA	0	0	0.06	0.13	0.13	0.13	0.13	0.13	0.13	0.13
AA	0.02	0.06	0.08	0.11	0.15	0.19	0.24	0.32	0.44	0.67
A	0.03	0.07	0.11	0.16	0.25	0.33	0.44	0.55	0.73	0.73
BBB	0.2	0.38	0.62	1.03	1.49	1.87	2.12	2.4	2.71	3.25
BB	0.83	2.39	4.32	5.9	7.44	9.12	10.52	11.5	12.95	13.78
B	6.06	12.37	16.74	19.78	22.15	24.21	26.69	28.57	29.4	30.45
CCC	27.07	35.12	40.36	44.55	47.73	49.52	50.94	51.73	54.09	55.73
Inv. grade	0.08	0.15	0.24	0.38	0.53	0.66	0.78	0.91	1.08	1.26
Spec. grade	4.45	8.53	11.72	14.08	16.08	17.94	19.83	21.19	22.46	23.47

All Industries and Countries
Pool: ALL (1995–2000), N. R. Adjusted

	Y1	Y2	Y3	Y4	Y5	Y6
AAA	0	0	0	0	0	0
AA	0.03	0.06	0.11	0.17	0.27	0.27
A	0.03	0.07	0.12	0.18	0.29	0.38
BBB	0.23	0.46	0.76	1.32	2.08	2.39
BB	0.85	2.46	4.99	7.35	9.72	12.06
B	5.78	12.64	17.79	21.76	25.1	27.57
CCC	27.78	35.96	40.96	46.68	48.81	52.26
Inv. grade	0.09	0.18	0.3	0.49	0.76	0.88
Spec. grade	4.16	8.5	12.32	15.49	18.3	20.73

Source: Standard & Poor's Risk Solutions.

EXHIBIT 3.4 Transition Matrix from Standard & Poor's Risk Solutions' CreditPro

One-Year Transition Matrix

All Industries and Countries
Pool: ALL (1981–2000), N. R. Adjusted

	AAA	AA	A	BBB	BB	B	CCC	D
AAA	93.65	5.83	0.4	0.09	0.03	0	0	0
AA	0.66	91.72	6.95	0.49	0.06	0.09	0.02	0.01
A	0.07	2.25	91.76	5.18	0.49	0.2	0.01	0.04
BBB	0.03	0.26	4.83	89.25	4.44	0.8	0.15	0.24
BB	0.03	0.06	0.44	6.66	83.23	7.46	1.04	1.07
B	0	0.1	0.32	0.46	5.72	83.62	3.84	5.94
CCC	0.15	0	0.29	0.88	1.91	10.28	61.23	25.26

Source: Standard & Poor's Risk Solutions.

credit risk. If this is the case, bank-assigned risk ratings would exhibit more upgrades and downgrades than rating agency assessments.

Empirical Analysis of Defaults   The most cited empirical analysis of defaults is the work done by Ed Altman at New York University. Professor Altman first applied survival analysis to cohorts of rated bonds in 1989 in a paper that appeared in the *Journal of Finance*. This analysis was subsequently updated in 1998.

The calculation of mortality rates proceeds as follows: From a given starting year and rating category, define the dollar value of bonds defaulting in year t as D and the dollar value of bonds *from the original pool* that were still around in year t (i.e., the "surviving population") as S. Then the marginal mortality rate in year t is

$$(\text{Marginal Mortality Rate})_t = \frac{D}{S}$$

Probabilities of Default Predicted Using Financial Statement Data

A number of models predict *current* default probabilities using financial statement data. The logical structure of this set of models is straightforward and can be thought of as proceeding in two steps:

1. Historical data on defaults (or ratings) is *related* to observable characteristics of individual firms. The observable characteristics are primar-

ily financial statement data. The relation between defaults and the financial statement data is obtained via a statistical estimation, such as regression analysis, discriminant analysis, maximum likelihood estimation, probit or logit estimation, neural networks, or proximal support vector machines.

2. Inputting current values of the observable characteristics of individual firms, the *relations* quantified in Step 1 are used to predict the likelihood of default (or a credit rating).

Regression Analysis

The most widely used technique for relating one variable to another (or to a group of other variables) is *regression analysis*. A linear regression—also referred to as "ordinary-least-squares" (OLS) estimation—estimates a linear relation between the dependent and independent (explanatory) variables by minimizing the sum of the squared errors.

It's simple to see how this works in the case of a single independent (explanatory) variable. Suppose we have the set of data on rainfall (the independent variable) and crop yield (the dependent) variable illustrated by the dots in the following diagram.

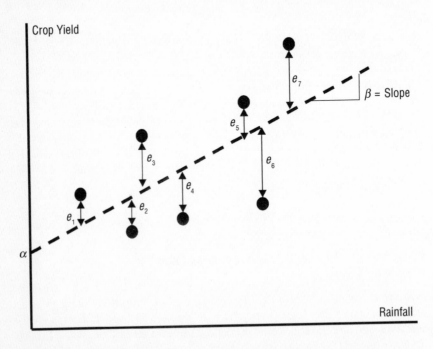

Linear regression provides an estimate of the straight line

$$(\text{Crop Yield}) = \alpha + \beta\,(\text{Rainfall})$$

This is accomplished by selecting the values of α (the intercept) and β (the slope) that will minimize the sum of the squared errors, where the errors are illustrated by the distances e_i in the diagram.

While it's not as easy to see in the case of several explanatory variables (i.e., a multivariate regression), the process is the same. If there are three explanatory variables—x_1, x_2, and x_3—the linear function that will be estimated is

$$y = \alpha + \beta_1 x_1 + \beta_2 x_2 + \beta_3 x_3$$

Regression analysis selects the values of the intercept (α) and the slope terms (β_1, β_2, and β_3) that will minimize the sum of the squared errors.

We would like to use OLS regression to estimate a probability of default equation

$$\text{Probability of Default} = \alpha + \beta_1 x_1 + \beta_2 x_2 + \beta_3 x_3$$

However, such an estimation is tricky, for two reasons.

1. The first reason comes from the fact that we need a data set (as large as possible) to estimate the regression coefficients. So this means we need to find a data set comprised of *predictors of the probability of default* or independent variables (the x's) and the dependent quantities—the probability of default for the firms in the data set. That immediately leads to a question: How does one observe a probability of default for a particular firm in the real world? The answer is that it is not possible. To directly observe probabilities for a particular firm, we would need to track a collection of identical firms. That is, if we could, we would look at 1,000 *identical* firms and see how many defaulted after going through identical economic conditions. This would lead to a "true" probability of default for a particular firm. But we have no way of doing this in reality, so we would need to look at pools of very similar firms. But this leads to the problem of scarcity of data, so in practice this is not feasible.
2. The second reason is that predicted default probability must be between zero and one. The likelihood of nonsensical probabilities increases with lower correlation of the inputs to default probability and for very high or very low credit quality obligors.

The way around these problems entails modeling *default events*, rather than modeling the *probability of default*. We will see several tools that do this in this section.

Since all the financial statement data models are rooted in Ed Altman's Z-score measure, we begin there.

Z-Scores and the ZETA®² Credit Risk Model—Zeta Services, Inc. Ed Altman's original Z-Score model was published in 1968. An expanded version of this approach, referred to as ZETA, was introduced in 1977.

The ZETA model relates historical defaults to firm-specific, financial statement data relating to capital structure, income stability, liquidity, profitability, ability to service debt, and size.

Model Structure/Analytics   The equation to be estimated in the Zeta Credit Risk model is

$$\text{Zeta} = V_1X_1 + V_2X_2 + V_3X_3 + V_4X_4 + V_5X_5 + V_6X_6 + V_7X_7$$

where the X_i are the financial statement data inputs (see section on Inputs) and parameters $V_1 \ldots V_7$ are estimated using a multivariate, discriminant analysis for a sample of bankrupt and nonbankrupt firms.

Discriminant Analysis

A limitation of ordinary linear models is the requirement that the dependent variable is continuous rather than discrete, but many interesting variables are categorical (discrete)—patients may live or die, firms may go bankrupt or stay solvent, and so on. Discriminant analysis is one of a range of techniques developed for analyzing data with categorical dependent variables.

The purpose of discriminant analysis is to predict membership in two or more mutually exclusive groups from a set of predictors. Applied in this context, we want to predict whether firms will default over a specified period based on knowledge of their asset size, capital structure, EBITDA, and so on.

Discriminant analysis is not a regression model. Rather, it is the inverse of a one-way multivariate analysis of variance (ANOVA). That is, instead of minimizing the sum of squared errors, discriminant analysis maximizes the ratio of "between group variance" to "within group variance" (where the groups could be "those that default" and "those that survive"). Mathematically, for two-category dependent variables (e.g, default/no-default), ANOVA and discriminant analysis are the same. The discriminant function is the linear combination of the independent variables that yields the largest mean differences between the groups.

If the *discriminant score* of the function is *less than or equal to the cutoff score*, the case is classed as 0; if it is *above the cutoff score*, it is classed as 1.

To make this more concrete, let's look at a simple case. We first need to decide what time horizon to use for the default event. Suppose we decide on a one-year time horizon. Then, we need to use the values of the predictor variables (i.e., financial data) of each firm a year prior to the event of default. Though it is less clear as to what time point to use for collecting the financial data of nondefaulting firms, one might choose some sort of consistent scheme (for example, using averages of financial data for the different one-year prior to default time points).

Suppose our default model has just one predictor variable—a financial ratio—and we want to estimate the relation between this variable and default, using a database of 40 defaults and 400 nondefaults. In the regression, we set $y = 1$ for default and $y = 0$ for no default and we weight each default by the multiple of nondefaults to defaults (i.e., 10). The resulting regression equation is shown in the following diagram.

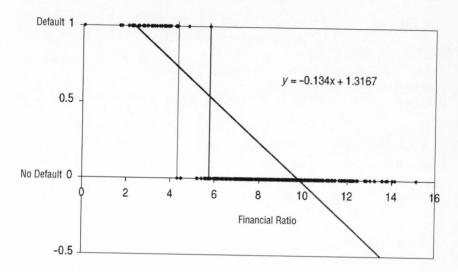

Finally, we must specify the *cutoff score* to classify new (i.e., out-of-sample) cases as either defaulting or not defaulting. For this illustration, the cutoff point would probably lie somewhere between the left vertical line (passing through the minimum financial predictor value among the nondefaults) and the right vertical line (passing through the maximum financial predictor value among the defaults). For this illustrative model, if the higher cutoff (left vertical line) were used, there are two firms that actually defaulted (out of 40) that would be classified as no-defaults while all the no-defaults would be classified as no-default. If the right vertical line were used as a cutoff (lower cutoff score), 10 nondefaulting firms (out of 400) would be classified as defaulting, while all defaulting firms would be classified as defaulting. (We will return to this in the next box.)

Scores predicted in discriminant analysis are linear in the explanatory variables.

Altman (2000) claims the following accuracy results from back testing of the model.

Years Prior to Event	Bankruptcies Correctly Predicted	Non-Bankruptcies Correctly Predicted
1	96.2%	89.7%
2	84.9	93.1
3	74.5	91.4
4	68.1	89.5
5	69.8	82.1

Note that column 2 is related to Type 1 errors, while column three indicates Type 2 errors.

TYPE 1 AND TYPE 2 ERRORS

In any estimation process, errors are always a possibility. Statisticians talk about two types of errors.

The Type 1 error is the more serious. Since it makes its decision on the basis of evidence presented to it, a jury can make an error; and the most serious error—the Type 1 error—would be to convict an innocent person. In the realm of probabilities of default, the Type 1 error would be that the model has predicted no default when in actuality that company later did default.

In the jury example, the Type 2 error would be to acquit a guilty person. In probabilities of default, the Type 2 error occurs when the model predicts default for a company that does not default.

The problem is that actions designed to reduce Type 1 errors will increase Type 2 errors.

To illustrate this, look again at the illustrative model used in the preceding box. The higher cutoff (left vertical line) would give an *in-sample* Type 1 error of 5% ($2/40 = 0.05$) and a Type 2 error of 0%. The lower cutoff would result in a Type 1 error of 0% and a Type 2 error of 2.5% ($10/400 = 0.025$). This lower cutoff is considered more conservative than the higher one and would more likely be used to classify firms.

Zeta Services also compares the average ZETA scores of the model to companies within a credit rating:

S&P Rating	Average Zeta Score
AAA	9.1
AA	7.3
A	5.1
BBB	2.8
BB	0.5
B	−2.1
CCC	−5.0
CC	−7.5
C	−8.0

Zeta Services asserts that they "are not interested in bankruptcy per se, but feel that it is an unequivocal credit standard. The ZETA model compares a company's operating and financial characteristics to those firms which have already failed." Zeta Services summarizes the relevance of bankruptcy to credit modeling by the following.

■ Bankruptcy is a relatively objective standard.
■ Bankruptcy is valuable for study because it facilitates empirical determination of financial characteristics that separate bankrupt companies from non-bankrupt ones.
■ The result of statistically testing bankrupt companies is a series of equations that calculate a credit score for any industrial company about which there is adequate information.
■ In practice, low-scoring companies have a much higher incidence of bankruptcy than high-scoring companies.
■ Bankruptcy is correlated with other pre-bankruptcy liquidity problems, such as passing on common and preferred dividends, loan restructuring, forced sale of assets, and self-liquidation. These pre-bankruptcy problems are much more highly associated with low ZETA credit score companies than high-scoring companies.

Applicability ZETA scores are applicable to both public and private non-financial firms. Zeta Services notes that the application should not be applied to the financial statements of banks, finance companies, insurance companies, municipals, real estate development/management, savings and loans, broker/dealers, and nonprofits.

Inputs The ZETA credit risk model uses the following borrower financial statement data and ratios as inputs:

■ Return on Assets (EBIT/Total Assets)
■ Standard error of estimate around a 5- to 10-year trend in (1).
■ Debt service (EBIT/Total Interest Payments)
■ Cumulative Profitability (Retained Earnings/Total Assets)
■ Liquidity, measured by the Current Ratio
■ Capitalization (Common Equity/Total Capital). A 5-year average is used.
■ Log(Total Assets)

(Altman's original Z-Score Model related defaults to five financial statement variables or ratios: working capital/total assets, retained earnings/total assets, earnings before interest and taxes/total assets, market value of equity/book value of total liabilities, and sales/total assets.)

Database ZETA provides databases of pre-calculated scores that are included in the software licenses and are divided into two groups: (1) bond rating database and (2) industry database. Each database receives monthly and quarterly reports. They are organized as follows.

1. Bond rating database
   - High yield bonds (350 companies rated)
   - Convertible bonds (425 companies rated)
   - High grade bond database (375 companies rated)
2. Industry database is sorted into
   - 1,700 industries (4-digit SIC)
   - 300 groups (3-digit SIC)
   - 70 major industrial groups (2-digit SIC)

The quarterly reports include alphabetic listing of companies, a ranked listing (from highest ZETA score to lowest), 3 (industrial) or 10 (bonds) years' credit profile for each company, and for the bonds, a differential report highlighting the differences in credit judgment between ZETA and S&P and Moody's.

Outputs   The output is a numerical credit score that may be mapped to any existing rating system (i.e., bond ratings, regulatory ratings, or ratings defined by individual banks or other financial institutions). This allows Zeta Services to create a correspondence between public debt ratings and ratings assigned to private companies by banks or others. Zeta Services also estimates the probability of default associated with its ZETA credit scores by tracking the record of scores compared with nonfinancial corporate bonds defaulting since 1986.

CreditModel—Standard & Poor's Risk Solutions   CreditModel is an Internet-delivered product designed to empirically replicate the judgments made by S&P's own industry-specialized credit rating analysts. It was developed by analyzing relationships between financial data and ratings within each sector. The result was a series of scoring models that embody Standard & Poor's views of credit in specific industries and regions. The interpretation of the financial data is shaped by S&P's experience and views of the sector.

Model Structure   There are 26 distinct models, each applicable to companies in specific industries and regions. Certain models, such as the one for European retailers, are devoted to scoring companies in one region. Other models are used for both North American and European firms. An airline model is applicable to firms in Europe, North America, and Japan.

The models evaluate each input in the context of other inputs, recognizing nonlinear relationships.

All models are systematically validated. From the data required to develop each model, a representative sample is held back. This holdback sample, or validation set, as well as the training data, are used to test the models. Scores generated during the tests are compared to the actual Standard & Poor's ratings for the test companies.

As illustrated in Exhibit 3.5, S&P indicates that about 96% of the test scores obtained from CreditModel fell within two rating notches of the actual rating.

All models are tested at least once a year, as new financial data become available. In addition, models are periodically revised to incorporate more recent financial data and Standard & Poor's evolving views of credit risk.

EXHIBIT 3.5 Performance of CreditModels Training and Validation Samples (1997–2000)

Model	Score = Rating	Score within 1 Notch	Score within 2 Notches	Correlation Coefficient	Sample Size
Chemicals[1]	67.08%	88.20%	96.89%	0.9709	161
Consumer Products, Branded[1]	82.81%	95.48%	97.29%	0.9876	221
Consumer Products, Other[1]	67.78%	93.70%	97.78%	0.9760	270
Drugs[1]	80.32%	88.15%	93.43%	0.9788	137
Electronic Media[1]	80.12%	93.98%	96.39%	0.9649	166
Food Stores & Restaurants[1]	78.10%	92.70%	96.35%	0.9795	137
Forest & Building Products[1]	55.00%	88.64%	96.82%	0.9634	220
Healthcare Services[1]	64.23%	88.62%	96.75%	0.9763	123
Metals[1]	78.80%	86.96%	96.20%	0.9744	184
Retail[1]	53.72%	84.83%	92.45%	0.9308	294
Aerospace and Defense[2]	63.76%	83.89%	92.62%	0.9595	149
Airline[3]	69.54%	90.61%	92.47%	0.9523	93
Automotive[2]	55.95%	88.10%	97.02%	0.969	168
Energy[2]	76.47%	92.38%	96.78%	0.9726	249
High-Tech Manufacturers[2]	57.49%	83.62%	91.29%	0.9362	287
Hotel & Gaming[2]	72.34%	95.21%	98.40%	0.9778	188
Industrial Products[2]	66.18%	93.24%	97.35%	0.9703	340
Print Media[2]	67.08%	87.85%	97.08%	0.9705	131
Services for Business & Industry[2]	73.15%	90.39%	97.29%	0.9667	406

[1]North America only
[2]North America and Europe
[3]North America, Europe, and Japan
Source: Standard & Poor's Risk Solutions.

Analytics CreditModel was originally based on a collection of neural network models. In 2002, S&P Risk Solutions replaced the neural network models with proximal support vector (PSV) models.

In 2002, S&P indicated that the decision to switch to proximal support vector (PSV) machine classifier models was based on speed, accuracy, and robustness. S&P claims that "solutions are stable with respect to small changes in the data. A small change in an input will not result in a large score change."

Neural Network and Proximal Support Vector Models

NEURAL NETWORKS

Neural networks are behavior models that "learn" behavior through so-called "neural nets." A neural net that is ignorant at the beginning "learns" its pattern or "direction" from a collection of many examples. In the case of CreditModel, historical financial information (10 inputs) and the risk rating of the firm are used as learning examples. A statistical model is built as a result of this learning process.

The following figure attempts to show the detail of the operation on a neural net process. Data on a particular firm is inputted into the neural net. The various pieces of data on the firms are filtered/transmitted through the connections, being modified until they reach the bottom of the network with a set of results (e.g., a rating).

Then how does the neural net actually "learn"? Once the data are inputted into the neural net, these values are "propagated" toward the output, predicted values. Initially the predicted values would most likely contain large errors. The computed "error values" (the difference between the expected value and the actual output value) are then "back-propagated" by backtracking the network connections—modifying the weights proportionally to each one's contribution to the total error value. These adjustments are repeated and in this manner the model is improved.

PROXIMAL SUPPORT VECTOR (PSV) MODELS

Development work on support vector models began more than 25 years ago. Support vector machines reduce the task of estimating a rating to an optimization problem, as neural network models do.

For the application we are considering, the modeling problem may be viewed as a series of classification problems. That is, given the data we have on a particular firm, we need to classify that firm according to membership in the 19 categories:

AAA
AA+ or Better
. . .
CCC– or Better

The output of these classification models can be used to determine a "score" for each of the firms. Support vector machines solve such classification problems.

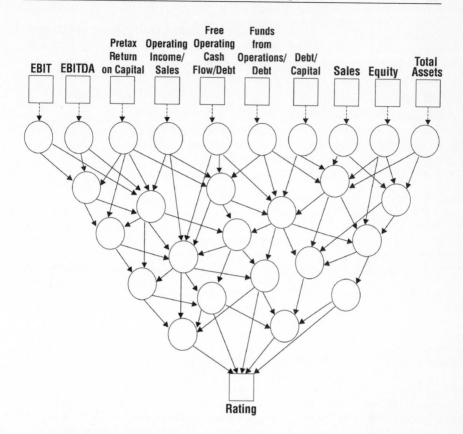

Rating

S&P claims that support vector models in general "will not get stuck in a solution that represents a local (false) optimum." The reason for this assertion is that the proximal support vector model classification decision surface has parameters that are solutions of a strictly convex optimization problem (see Fung and Mangasarian, 2001). Such problems have a unique global optimum. There is only one global optimum that can reliably be found numerically. This means that "a small change in the training data will not result in a large change in the model."

Fung and Mangasarian have shown that support vector models have successfully solved problems that have stumped neural network models.

The PSV classifiers are a type of improved support vector models (i.e., Fung and Mangasarian indicate that PSV models are related to support vector machines and have comparable accuracy, but are faster.

Applicability   CreditModel currently evaluates nonfinancial firms based in North America, Japan, and western Europe. S&P asserts that CreditModel is effective for publicly and privately owned firms with revenues of at least $50 million ($75 million for North American and European firms).

S&P asserts that CreditModel can be used to:

- Determine a credit score for a single company or for every company in a portfolio.
- Efficiently screen new borrowers, counterparties, or customers.
- Identify marginal credits for more intensive review.
- Benchmark internal credit scoring systems against a globally recognized standard for which default rates are published.
- Perform sensitivity analysis.
- Evaluate the consistency of internal credit ratings.
- Analyze credits for securitization.

Inputs   While the required data inputs vary slightly by region and industry, the following list generally summarizes the inputs required:

> Earnings Before Interest and Taxes (EBIT) interest coverage
> Earnings Before Interest, Taxes, Depreciation, and Amortization (EBITDA) interest coverage
> Pretax return on capital
> Operating income/sales
> Free operating cash flow/total debt
> Funds from operations/total debt
> Total debt/capital
> Sales
> Equity
> Total Assets

All CreditModel financial data entries are automatically provided by Standard & Poor's Compustat® for more than 13,000 public companies. Users are able to modify these data. Companies may be scored individually or in a batch. For private firms, data are entered manually. The model is able to *impute* values for inputs that may not be available to the user, based on the other given inputs to CM.

A user manual, including a glossary of financial terms and formulas for the ratios, is provided within the system.

Output   CreditModel scores are represented with S&P rating symbols—but shown in lowercase to indicate they are quantitatively derived *estimates* of S&P's credit ratings. As a CreditModel score is an estimate of a Standard & Poor's credit rating, the default rates associated with ratings may be reasonably applied to CreditModel scores. In fact, a very high correlation between CreditModel scores and Standard & Poor's credit ratings has been demonstrated. For each score, the associated one-year, three-year, and five-year default rates from Standard & Poor's most recent historical default study are displayed on the score report. (The default probabilities in CreditModel are the actual historical average cumulative incidence of default for each rating.) S&P states that "Standard & Poor's default studies have found a clear correlation between credit ratings and default risk: the higher the rating, the lower the probability of default."

In addition to these implied default probabilities, the output of Credit-Model also indicates the three *inputs* that have the most influence on the credit score. This is what they call "input sensitivity ranking." One drawback of CreditModel is that it cannot provide any greater resolution to creditworthiness than the 19 S&P ratings.

Default Filter—S&P Risk Solutions   Default Filter is a hybrid model that relates probabilities of default to credit factor information (including financial information) on the obligor and to user-defined macroeconomic variables. It was initially developed by Bankers Trust Company, and was originally targeted for pricing credit risk in emerging markets where obligor information is scarce. Default Filter was acquired by S&P Risk Solutions in the summer of 2002.

Model Structure/Analytics   The model structure is comprised of three main elements:

1. Statistical diagnostic tools to guide users in building homogeneous representative historical databases to be used for validation purposes and ongoing data controls.
2. Credit factor data optimization routine made up of several optimization loops and loosely based on neural network processing principles. (When reviewing this section prior to publication, S&P Risk Solutions stressed that it is not a neural network.)
3. Impact of future anticipated macroeconomic conditions defined in terms of change in the GDP, sectorial growth rate in any country, foreign exchange rate, and interest rates.

The first two are used to relate default probabilities to credit factor (including financial) information, while the third element is like a macrofactor model.

Default Filter is able to use as an input any credit factor (financial, qualitative, business, or market price) that is historically available and is able to test their predictive power.

S&P Risk Solutions highlights the optimization routine of Default Filter. They argue that the optimization routine provides for stability of the coefficients associated to individual credit factors, where stability is defined in terms of the standard deviation of the coefficients. S&P Risk Solutions asserts that, as a result, Default Filter returns "the most stable logistic function that has the highest predictive power."

Default Filter borrows a number of processing principles from neural network processing techniques:

- The credit factors used as input are not usually linearly and independently related.
- There are potentially hidden "correlations" between credit factor variables and these "correlations" are not necessarily linear relationships.
- There is no known relationship between input and output. This relationship needs to be built through repeated layers of trials and errors that progressively retain positive trial experiences.
- The objective is to optimize the use of credit factor input to maximize an output.

However, S&P Risk Solutions stresses that Default Filter has characteristics that differentiate it from a neural network model:

- The credit factors used as input must pass the test of homogeneity/representativity before being used.
- Users are able to incorporate their own views and assumptions in the process.

The model is validated through both user-defined stress tests on individual obligors or portfolios and through the application of six back-test validation criteria to the default probability results:

1. Type 1 and Type 2 accuracy observed on out-of-sample dataset.
2. Using a user-defined number of (e.g., 100) randomly extracted out-of-sample datasets, the accuracy of the model is tracked to measure its stability. Each randomly extracted subset of the model is compared with that for two naive credit-risk predictive rules.
   - *Rule 1: There will be no default next year.*
   - *Rule 2: Probabilities of default next year are a function of the rate of default observed the previous year.*
3. Comparison of the observed portfolio (or individual rating class) default year the following year and of the compilation of the predicted portfolio default rate, measured as an arithmetic average of individual probabilities of default.
4. Percentage deviation of individual default probabilities for individual obligors if any of the random subset used for validation criteria 2 are used to calibrate the logistic function.

5. Number of credit factors retained in the system and sanity check on the signs assigned to each credit factor. (S&P Risk Solutions points out that this is of significance only if the user wants to convert the results of the logistic function into a linear function equivalent.)
6. Relationship between the most significant factor identified by the system and the resulting probabilities of default. (S&P Risk Solutions points out that this is significant if the user chooses to stress-test results using identified correlations between the most significant default drivers and all other inputs.)

Inputs   Any user-defined financial factors, qualitative factors, and market price related factors may be used as input into Default Filter, as long as they are available historically. Following is an illustrative example of some of the financial data that may be used within Default Filter's spreading tool.

Balance Sheet	Income Statement
Current Assets	Turnover
Cash and Securities	Gross Profit
Inventories	EBIT
Accounts Receivable	Interest Expense
Total Assets	Cash Dividend
Current Liabilities	Net Profit before Tax
Accounts Payable	Net Profit after Tax
Total Interest Bearing Debt	Cash Flow
Total Debt	
Total Liabilities	
Tangible Net Worth	

Users usually define different financial and/or qualitative factors per industry. Market price related factors often used include bond spread and equity volatility related measures.

Other inputs include recovery rate (either specified by the user or modeled by Default Filter), the hurdle RAROC rate, and the tax rate. There are also fields for scenario options, and percentage changes of the GDP, sectorial growth, foreign exchange rates, and interest rates for user-defined countries.

Database   The portal and in-house installation can make use of a comprehensive validation database of historical European and Asian default information. (A "data scrubbing" utility is included to maintain the accuracy of historical data and to track its representativity to any designated database.) These data are mostly used when a bank's own data are incomplete or insufficient.

The credit default database contains credit factors such as financial, qualitative or industrial factors, history of default, and industry and country information.

Outputs   Default Filter provides the default probability and an implied credit rating (in the S&P format). It also provides an estimate of loss under macroeconomic stress (either expected and/or unexpected). Default Filter can also provide joint probability recovery functions if historical data are available for validation.

Credit Rating System—Fitch Risk Management   Credit Rating System (CRS) produces long-term issuer ratings on a rating agency scale (i.e., AAA–C). In 2002, Fitch Risk Management purchased CRS from Credit Suisse First Boston, which had developed the models to support its credit function.

CRS currently contains models for private and public companies (excluding real estate companies) and utilities. Fitch Risk Management indicated that models for banks are under development. In order to compare this model with the other financial statement models in this section, this discussion focuses on the model CRS employs for private companies.[3]

CRS is a regression model that utilizes historic financial information to produce an "agency like" rating. The models were developed using agency ratings and historical financial data for approximately 1,300 corporates. The models for corporates do not contain differentiation by region. However, the models do take account of a company's industrial classification.

The corporate models use the following financial measures: ROA, Total Debt/EBITDA, Total Debt/Capitalization, EBITDA/Interest Expense, and Total Assets.

The CRS models are tested using a standard "hold out" process, in which the performance of the model estimated using the "build sample" is compared to randomly selected subsets of the "hold out sample." Fitch Risk Management indicates that the private model is within two notches of the agency ratings 81% of the time.[4] Fitch Risk Management notes that, when CRS differs from the ratings agencies, the agency ratings tend to migrate in the same direction as the model ratings.

CRS supports automatic uploading of financial data from the vendors of such information and also allows the user to manually input the data if they are unavailable from a commercial service. Regardless of the way the data are fed into the system, it automatically generates a comprehensive set of financial ratios, which are used to drive the rating model.

CRS produces ratings that are similar to long-term issuer ratings from the major rating agencies. It also provides the user with financial spreads including ratio calculations. And CRS identifies which financial measures are the model drivers. CRS also supports sensitivity analysis and side-by-side peer group comparisons.

RiskCalc for Private Companies—Moody's Risk Management Services The RiskCalc model from Moody's for non-publicly traded firms is generally labeled as a multivariate, *probit* model of default.

Probit and Logit Estimation

Earlier we talked about discriminant analysis, a way to classify objects in two or more categories—Zeta Services has one such implementation. The goal of that model is to predict bankruptcy over a one-or-more-year time horizon.

As we have argued earlier, to model probability of default directly using a linear regression model is not meaningful because we cannot directly observe probabilities of default for particular firms.

To resolve this problem, if one could find a function *f* that (1) depends on the individual default probability *p* but that also depends on the predictor variables (i.e., financial data or ratios) and (2) could take *any value* from negative infinity to positive infinity, then we could model *f* using a linear equation such as

$$f_j = \alpha_j + \beta_{1j}X_{1j} + \beta_{2j}X_{2j} + \ldots + \beta_{kj}X_{kj} \qquad (1)$$

where the subscript *j* refers to the *j*th case/firm. If, for the function f, we use the inverse standard normal cumulative distribution—$f_j \equiv N^{-1}[p_j]$—then the resulting estimation equation is called a *probit* model. If, for the function f, we use the logistic function—$f_j \equiv \ln[p_j/(1 - p_j)]$—the resulting estimation equation is called a "logit model." (Here $\ln(x)$ is the natural (i.e., to the base *e*) logarithm of *x*.)

If we solve for the probability p_j, we obtain the estimation models:

$$\text{Probit model:} \qquad p_j = N[f_j] \qquad (2)$$

$$\text{Logit model:} \qquad p_j = \frac{1}{1 + \exp(-f_j)} \qquad (3)$$

For both equations, if *f* approaches minus infinity, *p* approaches zero and if *f* approaches infinity, *p* approaches 1, thus ensuring the boundary conditions of *p*. The following diagram shows both functions plotted with probability on the horizontal axis. Notice the similarity in the *shapes* of the two curves.

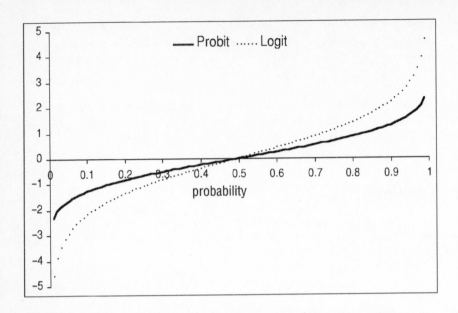

The most widely used method of estimating the k factor loadings $(\beta_1 \ldots \beta_k)$ is by performing a maximum likelihood estimation (MLE). This entails finding the maximum of the product of all default probabilities for defaulted firms and survival probabilities (by definition survival probability plus default probability equals one) for nondefaulted firms:

$$Likelihood \equiv L = \prod_{j=1}^{n}\left((p_j)^{y_j}(1-p_j)^{1-y_j}\right) \tag{4}$$

where

 j is the index of the firm
 p_j is determined by the predictor variables (i.e., the financial ratios) through the logit
   or probit functions
 $y_j = 1$ indicates firm j defaulted
 $y_j = 0$ indicates firm j did not default, and
 n is the number of firms in the data set used to estimate the relation.

These n cases could be randomly chosen firms from across all industries, or if one wished to focus on one industry, then from across sectors in the industry. The important point here is that one needs to have a database that is large enough to cover a good number of default events (e.g., at least 100).

One then maximizes the *logarithm* of the likelihood L, given by

$$\ln[L] = \sum_{j=1}^{n}\left(y_j \ln[p_j] + (1-y_j)\ln[1-p_j]\right)$$

where

> y_j is the observed default in the training dataset for the jth firm and is equal to 1 if the firm has defaulted or 0 if it has not, and
>
> p_j is the probability of default determined from the regression equations (1) and either (2) or (3).

Let's look at an example of using equation (3). Suppose $n = 6$ and $(y_1, \ldots, y_6) = (0, 1, 0, 0, 1, 0)$; then the likelihood equation (4) becomes

$$L_1 = (1 - p_1)(p_2)(1 - p_3)(1 - p_4)(p_5)(1 - p_6)$$

Finding the maximum of this equation entails finding a set of factor loadings such that the probability of default is maximized for a defaulting firm and minimized (i.e., $1 - p_j$ is maximized) for a nondefaulting firm. Remember that each p_j is determined by the estimated coefficients $(\beta_1 \ldots \beta_k)$, the financial ratios X_{ij} for the particular (jth) case, and either the cumulative standard normal distribution [probit model—equation (2)] or the logistic function [logit model—equation (3)].

The constant coefficient is determined directly by the equation

$$\ln[L_0] = n_0 \ln\left[\frac{n_0}{n}\right] + n_1 \ln\left[\frac{n_1}{n}\right]$$

where

> $\ln(L_0)$ is the natural log of the (logit or probit) likelihood of the null model (intercept only)
>
> n_0 is the number of observations with a value of 0 (zero = no default)
>
> n_1 is the number of observations with a value of 1 (= default) and
>
> n is the total number of observations.

There are several computational methods (optimization algorithms) to obtain the maximum likelihood (Newton–Raphson, quasi-Newton, Simplex, etc.).

Moody's claims that the model's key advantage derives from Moody's unique and proprietary middle market private firm financial statement and default database—Credit Research Database (see Falkenstein, 2000). This database comprises 28,104 companies and 1,604 defaults. From this database and others for public firms, Moody's also claims that the relationship between financial predictor variables and default risk varies substantially between public and private firms.

The model targets middle market (asset size > $100,000) private firms (i.e., about 2 million firms in the United States), extending up to publicly traded companies. The private firm model of RiskCalc does not have industry-specific models.

While inputs vary by country, RiskCalc for Private Companies generally uses 17 inputs that are converted to 10 ratios.

Inputs	Ratios
Assets (2 yrs.)	Assets/CPI
Cost of Goods Sold	Inventories/COGS
Current Assets	Liabilities/Assets
Current Liabilities	Net Income Growth
Inventory	Net Income / Assets
Liabilities	Quick Ratio
Net Income (2 yrs.)	Retained Earnings/Assets
Retained Earnings	Sales Growth
Sales (2 yrs.)	Cash/Assets
Cash & Equivalents	Debt Service Coverage Ratio
EBIT	
Interest Expense	
Extraordinary Items (2 yrs.)	

Moody's observes that the input financial ratios are highly "nonnormally" distributed and consequently adds another layer to the probit regression by introducing transformation functions derived empirically on the financial ratios. The dependence of five-year cumulative default probabilities was obtained in a univariate nonparametric analysis. ("Nonparametric estimation" refers to a collection of techniques for fitting a curve when there is little a priori knowledge about its shape. Many nonparametric procedures are based on using the ranks of numbers instead of the numbers themselves.) This process determines a *transformation* function T for each ratio x_i. These transformation functions were obtained from Moody's proprietary private firm defaults database.

Thus, the full probit model estimated in RiskCalc is

$$\text{Prob(Default)} = N[\beta' \times T(x)]$$

where β' is the row vector of 10 weights to be estimated, $T(x)$ is the column vector of the 10 transformed financial ratios, and $N[\ldots]$ is the cumulative standard normal distribution function.

Private Firm Model—Moody's KMV   While this discussion is appropriately located under the heading of the models that rely on financial statement data, it may be easier to understand this model if you first read the description of the Moody's KMV public firm model (i.e., Credit Monitor[5] and CreditEdge) in the next section of this chapter. The public firm model was developed first; and the Private Firm Model was constructed with the same logic.

The approach of the Private Firm Model is based on dissecting market information in the form of valuations (prices) and volatility of valuations (business risk) as observed among public firms. This so-called "comparables model" recognizes that values will change over time across industries and geographical regions in a way that reflects important information about future cash flows for a private firm, and their risk. Moody's KMV justifies this approach for various reasons. Moody's KMV asserts:

> *Private firms compete with public firms, buy from the same vendors, sell to the same customers, hire from the same labor pool, and face the same economic tide. Investment choices reflected in market trends and the cash payoffs from these choices influence management decision-making at both private and public firms. A private firm cannot exist in a vacuum; the market pressures on its business ultimately impact it. Ignoring market information and relying entirely on historical financial data is like driving while looking in the rear view mirror: it works very well when the road is straight. Only market information can signal turns in the prospects faced by a private firm. (KMV, 2001)*

The input window for the Private Firm Model is the same as for the Moody's KMV public firm model (Credit Monitor), except that the input market items are not used. In the absence of market equity values, asset value and volatility have to be estimated on the basis of the "comparables analysis" discussed previously and characteristics of the firm obtained from the balance sheet and income statement.

Exhibit 3.6 depicts the drivers and information flow in the Private Firm Model.

The Private Firm Model (like Credit Monitor for public companies, to be described in the next section) has three steps in the determination of the default probability of a firm:

1. Estimate asset value and volatility: The asset value and asset volatility of the private firm are estimated from market data on comparable companies from Credit Monitor coupled with the firm's reported operating cash flow, sales, book value of liabilities, and its industry mix.
2. Calculate the distance to default: The firm's distance to default is calculated from the asset value, asset volatility, and the book value of its liabilities.
3. Calculate the default probability: The default probability is determined by mapping the distance to default to the default rate.

In the Private Firm Model, the estimate of the value of the firm's assets depends on whether the firm has positive EBITDA. Moody's KMV

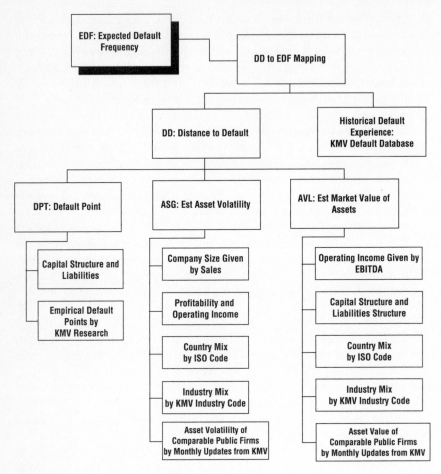

EXHIBIT 3.6 Private Firm Model Drivers
Source: KMV (2001).

argues that EBITDA acts as a proxy for cash a firm can generate from its operations.

The Private Firm Model translates a firm's cash flow into its asset value by using a "multiples approach." According to the KMV documentation,

> *the multiples approach is consistent across all industries, though the size of the multiple will be driven by the market's estimation of the future prospects in each sector, and will move as prospects change. The firm-specific information for the private firm's asset value comes from*

the cash flows it reports. That is, the multiples approach uses the em-
pirical observation that the higher the EBITDA, the greater the value
the market places on the firm. (KMV, 2001)

KMV measures the multiples for country and industry separately, allowing for separate evaluation of the industry and country influences. To
estimate the value of a private firm's assets, the model uses the median
value from firms in the same region and industry with similar cash flow. In
Exhibit 3.7, the filled circles illustrate the relationship between observed
market asset values and cash flows of public firms in one of 61 KMV sectors (North American Steel & Metal Products), and the unfilled circles indicate the Private Firm Model estimates of asset value for each of those
firms, based on treating each as the typical firm in that sector.

In the Private Firm Model, the estimate of asset *volatility* for private
firms is the measure of business risk. Moody's KMV notes that the direct
calculation of the volatility of the market value of assets would usually
require a time series of asset value observations—a technique that is not
feasible for private firms. Instead, Moody's KMV uses another "comparables approach."

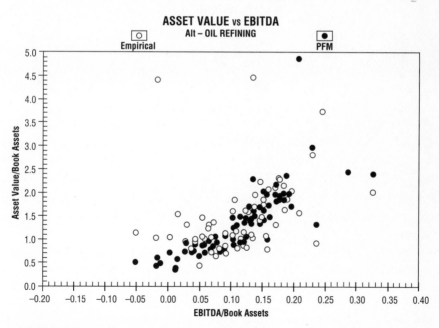

EXHIBIT 3.7   Relation of Asset Value to EBITDA
©2002 KMV LLC.

Moody's KMV argues that, in general, asset volatilities are relatively stable through time and that reestimation is necessary only when industries undergo fundamental changes.

Moody's KMV further argues that a firm's asset volatility is determined by its industry, size, and the region in which it does business.

■ Moody's KMV argues that, for a given size of a firm, the assets of a bank are less risky than those for a beverage retailer, which are, in turn, less risky than the assets of a biotechnology firm. Moody's KMV argues that, in general, growth industries have riskier assets than mature industries.

■ Exhibit 3.8 shows the relationship between observed asset volatility and size for public companies that produce construction materials. The vertical axis shows asset volatility and the horizontal axis shows company size, as measured by sales. Exhibit 3.8 provides an example of an industry in which the larger the firm, the more predictable the cash flows and the less variable the asset value. Moody's KMV argues that larger firms have more diversification (across cus-

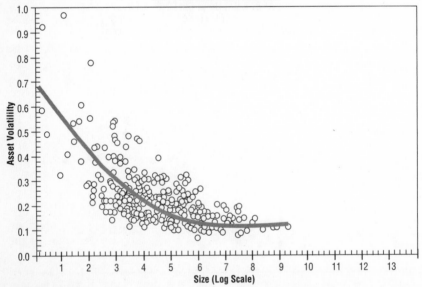

EXHIBIT 3.8   Relation of Volatility of Asset Values to Size of the Firm
©2002 KMV LLC.

tomers, product lines, and regions), so there is less likelihood of a single event wiping out the entire firm.

For each region, Moody's KMV uses the public comparables to estimate a nonlinear relationship between asset size and asset volatility by industry. A line—such as the one in Exhibit 3.8—represents the median firm's asset volatility, given its size, industry, and geographic region. Moody's KMV calls this median volatility "modeled volatility."

However, Moody's KMV modifies this "modeled volatility" by including characteristics specific to the firm. Moody's KMV argues that companies with very high or very low EBITDA relative to their industry tend to be more volatile.

Summary of Financial Statement Data Models   Our discussion of the six financial statement models is summarized in Exhibit 3.9. Exhibits 3.10 and 3.11 summarize the data inputs used by the different models.

Probabilities of Default Implied from Equity Market Data

Credit Monitor and CreditEdge™—Moody's–KMV   In 1991 the KMV Corporation introduced Credit Monitor, a product that produces estimates of the probability of default (referred to as Expected Default Frequency™ or EDF)[6] for publicly traded firms by implying the current market value of the firm's assets and the volatility of the value of those assets from equity market data. In 2002 Moody's acquired KMV and the KMV models were redesignated as Moody's–KMV models.

Moody's–KMV CreditEdge is accessed over the Web and is targeted at the active portfolio manager. Users receive EDF and stock price information updated daily. The interactive format allows users to track company-specific news, set EDF driven alerts on companies in their portfolios, capture current financial data, and be informed of corporate filings.

The Merton Insight   The Moody's–KMV model is based on the "Merton insight," which is that debt behaves like a put option on the value of the firm's assets.

To explain this insight, let's think about a very simple firm financed with equity and a single debt issue that has a face value of $100. Also let's think about a one-year horizon (i.e., imagine that, one year from now, that firm could be liquidated).

EXHIBIT 3.9 Summary of Financial Statement Models

MODEL	Theoretical Underpinning	Model Analytics	Applicability	Inputs
ZETA Credit Scores	Empirical relation between historical defaults and firm-specific financial statement data	Discriminant Analysis	Public and private corporates (U.S. accounting standards). No banks/fin. institutions and insurance companies.	7 financial statement items (or ratios) for the obligor
S&P's CreditModel	Empirical relation of credit ratings to industry, region, and financial data	Proximal Support Vector Model 26 industry and region-specific models	Non-financial public and private firms with revenues >$75 mm	8–11 financial stmt. items and ratios Business risk indicators in some models
S&P's Default Filter	Uses borrower credit information and macroeconomic forecasts	Neural Network Impact of anticipated macro factors through changes in GDP, interest rate, FX	Public and private firms (middle market to large corporates)	11 balance sheet and 8 income statement items, along with macroeconomic data
Fitch Risk Management's Credit Rating System	Empirical relation of long-term issuer ratings to financial and market data	Multivariate Statistical Model	Public and private non-financial firms	Up to 11 financial statement items (and equity data for public firms)
Moody's RiskCalc for Private firms	Empirical relation of default probabilities to financial data	Probit Model	Private firms with at least $100,000 in assets	17 balance sheet and income statement items, used in 10 ratios
Moody's–KMV Private Firm Model	Similar to Credit Monitor: Distance to default calculated from estimates of asset value and volatility	Multivariate statistics to determine asset volatility from sales, industry, and asset size	Non-financials	"Peer" (public) company equity data; financial statement data

EXHIBIT 3.10 Summary of Balance Sheet Data Used by Financial Statement Models

Input	ZETA Credit Scores	S&P's Credit Model	S&P's Default Filter	Fitch Risk Management's Credit Rating System	Moody's RiskCalc for Private Firms	Moody's–KMV Private Firm Model
Cash and short-term securities			✓		✓	
Receivables			✓		✓	
Inventories			✓		✓	
Current assets	✓		✓		✓	
Long-term assets	✓				✓	
Total assets	✓	✓	✓	✓		
Short-term debt	✓	✓	✓	✓		✓
Payables			✓			
Total current liabilities	✓			✓	✓	✓
Long-term debt and capital leases	✓	✓			✓	
Other long-term liabilities	✓				✓	
Total liabilities	✓	✓	✓	✓	✓	✓
Book equity	✓	✓	✓	✓	✓	

EXHIBIT 3.11 Summary of Income Statement and Other Data Used by Financial Statement Models

Input	ZETA Credit Scores	S&P's Credit Model	S&P's Default Filter	Fitch Risk Management's Credit Rating System	Moody's RiskCalc for Private Firms	Moody's–KMV Private Firm Model
Income Statement						
Sales (turnover)		✓	✓		✓	✓
Operating income		✓				
Cost of goods sold		✓	✓		✓	✓
Depreciation		✓	✓			
EBIT or EBITDA	✓	✓	✓	✓	✓	✓
Net interest payments	✓	✓	✓		✓	
Gross interest expense				✓		
Funds from operations				✓		
Other Fin. Stmt. Measures						
Retained earnings	✓				✓	
Capitalization	✓	✓				

How much would the equity be worth when the firm is liquidated? It depends on the value of the assets:

■ If the value of the assets is below the face value of the debt, the equity is worthless: If the assets are worth $50 and the face value of the debt is $100, there is nothing left for the equity holders.

■ It is only when the value of the assets exceeds the face value of the debt that the equity has any value.
   If the value of the assets is $101, the equity is worth $1.
   If the value of the assets is $102, the value of the equity will be $2.

The resulting trace of the value of the equity—the bold line in Panel A of Exhibit 3.12—is equivalent to a long position on a call option on the value of the firm's assets. That remarkable insight is attributed to Fischer Black and Myron Scholes.

Panel A: The Value of Equity

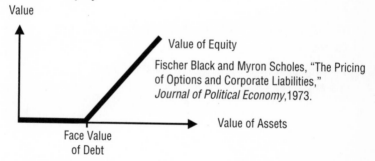

Panel B: The Value of Debt

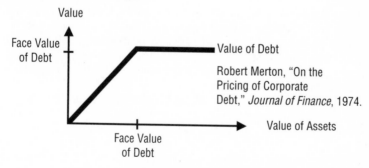

EXHIBIT 3.12   Merton Insight

How much would the debt be worth? It again depends on the value of the assets:

■ If the value of the assets is equal to or below the face value of the debt, the value of the debt will be equal to the value of the assets. If the value of the assets turns out to be $50, the debt holders will get all the $50, because the debt holders have the senior claim. If the assets are worth $75, the debt is worth $75. If the assets are worth $100, the debt is worth $100.

■ If the value of the assets is greater than the face value of the debt, the value of the debt will be equal to its face value. If the value of the assets gets higher than the face value of the debt, the bondholders don't get any more—the additional value accrues to the equity holders. So the value of the debt remains at $100.

The resulting trace of the value of the equity—the bold line in Panel A of Exhibit 3.12—is equivalent to a short position on a put option on the value of the firm's assets. That is Robert Merton's insight.

Holding equity is equivalent to being long a call on the value of the assets.

Holding debt is equivalent to being short a put on the value of the firm's assets.

A Second-Generation Merton-Type Model

There is a problem with implementing the Merton insight directly. To do so, we would need to specify not only the market value of the firm's assets and the volatility of that value but also the complete claim structure of the firm. And that latter problem keeps us from actually implementing the Merton insight itself.

Instead, the KMV model actually implements an extension of the Merton model proposed by Francis Longstaff and Eduardo Schwartz.

The Merton approach posits that a firm will default when asset value falls below the face value of the debt. That is not what we actually observe empirically. Instead, we observe that, when a firm defaults, the value of the assets is considerably below the face value of the claims against the firm.

To deal with this, Longstaff and Schwartz specified a value K below the face value of the firm's debt. And default occurs when the value of the assets hits this value K.

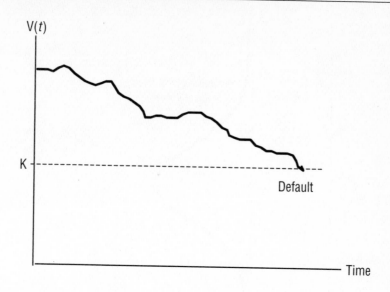

The primary consequence of this change is that the model is now able to be implemented.

Logic of the KMV Approach In order to operationalize the Merton approach, we need to know three things: (1) the value of the firm's assets, (2) the volatility of those assets, and (3) leverage.

Exhibit 3.13 illustrates how KMV's Credit Monitor works. In this diagram, the vertical axis measures values. (To be precise, in the KMV model, all values are expressed as the natural logarithm of the value itself.) The horizontal axis measures time. We evaluate the firm (i.e., pretend that we liquidate the firm) at a point in the future; for this illustration, we use one year from now.

To get started in Exhibit 3.13, we need some current data:

- *Current market value of the firm's assets.* Note that this is the market value of the assets, not the book value. Finding this value is one of the tricks in this approach that we will see when we look at the implementation.
- *Rate of growth of the value of the firm's assets.*
- *Default point.* This is the value that will trigger default and is the point we identified as *K* in the preceding box. In this second-generation Merton model, if the value of the firm's assets falls below this "default point," the firm will default.

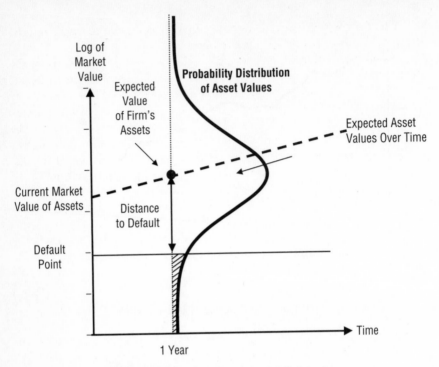

EXHIBIT 3.13   Logic of KMV's Credit Monitor

Using the current market value of the firm's assets and the rate of growth of that value, we can obtain the expected market value for the firm's assets in the future (the dashed line in Exhibit 3.13). The expected market value of the firm's assets one year from now is indicated by the dot in Exhibit 3.13. Note that the expected value of the assets exceeds the default point. A way of expressing what is implied in the diagram is: "*On average*, this firm doesn't have a problem, because the value of the assets *on average* exceeds the default point."

But portfolio managers don't work in an "on average" world. It doesn't matter that on average the firm will not default. What matters is the likelihood that the firm will default in a specific period. So in addition to knowing the expected value, we also need to know the dispersion about the mean. That is, we want to see the distribution of asset values (actually the distribution of the *logarithm* of asset values). This distribution is shown with the bold line in Exhibit 3.13 (This is a two-dimensional representation of a three-dimensional argument. The distribution is actualy rising out of the page.) To get the distribution, we need, at a minimum, a measure of the variance of the returns of the market value of the assets.

This distance between the expected market value of the assets and the default point is called the *distance to default*.

If the distribution of asset value returns is a normal distribution, the determination of the probability of default—which is referred to as *expected default frequency (EDF)* in KMV's model—would be a relatively simple statistics exercise. In the context of Exhibit 3.13, we want to know the percentage of the distribution of asset value returns that fall below the default point. With a normal distribution, we would need to measure the *distance to default* in terms of x number of standard deviations of the distribution of asset values (remember that the standard deviation is the square root of the variance). Then, we would look up in a Z table (a standard normal table) the percentage of the area of a standard normal distribution that lies beyond x standard deviations.

Note, however, that KMV does not use a normal distribution when it calculates EDFs. Once *distance to default* is calculated as a number of standard deviations, that number is taken to a proprietary data set that KMV has built. (We return to this when we discuss implementation.)

Implementing the KMV Approach

Step 1: Estimate asset value and volatility of asset value. To calculate the market value of the firm's assets and its volatility, KMV uses the Black–Scholes insight that equity is equivalent to a call on the value of the firm's assets. Exhibit 3.14 shows how this insight is implemented:

■ The first line in Exhibit 3.14 is the Black–Scholes option pricing equation for a call option on equity. In this equation, the notation $N\{d_1\}$ and $N\{d_2\}$ denote cumulative standard normal distribution on d_1 and d_2. (We return to talk about d_1 and d_2 in a moment.) And the effect of multiplying the exercise price by e^{-rT} is to discount the exercise price. (This is called "continuous" discounting.)

EXHIBIT 3.14   Implementing the Black–Scholes Insight

Call Option on Equity	$= (\text{Share Price}) \times N\{d_1\} - (\text{Exercise Price}) \times e^{-rT} \times N\{d_2\}$
Call Option on Asset Value	$= (\text{Asset Value}) \times N\{d_1\} - (\text{Default Point}) \times e^{-rT} \times N\{d_2\}$

■ The second line in Exhibit 3.14 is the corresponding Black–Scholes equation for a call option on the value of the firm's assets. Note that Asset Value replaces Share Price and Default Point replaces Exercise Price.

The second line in Exhibit 3.14 *implies* that if I know the value of the firm's equity and the default point, I should be able to use a Black–Scholes model to back out the market value of the assets. However, there is a complication, which arises from d_1 and d_2. In the Black–Scholes equation for a call option on equity (the first line in Exhibit 3.15), d_1 and d_2 are both functions of the share price, the exercise price, the time to maturity of the option, the risk-free interest rate corresponding to the time to maturity, and the volatility of the equity price. That means that, in the Black–Scholes equation for a call option on the value of the firm's assets (the second line in Exhibit 3.14), d_1 and d_2 will be functions of the *market value of the firm's assets*, the default point, the time to maturity of the option, the risk-free interest rate corresponding to the time to maturity, and the *volatility of the market value of the firm's assets*. That is, the equation in the second line in Exhibit 3.14 involves two unknowns—the market value of the assets and the volatility of the market value of assets. So we've got one equation and two unknowns . . . the algebra doesn't work. To resolve this problem, KMV uses an iterative procedure to calculate the market value of the firm's assets and the volatility of that number:

■ Seed the process with an initial guess about the volatility of the asset value.
■ Generate a time series of implied asset values that correspond to the time series of actual observed equity values.
■ Calculate a new asset volatility from the implied asset values and compare with previous asset volatility.
■ Repeat until the process converges.

Another Solution

KMV used an iterative procedure to get around the "one equation and two unknowns" problem. Actually, there is a second equation that could resolve this problem.

The second equation would be obtained using Ito's lemma on the equity and assuming equity and asset values follow the same random variable. Equity value (E) and asset value (A) would then be related through the equation

$$\sigma_E E = N(d_1)\sigma_A A$$

where

$$d_1 = \frac{\left[\ln\left(\dfrac{A}{DPT}\right) + \left(r + \dfrac{1}{2}\sigma_A^2\right)(T - t)\right]}{\sigma_A (T - t)^{1/2}}$$

and *DPT* is the default point, *r* is the risk-free interest rate, σ_A is the asset volatility, σ_E is the equity volatility, *t* is the current time and *T* is a horizon time for calculating the default probability (e.g., *T* = 1 year).

Combining this equation with that in Exhibit 3.14, the two simultaneous equations could then be solved iteratively.

Step 2: Calculate the distance to default. Earlier we noted that the available empirical evidence suggests that firms continue to pay on liabilities even after the value of their assets has fallen below the face value of the firm's fixed claims. In terms of implementing the theory, that piece of empirical evidence means that the default point will be less than the value of the fixed claims. To implement this, KMV defines the default point as all the firm's current liabilities and half of its long-term debt.

Then, the distance to default is[7]

$$DD = \frac{\ln(A) - \ln(DPT)}{\sigma_A}$$

where

A = Estimated market value of assets
DPT = Current liabilities + ½ (long-term debt)
σ_A = Annual asset volatility in percentage terms

Step 3: Calculate the default probability. Once we have the distance to default, we need to map that into a probability of default—what KMV calls *expected default frequency (EDF)*.

As we noted earlier, if asset returns were normally distributed, we could look up the default probability in a statistics book. In reality, the actual distribution of asset returns has *fat tails*.

Consequently, KMV uses a proprietary empirical distribution of default rates. This distribution is created from a large database of defaulting firms. It contains the distance to default data for many firms for many years prior to default.

Given the estimate of *DD*, the KMV model looks up the probability of default—the EDF—in their proprietary probability table.

To get some insight into how this process works, let's use one of KMV's own illustrations.

KMV's EDFs

At the time this illustration was developed, the financials of the two companies were very similar: The market value of the assets (obtained using equity market data in Step 1) were both about $24–$25 billion. The default points (i.e., all the current liabilities and ½ long-term debt) were both about $3.5 billion. So the market net worth of the two companies was very similar—$21–$22 billion.

	Anheuser–Busch	Compaq Computer
Inputs		
Market Value of Assets	25.5	24.2
Default Point	3.6	3.4
Market Net Worth	21.9	20.8
Outputs		
Asset Volatility	13%	30%
Default Probability (per annum)	0.02%	0.20%

But we know that the likelihood of the two firms defaulting should not be the same. Where is the difference going to be? The difference is in the volatility of the asset values. The volatility of the asset value for the brewer was significantly larger—and it better be if any of this is to make sense. That difference in the volatility of asset value leads to the default probabilities being very different. Note that both the EDFs are very small default probabilities: $2/10$ of 1% and $2/100$ of 1%. But they are different by a factor of 10. The larger volatility of asset value for the computer maker translates into a higher probability of default.

Accuracy of the KMV Approach The most convincing comparison of the accuracy of alternative probability of default measures would be a comparison done by a disinterested third party—an academic or a supervisor. I am not aware of any such third-party comparisons. That being said, we are left with the comparisons provided by the vendors of the models.

Exhibit 3.15 is an accuracy profile created by KMV that compares the accuracy of KMV's EDFs with the accuracy of external debt ratings. The fact that the white bars are higher than the black bars indicates that KMV's EDFs were more accurate in predicting defaults than were the bond ratings.

Creating an "Accuracy Profile"

To create an "accuracy profile" like those presented in Exhibit 3.15, you would begin by ranking the obligors by the probability of default assigned by the model—*from highest to lowest probability of default*.

The points on the "accuracy profile" (the bars in Exhibit 3.15) are plotted as follows:

1. The x value (horizontal axis) = the x% of the obligors with the highest predicted probabilities of default.
2. The y value (vertical axis) = the percentage of actual defaults in the entire sample that are in the group being examined (determined by x).

Note that this process guarantees that $y = 100$% when $x = 100$%.

Once the points (bars) are plotted, the models can be compared:

If the model is "perfect," y will reach 100% when x is equal to the percentage of actual defaults in the entire sample.
If the model is "less perfect," y will reach 100% later.
If the model is "purely random," y will not reach 100% until $x = 100\%$ and the accuracy profile will be a straight line.

BondScore—CreditSights   BondScore by CreditSights is a hybrid model (i.e., a combination of two types of models. It combines two credit risk modeling approaches to estimate probability of default for a firm:

1. A structural model based on Merton's option-theoretic view of firms, wherein default would occur if the value of the firm's assets falls below some critical value.
2. A statistical model in which historical financial data on the firm are related to default experience.

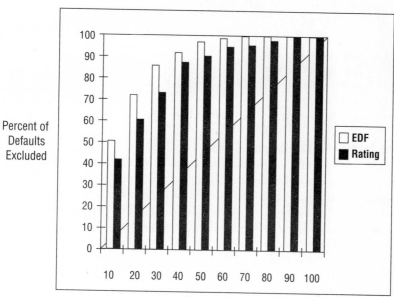

Default Predictive Power
EDF and Bond Ratings
Rated Universe

EXHIBIT 3.15   Accuracy Profile Comparing KMV to External Bond Ratings
©2002 KMV LLC.

In this way, it is very similar to Moody's RiskCalc for Public Companies. BondScore hence derives an empirical relation of default probabilities to financial data *and* market value/equity data. The type of statistical model used is a *logistic regression* (see box on probit/logit models), also as is done in Moody's RiskCalc for Public Companies. The database used for the estimation of the model parameters was from 2,122 firms (representing 14,167 firm-years).

BondScore was developed using default data from several sources and statistical analysis of default probability with multiple inputs/drivers. Because the model is intended to best predict default for rated issuers of public or private debt, the estimation sample includes only companies that held agency ratings (although ratings themselves are not a predictor in the model). Analysts advised on initial selection of candidate variables from which the drivers of the model were drawn, but performed no data biasing/correcting.

The predictors used in BondScore consist of seven financial statement items [taken from trailing four quarters from Compustat (fundamental financial data), current equity information (market capitalization), and Compustat annuals (earnings volatility)] and the trailing 24 months of equity volatility:

1. Leverage [debt including 8X leases/(Current market value + Debt)]
2. Margins [Earnings before interest, taxes, depreciation, and amortization (EBITDA)/Sales]
3. Asset turnover (Sales/Assets)
4. Liquidity (quick ratio)
5. Size [Log (relative assets)]
6. Volatility of past cash flows (standard deviation of past 10 years EBITDA/Assets)
7. Residual Equity Volatility (standard deviation of error in beta equation)

CreditGrades™—RiskMetrics Group   CreditGrades, developed by the RiskMetrics Group and a consortium of financial institutions (Deutsche Bank, Goldman Sachs, and JPMorgan Chase), was released in 2002. It differs in two important respects from the other models described in this section.

The first difference is the goal of the model. The other models we discussed are designed to produce accurate estimates of probabilities of default and to distinguish firms about to default from healthy firms. As such, the models are estimated on proprietary default databases. (We noted that Moody's–KMV Credit Monitor contains one such large proprietary database.) The CreditGrades model, on the other hand, is designed to track credit spreads and to provide a timely indication of when a firm's credit becomes impaired. Parameter estimates and other model decisions are made based on the model's ability to reproduce historical default swap spreads. That is, the modeling aims differ—accurate spreads versus accurate default probabilities—and the estimation data sets differ—market spreads versus actual defaults.

A second difference is in how the model input parameters are derived. The current approaches take literal interpretations of the structural model approach. Consequently, there is a significant emphasis on how to calculate certain fundamental but unobservable parameters, notably the value and volatility of a firm's assets. The CreditGrades approach is more practical, bypassing strict definitions in favor of simple formulas tied to market observables. As a result, the CreditGrades model can be stated as a simple formula based on a small number of input parameters, and sensitivities to these parameters can be easily ascertained.

Probabilities of Default Implied from Market Credit Spread Data

In 1995 Robert Jarrow and Stuart Turnbull introduced a model of credit risk that derives the probability of default from the spread on a firm's risky debt. The Jarrow–Turnbull model and extensions are widely used for pricing credit risk; however, the probabilities derived are not typically used for risk management (except for marking-to-market) because they contain a liquidity premium.

Sources of Probabilities of Default Implied from Market Credit Spread Data

To get this discussion started, let's look at some probabilities of default that were implied from credit spreads observed in the debt market. Savvysoft, a vendor of derivative software, sponsors a site called freederivatives.com. Exhibit 3.16 reproduces a page from that website.

Note the matrix where the columns are banks, finance, industrial companies, and utilities and the rows are Moody's ratings. Suppose you were to click on the BAA2 industrial cell. What do you expect to see? You probably would expect to see a table of default probabilities—the one-year probability, the two-year probability, and so on. However, as illustrated in Exhibit 3.17, instead of getting one table, you would actually get 10 tables.

The differences in the 10 tables are the recovery rate; each of the tables relates to a different recovery rate. For example, the one-year probability of default for a recovery rate of 10% is 1.65%, while the one-year probability of default for a recovery rate of 70% is 4.96%. I hope you see from the preceding that, if you are going to imply probabilities of default from credit spreads, the recovery rate will be crucial.

Mechanics of Implying Probability of Default from Credit Spreads

Two credit spreads are illustrated in Exhibit 3.18. One of the spreads is the spread over U.S. Treasuries and the other is the spread over the London Interbank Offer Rate (LIBOR).

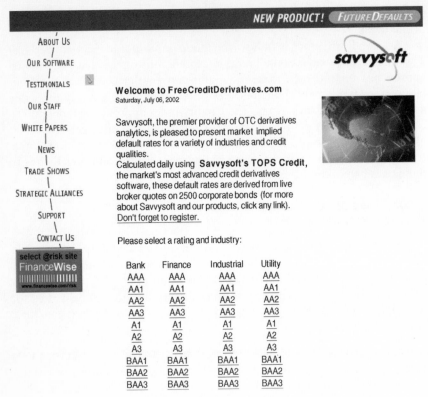

EXHIBIT 3.16   FreeCreditDerivatives.com Sponsored by Savvysoft

What is the credit spread? Clearly, it must represent compensation for the risk of default. (I expect to lose, on average, a certain amount of my portfolio to defaults so the credit spread must be enough to compensate for the losses I *expect* to experience.) But that's not all it is. The credit spread also must reflect compensation for the lack of liquidity. After all, other things equal, investors will demand a higher spread on illiquid assets. (A Ford Motor bond would be more liquid than a loan to Ford. A loan to Ford Motor—which could be syndicated or traded in the secondary market—is more liquid than a loan to ACME Mouse Pads.) And there may well be other things reflected in the credit spread,

Credit Spread = Compensation for Risk of Default
+ Compensation for Lack of Liquidity + ???

That being said, from here out, we will treat the spread as compensation for bearing credit risk. This is clearly not absolutely true for either of the spreads illustrated in Exhibit 3.18. But it might be more correct for the

TOPS Credit
Market Implied Default Probabilities
Updated Thursday, July 04, 2002 1:02 am EST

BAA2 INDUSTRIAL
Note: Default probabilities are calculated using recovery rates from 0 to .9 . . .

Recovery Rate: 0	
Term	Probability
1	0.0149
2	0.0180

Recovery Rate: .1	
Term	Probability
1	0.0165
2	0.0200

Recovery Rate: .7	
Term	Probability
1	0.0496
2	0.0599

EXHIBIT 3.17   Implied Probabilities of Default from FreeCreditDerivatives.com

spread over LIBOR than for the spread over Treasuries, because the spread of LIBOR over Treasuries (called the treasuries—eurodollar spread or the "TED spread") picks up some of the liquidity.

The reason we want to treat the credit spread as entirely default risk is because we can then define the difference in price (or yield spread) between a corporate bond and an otherwise equivalent credit-risk-free benchmark as compensation for bearing credit risk.

$$\text{Credit Risk} \longrightarrow \text{Credit Spread} = \text{Amount at Risk} \times \text{Probability of Default}$$

A model can be used to derive the default probability implied by current spreads. This probability is called a "risk neutral" probability because

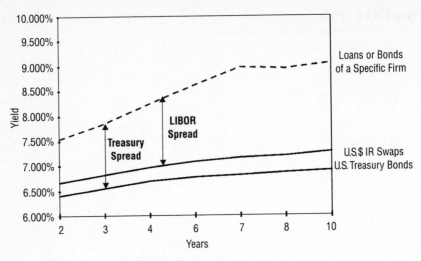

EXHIBIT 3.18   Credit Spreads

it reflects investors' risk aversion. In Exhibit 3.19, the price of a risky bond is modeled as the present value of its *expected* cash flows at maturity.

$CORP_1$ is the price of a risky, one-year zero coupon bond. (We use a zero coupon instrument because they are the easiest to deal with.) $BENCH_1$ is the price of a one-year zero coupon Treasury (the risk-free bond) that has the same face value as the risky bond. That risky bond has a risk-free component—the recovery amount. The holder of the corporate bond will get that amount regardless of whether the issuer of the bond defaults or not:

- If the issuer of the risky bond defaults, the holder of the corporate bond receives $RR \times BENCH_1$ where RR is the recovery rate.
- If the issuer of the risky bond does not default, the holder of the corporate bond receives $BENCH_1$.

As the preceding equation makes clear, to value the risky bond, we need the probability of default, q. That is, if I know $BENCH_1$, RR, and q, I could calculate the value of the risky bond.

But we can also do the reverse. That is, if we know the market price of the risky bond, $CORP_1$, and the market price of the Treasury, $BENCH_1$ (both of which are observable), and if we also know the recovery rate, RR, we could calculate—*imply*—the probability of default, q.

And that is precisely how this technique works. We *observe* the market prices of the risky bond and the risk-free bond. Next, we *assume* a recovery rate. Then, we *solve* for the probability of default.

EXHIBIT 3.19   Credit Spreads

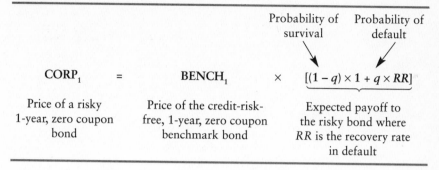

Probability of survival — Probability of default

$$CORP_1 = BENCH_1 \times [(1 - q) \times 1 + q \times RR]$$

Price of a risky 1-year, zero coupon bond   Price of the credit-risk-free, 1-year, zero coupon benchmark bond   Expected payoff to the risky bond where RR is the recovery rate in default

---

THE HEROIC ASSUMPTION

At this point some of you may be thinking that this discussion reinforces everything you have ever heard about economists: *If he's going to make such a heroic assumption, why doesn't he just assume what the probability of default is and be done with it?*

As was mentioned at the outset of this section, this approach is widely used for pricing credit risk (i.e., pricing credit derivatives). In Chapter 6, we return to this topic and I show you that, in the case of pricing credit derivatives, the effect of that heroic-appearing assumption is minimal.

Let's see how this technique would work. For simplicity, let's use continuously compounded interest rates. If the risk-free interest rate is r, we can express the price of the risk-free, zero-coupon bond as

$$BENCH_1 = e^{-rt}$$

and the price of the risky zero coupon bond as

$$CORP_1 = e^{-(r + s)t}$$

where s is the *credit spread*.

Incorporating these values into our model of default probability

$$e^{-(r + s)t} = e^{-rt} [(1 - q) + q \times RR]$$

Doing some algebra, we can rearrange the equation as

$$e^{-st} = 1 - q + q \times RR = q(RR - 1) + 1$$

or as

$$1 - e^{-st} = q(1 - RR)$$

So the probability of default is

$$q = \frac{1 - e^{-st}}{1 - RR}$$

Example

Suppose we observe the following market rates:

Risky one-year, zero-coupon rate	5.766%
Risk-free, one-year, zero-coupon rate	5.523%

It follows that the forward credit spread (continuously compounded) is

$$5.766 - 5.523 = 0.243\%$$

If our best guess about the recovery rate were 10%, the probability of default implied by the credit spread would be

$$q_{1\,yr} = \frac{1 - e^{-s}}{1 - RR} = \frac{1 - e^{-0.00243}}{1 - 0.1} = 0.2697\%$$

However, if our best guess about the recovery rate had been 70%, the probability of default implied by the credit spread would be

$$q_{1\,yr} = \frac{1 - e^{-s}}{1 - RR} = \frac{1 - e^{-0.00243}}{1 - 0.7} = 0.8090\%$$

Note how the different probabilities of default calculated in the preceding example mirror the probabilities of default from FreeCreditDerivatives.com that we show at the beginning of this section. If the assumed loss given default *decreases* threefold, the probability of default *increases* threefold [i.e., the probability of default is inversely proportional to the loss given default (or 1 − recovery)].

Survey Results

To provide some insight into what financial institutions are actually doing with respect to measures of probability of default, we provide some results from the *2002 Survey of Credit Portfolio Management Practices*.

2002 SURVEY OF CREDIT PORTFOLIO MANAGEMENT PRACTICES

We asked all institutions that participated in the survey to answer the following question.

Please rate the following source of probabilities of default in terms of their importance to calibrating your internal rating system. (*Scale of 1–6; 1 being the most important*)

	Percent Indicating They Use This Source	Importance Ranking (Average)
Bond migration studies (e.g, Moody's, S&P, Altman)	78%	2.1
KMV's Credit Monitor (i.e., EDFs)	78%	2.0
Moody's RiskCalc	23%	2.8
S&P's CreditModel	10%	3.5
Probabilities of default implied market credit spread data	30%	3.4
Internal review of portfolio migration	80%	1.6

Later in the questionnaire, we asked those respondents who reported that they use a credit portfolio model the following quesiton, which is very similar to the preceding question. The percentages reported are percentages of the number that answered this question.

What is the primary source of probabilities of default used in your portfolio model?

Bond migration studies (e.g. Moody's, S&P, Altman)	30%	*Since some*
KMV's Credit Monitor (i.e., EDFs)	42%	*respondents*
Moody's RiskCalc	3%	*checked more*
S&P CreditModel/CreditPro	3%	*than one, the*
Probabilities of default implied from term structures of spread	0%	*total adds to more than*
Internal review of portfolio migration	30%	*100%.*

RECOVERY AND UTILIZATION IN THE EVENT OF DEFAULT

Recovery in the Event of Default

Exhibit 3.20 summarizes what I know about sources of data on recovery in the event of default.

There are two types of industry studies. The first type looks at ultimate recovery—the actual recovery after a defaulted obligor emerges. "Emergence" can be defined as curing a default, completing a restructuring, finishing liquidation, or emerging from bankruptcy. The other common definition of "recovery" is the trading price of the defaulted instrument after default, usually 30–60 days.

Ultimate Recovery Data—S&P PMD Loss Database   One industry study based on ultimate recovery is the Portfolio Management Data (PMD) database. (PMD is a unit of Standard & Poor's.) The S&P PMD database contains recovery data for 1600+ defaulted instruments from 450+ obligors. All instrument types—including bank loans—are covered for each default event. The database comprises U.S. data from 1987 forward. The data were collected via a detailed review of public bankruptcy records and Securities and Exchange Commission (SEC) filings, as well as multiple pricing sources. The details provided include collateral type and amount above and below each tranche of debt on the balance sheet.

Exhibits 3.21 and 3.22 provide some illustrative data from the S&P PMD database. Exhibit 3.21 shows that the type of instrument matters, by comparing recovery rates (mean and standard deviation) for various types of instruments.

Exhibit 3.22 shows that the industry in which the obligor is located matters, by comparing mean recovery rates for various industries. The industries' shown are those that had nine or more observations.

The S&P PMD database lends itself to statistical analyses. In 2000, Standard & Poor's used the S&P PMD database to identify the determinants of recovery. That research identified four statistically significant de-

---

EXHIBIT 3.20   External Data on Recovery in the Event of Default

---

Recovery studies based on ultimate recovery
- PMD loss database
- Fitch Risk Management's Loan Loss Database

Recovery studies based on secondary market prices
- Altman and Kishore (1996)
- S&P bond recovery data (in CreditPro)
- Moody's bond recovery data

EXHIBIT 3.21 Recovery Rates by Instrument
(1988–2001) from Standard & Poor's LossStats™

	Recovery (%)	Standard Deviation (%)	Count
Bank loans	83.5	27.2	529
Senior secured notes	68.6	31.8	205
Senior unsecured notes	48.6	36.1	245
Senior subordinated notes	34.5	32.6	276
Subordinated notes	31.6	35.0	323
Junior subordinated notes	18.7	29.9	40

Source: Standard & Poor's Risk Solutions.

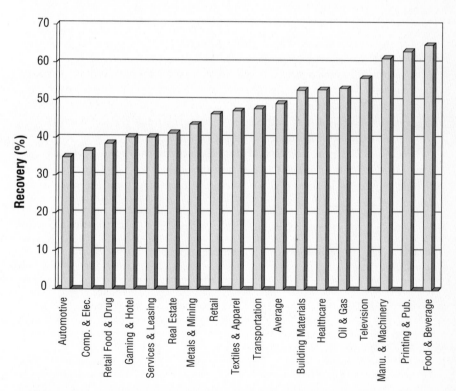

EXHIBIT 3.22 Average Overall Recovery by Industry from Standard & Poor's
LossStats
Source: Standard & Poor's Risk Solutions.

terminants of recovery: the seniority of the facility, the amount of collateral, the amount of time the obligor spends in default, and the size of the debt cushion. (The R-squared was 48%.) Such results lead to questions about the importance of structuring. Exhibit 3.23 illustrates the way that the S&P PMD data can be sliced and diced to analyze specific questions.

Ultimate Recovery Data—Fitch Risk Management Loan Loss Database   Originally developed by Loan Pricing Corporation, the Loan Loss Database was acquired by Fitch Risk Management (FRM) in 2001. FRM is now responsible for all aspects of the database management including data collection, audit, analysis, and user support. The Loan Loss Database is an interbank database, which as of September 2002 contains information on approximately 70,000 nondefaulted commercial loans and 4,800 defaulted commercial loans collected from more than 30 different lending institutions. This proprietary database contains an extensive data sample of both private and public commercial loan data and provides banks with a comprehensive view of the loan migration, default probability, loan utilization, and recovery-given-default parameters of the commercial loan market.

In the case of loans FRM argues that recovery rates based on actual post-default payment experiences are more relevant than those obtained from secondary market prices. This is because the secondary loan markets are relatively illiquid and only applicable to larger, syndicated loans. In addition to broadly syndicated loans, the Loan Loss Database contains extensive data on smaller loans and permits the user to analyze the data using a number of variables including borrower or facility size.

FRM collects post-default payment data on all the defaulted loans contained in the Loan Loss Database. The sum of the present value of all post-default payments is then divided by the outstanding loan amount at the date of default to provide the recovery rate for the defaulted loan.

EXHIBIT 3.23   The Importance of Structuring from Standard & Poor's LossStats

	Recovery (%)	Standard Deviation (%)	Count
All bank debt	84.1	25.7	423
Any debt cushion	85.7	23.9	385
Any debt cushion & any collateral	86.7	23.2	343
50% debt cushion & any collateral	93.5	16.6	221
50% debt cushion & all assets	94.4	16.2	154

Source: Standard & Poor's Risk Solutions.

Because it has data on loans, the FRM Loan Loss Database is able to look at differences in recovery rates for loans versus bonds. The data in Exhibit 3.24 are similar to those from S&P PMD (see Exhibit 3.21).

FRM calculates average recovery rates by several classifications, such as collateral type, defaulted loan amount, borrower size, borrower type, and industry of the borrower. Subscribers to the Loan Loss Database receive all the underlying data points (except for borrower and lender names) so they can verify the FRM calculated results or perform additional analysis using alternative discount rates or different segmentation of the data.

Exhibit 3.25 illustrates the bimodal nature of the recovery rate distribution that is estimated by FRM's Loan Loss Database. A significant number of loans to defaulted borrowers recover nearly all the defaulted exposure; and a significant number of loans to defaulted borrowers recover little or none of the defaulted exposure. This evidence suggests that it is preferable to incorporate probability distributions of recovery levels when generating expected and unexpected loss estimates through simulation exercises, rather than use a static average recovery level, since the frequency of defaulted loans that actually recover the average amount may in fact be quite low.

Studies Based on Secondary Market Prices—Altman and Kishore   In 1996 Ed Altman and Vellore Kishore published an examination of the recovery

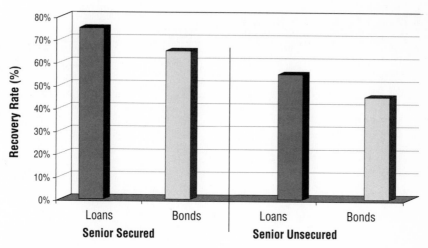

EXHIBIT 3.24   Fitch Risk Management Loan Loss Database: Recovery on Loans vs. Bonds
Source: Fitch Risk Management Loan Loss Database.
Data presented are for illustration purposes only, but are directionally consistent with trends observed in Fitch Risk Management's Loan Loss Database.

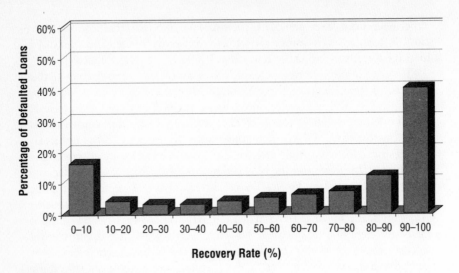

EXHIBIT 3.25 Fitch Risk Management Loan Loss Database: Distribution of Loan Recovery Rates
Source: Fitch Risk Management Loan Loss Database.
Data presented are for illustration purposes only, but are directionally consistent with trends observed in Fitch Risk Management's Loan Loss Database.

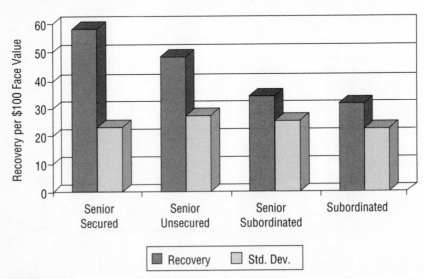

EXHIBIT 3.26 Altman & Kishore: Recovery on Bonds by Seniority
Source: Altman and Kishore, *Financial Analysts Journal*, November/December 1996. Copyright 1996, Association for Investment Management and Research. Reproduced and republished from *Financial Analysts Journal* with permission from the Association for Investment Management and Research. All rights reserved.

experience on a large sample of defaulted bonds over the 1981–1996 period. In this, they examined the effects of seniority (see Exhibit 3.26) and identified industry effects (see Exhibit 3.27).

As we note in Chapter 4, the Altman and Kishore data are available in the RiskMetrics Group's CreditManager model.

Studies Based on Secondary Market Prices—S&P Bond Recovery Data

S&P's Bond Recovery Data are available in its CreditPro product. This study updates the Altman and Kishore data set through 12/31/99. The file is searchable by S&P industry codes, SIC codes, country, and CUSIP numbers. The data set contains prices both at default and at emergence from bankruptcy.

What Recovery Rates Are Financial Institutions Using?

In the development of the 2002 *Survey of Credit Portfolio Management Practices,* we were interested in the values that credit portfolio managers were actually using. The following results from the survey provide some evidence—looking at the inverse of the recovery rate, *loss given default percentage.*

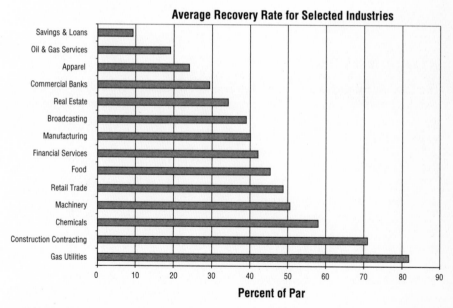

EXHIBIT 3.27   Altman & Kishore: Recovery on Bonds by Industry
Source: Altman and Kishore, *Financial Analysts Journal,* November/December 1996. Copyright 1996, Association for Investment Management and Research. Reproduced and republished from *Financial Analysts Journal* with permission from the Association for Investment Management and Research. All rights reserved.

2002 SURVEY OF CREDIT PORTFOLIO MANAGEMENT PRACTICES

Please complete the following matrix with typical LGD parameters for a new funded bank loan with term to final maturity of 1 year. (If your LGD methodology incorporates factors in addition to those in this table, please provide the LGD that would apply on average in each case.)

Average LGD parameter (%), rounded to nearest whole number

	Large Corporate Borrower	Mid-Market Corp Borrower	Bank Borrower	Other Financial Borrower
Senior Secured	33	35	31	28
Senior Unsecured	47	49	44	43
Subordinated Secured	47	47	38	44
Subordinated Unsecured	64	65	57	59

Utilization in the Event of Default

The available data on utilization in the event of default are even more limited than those for recovery. Given that there are so few data on utilization, the starting point for a portfolio manager would be to begin with the conservative estimate—100% utilization in the event of default. The question then is whether there is any evidence that would support utilization rates less than 100%.

As with recovery data, the sources can be characterized as either "internal data" or "industry studies."

Internal Data on Utilization

Study of Utilization at Citibank: 1987–1991   Using Citibank data, Elliot Asarnow and James Marker (1995) examined 50 facilities rated BB/B or below in a period between 1987 and 1991. Their utilization measure, loan equivalent exposure (LEQ), was expressed as a percentage of normally unused commitments. They calculated the LEQs for the lower credit grades and extrapolated the results for higher grades. Asarnow and Marker found that the LEQ was higher for the better credit quality borrowers.

Study of Utilization at Chase: 1995–2000 Using the Chase portfolio, Michel Araten and Michael Jacobs Jr. (2001) examined 408 facilities for 399 defaulted borrowers over a period between March 1995 and December 2000.

Araten and Jacobs considered both revolving credits and advised lines. They defined *loan equivalent exposure* (LEQ) as the portion of a credit line's undrawn commitment that is likely to be drawn down by the borrower in the event of default.

Araten and Jacobs noted that, in the practitioner community, there are two opposing views on how to deal with the credit quality of the borrower. One view is that investment grade borrowers should be assigned a higher LEQ, because higher rated borrowers tend to have fewer covenant restrictions and therefore have a greater ability to draw down if they get in financial trouble. The other view is that, since speculative grade borrowers have a greater probability of default, a higher LEQ should be assigned to lower grade borrowers.

Araten and Jacobs also noted that the other important factor in estimating LEQ is the tenor of the commitment. With longer time to maturity, there is a greater opportunity for drawdown as there is more time available (higher volatility) for a credit downturn to occur, raising its associated credit risk.

Consequently, Araten and Jacobs focused on the relation of the estimated LEQs to (1) the facility risk grade and (2) time-to-default.

The data set for revolving credits included 834 facility-years and 309 facilities (i.e., two to three years of LEQ measurements prior to default per facility).

Exhibit 3.28 contains the LEQs observed[8] (in boldface type) and predicted (in italics) by Araten/Jacobs. The average LEQ was 43% (with a standard deviation of 41%). The observed LEQs (the numbers in boldface type in Exhibit 3.28) suggest that

■ LEQ declines with decreasing credit quality. This is most evident in shorter time-to-default categories (years 1 and 2).
■ LEQ increases as time-to-default increases.

To fill in the missing LEQs and to smooth out the LEQs in the table, Araten/Jacobs used a regression analysis. While they considered many different combinations of factors, the regression equation that best fit the data (i.e., had the most explanatory power) was

$$LEQ = 48.36 - 3.49 \times (\text{Facility Rating}) + 10.87(\text{Time-to-Default})$$

where the facility rating was on a scale of 1–8 and time-to-default was in years. Other variables (lending organization, domicile of borrower, indus-

EXHIBIT 3.28   *Observed* and *Predicted* LEQs for Revolving Credits

	Years to Default				
	1	2	3	4	5–6
AAA/AA–	*56%*	12% *67%*	*78%*	*88%*	*99%*
A+/A–	79% *52%*	76% *63%*	84% *74%*	*85%*	*96%*
BBB+/BBB	94% *49%*	47% *60%*	42% *71%*	100% *82%*	*92%*
BBB/BB+	55% *45%*	52% *56%*	42% *67%*	38% *78%*	100% *89%*
BB	32% *42%*	45% *53%*	62% *64%*	76% *75%*	68% *85%*
BB–/B+	40% *38%*	50% *49%*	62% *60%*	63% *71%*	100% *82%*
B/B–	27% *35%*	40% *46%*	37% *57%*	98% *68%*	*79%*
CCC	25% *31%*	27% *42%*	9% *53%*	*64%*	*75%*

Source: Michel Araten and Michael Jacobs Jr. "Loan Equivalents for Revolving and Advised Lines." *The RMA Journal*, May 2001.

try, type of revolver, commitment size, and percent utilization) were not found to be sufficiently significant.

Using the preceding estimated regression equation, Araten/Jacobs predicted LEQs. These predicted LEQs are shown in italics in Exhibit 3.28.

In his review of this section prior to publication, Mich Araten reminded me that, when you want to apply these LEQs for a facility with a particular maturity t, you have to weight the $LEQ(t)$ by the relevant probability of default. The reason is that a 5-year loan's LEQ is based on the year it defaults; and it could default in years 1, . . . , 5. If the loan defaults in year 1, you would use the 1-year LEQ, and so on. In the unlikely event that the probability of default is constant over the 5-year period, you would effectively use an LEQ associated with 2.5 years.

Industry Studies

S&P PMD Loss Database   While the S&P PMD Loss Database described earlier was focused on recovery, it also contains data on revolver utilization at the time of default. This database provides estimates of utilization as a percentage of the commitment amount and as a percentage of the borrowing base amount, if applicable.

All data are taken from public sources. S&P PMD has indicated that it plans to expand the scope of the study to research the utilization behavior of borrowers as they migrate from investment grade into noninvestment grade.

Fitch Risk Management Loan Loss Database   The Fitch Risk Management (FRM) Loan Loss Database can be used as a source of utilization data as it contains annually updated transaction balances on commercial loans. In the FRM Loan Loss Database, the utilization rate is defined as the percentage of the available commitment amount on a loan that is drawn at a point in time. Users can calculate average utilization rates for loans at different credit ratings, including default, based on various loan and borrower characteristics, such as loan purpose, loan size, borrower size, and industry of the borrower.

FRM indicates that their analysis of the utilization rates of borrowers contained in the Loan Loss Database provides evidence that average utilization rates increase as the credit quality of the borrower deteriorates. This relation is illustrated in Exhibit 3.29.

What Utilization Rates Are Financial Institutions Using? As was the case with recovery, in the course of developing the questionnaire for the *2002 Survey of Credit Portfolio Management Practices*, we were interested in the values that credit portfolio managers were actually using. The following results from the survey provide some evidence.

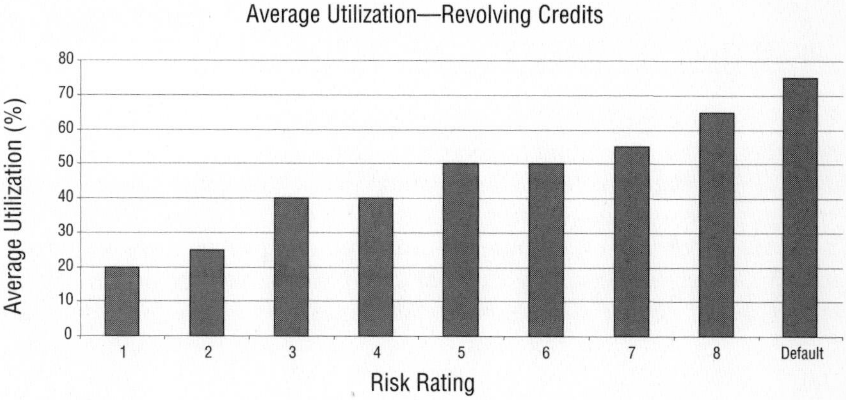

Average Utilization—Revolving Credits

EXHIBIT 3.29 Average Utilization for Revolving Credits by Risk Rating
Source: Fitch Risk Management Loan Loss Database.
Data presented are for illustration purposes only, but are directionally consistent with trends observed in Fitch Risk Management's Loan Loss Database.

2002 SURVEY OF CREDIT PORTFOLIO MANAGEMENT PRACTICES

(Utilization in the Event of Default/Exposure at Default) In the credit portfolio model, what credit conversion factors (or EAD factors or Utilization factors) are employed by your institution to determine utilization in the event of default for undrawn lines? Please complete the

(Continued)

2002 SURVEY OF CREDIT PORTFOLIO MANAGEMENT PRACTICES *(Continued)*

following table. (If your drawdown parameters are based on your internal ratings, please categorize your response by the equivalent external grade.)

	Average EAD factors (Utilization factors)					
	AAA/Aaa	AA/Aa	A/A	BBB/Baa	BB/Ba	B/B
Committed revolvers	59.14	59.43	60.84	60.89	62.73	65.81
CP backup facilities	64.39	64.60	65.00	66.11	63.17	66.63
Uncommitted lines	34.81	33.73	33.77	37.70	37.40	39.43

CORRELATION OF DEFAULTS

The picture I drew in Exhibit 3.1 indicates that *correlation* is something that goes into the "loading hopper" of a credit portfolio model. However, in truth, *correlation* is less like something that is "loaded into the model" and more like something that is "inside the model."

Default correlation is a major hurdle in the implementation of a portfolio approach to the management of credit assets, because default correlation cannot be directly estimated. Since most firms have not defaulted, the observed default correlation would be zero; but this is not a useful statistic. Data at the level of industry or rating class are available that would permit calculation of default correlation, but this is not sufficiently "fine grained."

As illustrated in Exhibit 3.30, there are two approaches. One is to treat correlation as an explicit input. The theoretical models underlying both

EXHIBIT 3.30 Approaches to Default Correlation

Correlation as an Explicit Input	Correlation as an Implicit Factor
• Asset value correlation (the KMV approach)	• Factor models
• Equity value correlation (the RMG approach)	• Actuarial models (e.g., Credit Risk+)

Moody's–KMV Portfolio Manager and the RiskMetrics Group's Credit-Manager presuppose an explicit correlation input. The other is to treat correlation as an implicit factor. This is what is done in the Macro Factor Model and in Credit Suisse First Boston's Credit Risk+.

Correlation as an Explicit Input

Approach Used in the Moody's–KMV Model   In the Moody's–KMV approach, default event correlation between company X and company Y is based on asset value correlation:

Default Correlation = f [Asset Value Correlation, $EDF_X(DPT_X)$, $EDF_Y(DPT_Y)$]

Note that default correlation is a characteristic of the obligor (not the facility).

AT THE END, ALL MODELS ARE IMPLICIT FACTOR MODELS

Mattia Filiaci reminded me that describing Portfolio Manager and CreditManager as models with explicit correlation inputs runs the risk of being misleading. This characterization is a more valid description of the theory underlying these models than it is of the way these models calculate the parameters necessary to generate correlated asset values.

For both CreditManager and Portfolio Manager, only the weights on the industry and country factors/indices for each firm are explicit inputs. These weights imply correlations through the loadings of the factors in the factor models.

Theory Underlying the Moody's–KMV Approach

At the outset, we should note that the description here is of the theoretical underpinnings of the Moody's–KMV model and would be used by the software to calculate default correlation between two firms only if the user is interested in viewing a particular value. Moreover, while this discussion is related to Portfolio Manager, *this discussion is valid for any model that generates correlated asset returns.*

An intuitive way to look at the theoretical relation between asset value correlation and default event correlation between two companies X and Y is summarized in the following figure.

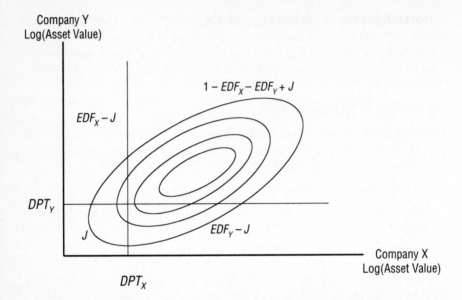

The horizontal axis measures company X's asset value (actually the logarithm of asset value) and the vertical axis measures company Y's asset value. Note that the default point for company X is indicated on the horizontal axis and the default point for company Y is indicated on the vertical axis.

The concentric ovals are "equal probability" lines. Every point on a given oval represents the same probability, and the inner ovals indicate higher probability. If the asset value for company X were uncorrelated with the asset value for company Y, the equal probability line would be a circle. If the asset values were perfectly correlated, the equal probability line would be a straight line. The ovals indicate that the asset values for companies X and Y are positively correlated, but less than perfectly correlated.

The probability that company X's asset value is less than DPT_X is EDF_X; and the probability that company Y's asset value is less than DPT_Y is EDF_Y. The joint probability that company X's asset value is less than DPT_X *and* company Y's asset value is less than DPT_X is J. Finally, the probability that company X's asset value exceeds DPT_X *and* company Y's asset value exceeds DPT_X is $1 - EDF_X - EDF_Y + J$.

Assuming that the asset values for company X and company Y are jointly normally distributed, the correlation of default for companies X and Y can be calculated as

$$\rho_{X,Y} = \frac{J - EDF_X \times EDF_Y}{EDF_X(1 - EDF_X)EDF_Y(1 - EDF_Y)}$$

This is a standard result from statistics when two random processes in which each can result in one of two states are correlated (i.e., have a joint probability of occurrence J).

Approach Used in the RiskMetrics Group's Model   The RiskMetrics Group's approach has a similar theoretical basis to that used in the Moody's–KMV model, but the implementation of correlation is simplified. Asset value returns are not directly modeled in a factor structure but are simulated using a correlation matrix of asset returns derived from returns on publicly available equity indices and country and industry allocations. (The user defines the time series.) Equity index return correlations in various countries and industries along with weights for each firm on the countries and industries determine asset value correlations (see Exhibit 3.31).

Correlation as an Implicit Factor

What we mean by correlation being implicit in a model is that there is no explicit input for any correlations or covariance matrix in the model. Intuitively, they are inside the model all the time—one might say they are "prebaked" into the model.

We now turn our attention to factor models, in which correlation between two firms is implied by the factor loadings of each firm on a set of *common factors*, and (if this is the case) by the correlations among the common factors.

Let's take a look at a simple factor model. We consider two cases: one in which the factors are independent, that is, they are uncorrelated, and the other in which they are not. Suppose some financial characteristic (e.g., continuously compounded returns—I am intentionally vague about this because some models use probability of default itself as the characteristic) of some obligor i depends linearly on two factors:

EXHIBIT 3.31   Comparison of the Moody's–KMV and RiskMetrics Group Approaches

Approach Used by Moody's–KMV Model	Approach Used by RiskMetrics Group's Model
• Asset value driven	• Equity index proxy
• Firms decomposed into systematic and non-systematic components	• Firms decomposed into systematic and non-systematic components
• Systematic risk based on industry and country of obligor	• Systematic risk based on industry and country of obligor and may be sensitive to asset size
• Default correlation derives from asset correlation	• Default correlation derives from correlation in the proxy (equity returns)

$$r_A = \mu_A + w_{A1} f_1 + w_{A2} f_2 + \varepsilon_A$$

where μ_A is the expected rate of return of obligor A, w_{A1} (w_{A2}) is the factor loading or weight on the 1st (2nd) factor

$$
\begin{aligned}
f_1 &\sim N(0, \sigma_1^2), \\
f_2 &\sim N(0, \sigma_2^2), \\
\varepsilon_A &\sim N(0, \sigma_A^2)
\end{aligned}
$$

σ_1 (σ_2) is the standard deviation of factor 1 (2), and σ_A is the firm-specific risk standard deviation.

If we assume that $\rho\ (f_1, f_2) \neq 0$, $\rho\ (f_1, \varepsilon_A) = 0$, and $\rho\ (f_2, \varepsilon_A) = 0$, then the correlation between two obligors A and B's returns are given by:

$$\rho(r_A, r_B) = \frac{w_{A1} w_{B1} \sigma_1^2 + w_{A2} w_{B2} \sigma_2^2 + (w_{A1} w_{B2} + w_{A2} w_{B1}) \sigma_1 \sigma_2 \rho(f_1, f_2)}{\sigma_{r_A} \sigma_{r_B}}$$

where

$$\sigma_{r_A} = (w_{A1}^2 \sigma_1^2 + w_{A2}^2 \sigma_2^2 + \sigma_A^2)^{\frac{1}{2}}$$

and similarly for obligor B. What is left is to determine the relationship between the correlation of the returns and the default event correlation for two obligors, as already discussed in the previous inset. We see that correlation depends both on the weights on the factors and on the correlation between the factors. It is possible to construct a model in which the correlation between the factors is zero (Moody's–KMV Portfolio Manager is one such example).

The Approach in the Macro Factor Model In a Macro Factor Model, the state of the economy, determined by the particular economic factors (e.g., gross domestic product, unemployment, etc.) chosen by the modeler, causes default rates and transition probabilities to change. Individual firms' default probabilities are affected by how much they depend on the economic factors. A low state of economic activity implies that the average of all default probabilities is high, but how each obligor's probability varies depends on its weight on each macrofactor. Default correlation thus depends on the similarity or dissimilarity across firms on their allocation to macrofactors, and on the correlations in the movements of the macrofactors themselves.

As with all the other models there is no explicit input or *calculation* of default correlation. (Default correlation is not calculated explicitly in *any* model for the purpose of calculating the loss distribution—only for user interest is it calculated.)

The Approach in Credit Risk+ Just as in the macrofactor models, in Credit Risk+, default correlation between two firms is maximized if the two firms are allocated in the same country or industry sector. Two obligors A and B that have no sector in common will have zero default event correlation. This is because no systematic factor affects them both. In the technical document, Credit Risk+ calculates an approximation for the default event correlation:

$$\rho_{AB} = \left(\sqrt{p_A p_B}\right) \sum_{k=1}^{n} w_{Ak} w_{Bk} \left(\frac{\sigma_k}{p_k}\right)^2$$

where there are n sectors, p_A (p_B) is the average default probability of obligor A (B), w_{Ak} (w_{Bk}) is the weight of obligor A (B) in sector k, and p_k and σ_k are the average default probability and volatility (standard deviation) of the default probability, respectively, in sector k:

$$p_k = \sum_{i=1}^{N} w_{ik} p_i \text{ and } \sigma_k = \sum_{i=1}^{N} w_{ik} \sigma_i$$

There are N obligors in the portfolio and the weights of each obligor on a sector satisfy

$$\sum_{k=1}^{n} w_{ik} = 1$$

Note that Credit Risk+ has introduced the concept of a volatility in the default rate itself. This is further discussed in the next chapter. Historical data suggest that the ratios σ_k/μ_k are of the order of unity. If this is the case, then the default correlation is proportional to the geometric mean $(= \sqrt{p_A p_B})$ of the two average default probabilities. In the next chapter we see that default correlations calculated in Moody's–KMV Portfolio Manager, for example, are indeed closer to the default probabilities than the asset value correlations.

NOTES

1. CreditPro™ is a registered trademark of The McGraw-Hill Companies, Inc.
2. ZETA® is the registered servicemark of Zeta Services, Inc., 615 Sherwood Parkway, Mountainside, NJ 07092.

3. For public companies, CRS employs a Merton-derived "distance to de-fault" measure requiring data on equity price and the volatility of that price. This type of modeling is discussed in the next section of this chapter.

4. Fitch Risk Management reports that the public model is within two notches of the agency ratings 86% of the time.

5. KMV® and Credit Monitor® are registered trademarks of KMV LLC.

6. Expected Default Frequency™ and EDF™ are trademarks of KMV LLC.

7. This assumes that $\mu - \frac{1}{2}\sigma_A^2$ is negligible, where μ is the expected return of the asset value. The probability that the asset value of a firm re-mains above its default point is equal to $N[d_2^*]$, where

$$d_2^* = \frac{\ln(A/DPT) + \left(\mu - \frac{1}{2}\sigma_A^2\right)(T - t)}{\sigma_A\sqrt{T - t}}$$

Note that d_2^* is the same as d_2 in the formulae in Exhibit 3.14 except that the expected return (μ) is replaced with the risk-free rate (r). $N[d_2^*]$ is called the probability of survival. Using a property of the standard normal cumulative distribution function, the probability of default (p_{def}) is

$$p_{def} = 1 - (\text{probability of survival}) = 1 - N[d_2^*] = N[-d_2^*]$$

This result is derived explicitly in the appendix to chapter 4, leading up to equation 4.18. Moody's-KMV asserts that $\mu - \frac{1}{2}\sigma_A^2$ is small com-pared to $\ln(A/DPT)$, so using one of the properties of logarithms and setting $t = 0$ and $T = 1$,

$$d_2^* \cong \frac{\ln(A) - \ln(DPT)}{\sigma_A}$$

which is the distance to default (DD) defined in the text.

8. Exhibit 3.28 does not give the reader any idea about the precision with which the LEQs are observed. Mich Araten reminded me that, in a number of cases, the observed LEQ is based on only one observation. The interested reader should see the original article for more.

CHAPTER 4

Credit Portfolio Models

While evaluation of the probability of default by an obligor has been the central focus of bankers since banks first began lending money, *quantitative* modeling of the credit risk for an individual obligor (or transaction) is actually fairly recent. Moreover, the modeling of the credit risk associated with *portfolios* of credit instruments—loans, bonds, guarantees, or derivatives—is a very recent development.

The development in credit portfolio models is comparable—albeit with a lag—to the development of market risk models [Value at Risk (VaR) models]. When the VaR models were being developed in the early 1990s, most large banks and securities firms recognized the need for such models, but there was little consensus on standards and few firms actually had full implementations. The same situation exists currently for credit risk modeling. The leading financial institutions recognize its necessity, but there exist a variety of approaches and competing methodologies.

There are three types of credit portfolio models in use currently:

1. Structural models—There are two vendor-supplied credit portfolio models of this type: Moody's–KMV Portfolio Manager and RiskMetrics Group's CreditManager.
2. Macrofactor models—McKinsey and Company introduced Credit PortfolioView in 1998.
3. Actuarial ("reduced form") models: Credit Suisse First Boston introduced Credit Risk+ in 1997.

In addition to the publicly available models noted above, it appears that a number of proprietary models have been developed. This point is illustrated by the fact that the ISDA/IIF project that compared credit portfolio models identified 18 proprietary (internal) models (IIF/ISDA, 2000). Note, however, that proprietary models were more likely to exist for credit card and mortgage portfolios or for middle market bank lending (i.e., credit scoring models).

The first generations of credit portfolio models were designed to reside on PCs or workstations as stand-alone applications. While centralized applications are still the norm, more products will be available either over the Web or through a client/server link.

STRUCTURAL MODELS

The structural models are also referred to as "asset volatility models." The "structural" aspect of the models comes from the fact that there is a story behind default (i.e., something happens to trigger default).

The structural (asset volatility) models are rooted in the Merton insight we introduced in Chapter 3: *Debt behaves like a put option on the value of the firm's assets.* In a "Merton model," default occurs when the value of the firm's assets falls below some trigger level; so default is determined by the structure of the individual firm and its asset volatility. It follows that default correlation must be a function of asset correlation.

Implementation of a structural (asset volatility) model requires estimating the market value of the firm's assets and the volatility of that value. Because asset values and their volatilities are not observable for most firms, structural models rely heavily on the existence of publicly traded equity to estimate the needed parameters.

Moody's–KMV Portfolio Manager[1]

The Moody's–KMV model, Portfolio Manager, was released in 1993.

Model Type   As noted above, the Moody's–KMV's model (like the other publicly available structural model) is based on Robert Merton's insight that debt behaves like a short put option on the value of the firm's assets—see Exhibit 4.1.

With such a perspective, default will occur when the value of the firm's assets falls below the value of the firm's debt (or other fixed claims).

Stochastic Variable   Since KMV's approach is based on Merton's insight that debt behaves like a short put on the value of the firm's assets, the stochastic variable in KMV's Portfolio Manager is the value of the firm's assets.

Probability of Default   While the user could input any probability of default, Portfolio Manager is designed to use EDFs obtained from Moody's–KMV Credit Monitor or Private Firm Model (see Exhibit 4.2).

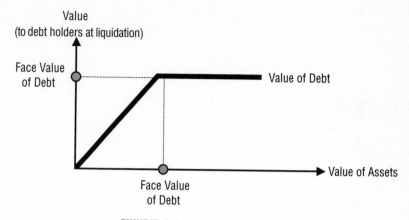

EXHIBIT 4.1   The Merton Insight

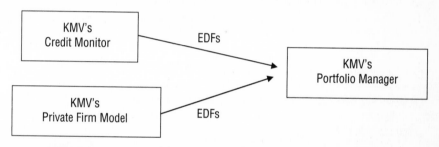

EXHIBIT 4.2   Sources of Probability of Default for Portfolio Manager

Default Correlation   *Since a full discussion of the manner in which default correlation is dealt with in the Moody's–KMV approach is relatively technical, we have put the technical details in the appendix to this chapter. Readers who do not wish to delve into the technical aspects that deeply can skip that appendix without losing the story line.*

The theory behind default correlation in Portfolio Manager was described in Chapter 3. The basic idea is that, for two obligors, the correlation between the values of their assets in combination with their individual default points will determine the probability that the two firms will default at the same time; and this joint probability of default can then be related to the default event correlation.

In the Moody's KMV model, default correlation is computed in the Global Correlation Model (GCorr)[2], which implements the asset-correlation approach via a factor model that generates *correlated* asset returns

$$r_A(t) = \beta_A r_{CI,A}(t)$$

where

$r_A(t)$ = the return on firm A's assets in period t, and
$r_{CI,A}(t)$ = the return on a *unique* custom index (factor) for firm A in period t.

The custom index for each firm is constructed from industry and country factors (indices). The construction of the custom index for an individual firm proceeds as follows:

1. Allocate the firm's assets and sales to the various *industries* in which it operates (from the 61 industries covered by the Moody's–KMV model).
2. Allocate the firm's assets and sales to the various *countries* in which it operates (from the 45 countries covered by the Moody's–KMV model).
3. Combine the country and industry returns.

To see how this works, let's look at an example.

Computing *Unique* Custom Indices for Individual Firms

Let's compute the custom indices for General Motors and Boeing.
The first step is to allocate the firms' assets and sales to the various *industries* in which they operate:

Industry Decomposition of GM and Boeing Co.

Industry	General Motors	Boeing Co.
Finance companies	51%	12%
Automotive	44%	
Telephone	3%	
Transportation equip.	1%	
Unassigned	1%	18%
Aerospace & defense		70%

Industry weights are an average of sales and assets reported in each industry classification (e.g., SIC code).
©2002 KMV LLC.

KMV supplies allocations to industries for each obligor. The user can employ those allocations or elect to use her or his own allocations.
The second step is to allocate each firm's assets and sales to the various *countries* in which it operates:

Country Decomposition of GM and Boeing Co.

Country	General Motors	Boeing Co.
USA	100%	100%

©2002 KMV LLC.

As with the industry allocations, KMV supplies allocations to countries for each obligor, but the user can elect to use her or his own allocations.

Next, the country and industry returns are combined. That is, the industry and country weights identified in Steps 1 and 2 determine the makeup of the custom indices.

$$\text{Return on the custom index for GM} = 1.0r_{us} + .51r_{fin} + .44r_{auto} + .03r_{tel} + .01r_{trans} + .01r_{un}$$

$$\text{Return on the custom index for Boeing} = 1.0r_{us} + .12r_{fin} + .18r_{un} + .70r_{aerodef}$$

As we will describe below, the component returns—e.g., r_{fin} for finance companies—are themselves constructed from 14 uncorrelated global, regional, and industrial sector indices.

As we note at the beginning of this subsection, in the Moody's–KMV approach, the correlation of default events for two firms depends on the asset correlation for those firms and their individual probabilities of default. In practice, this means that default correlations will be determined by the R^2 of the factor models and the EDFs of the individual companies. To make this a little more concrete, let's return to the example using GM and Boeing.

Measuring Asset Correlation in *Portfolio Manager*

Given the definition of the *unique* composite indices for GM and Boeing in an earlier box, the *Global Correlation Model* will use asset return data for GM, Boeing, and the 120 (= 61 + 45 + 14) factors to estimate two equations:

$$r_{GM}(t) = \beta_{GM}r_{CI,GM}(t) + \varepsilon_{GM}(t)$$
$$r_{BOEING}(t) = \beta_{BOEING}r_{CI,BOEING}(t) + \varepsilon_{BOEING}(t)$$

The output from this estimation is as follows:

	General Motors	Boeing
Asset volatility	6.6%	18.3%
R-squared	53.5%	42.4%
Correlation of asset returns	0.440	
Correlation of EDF	0.064	

©2002 KMV LLC.

Of the above values, only R^2 is sent to the simulation model in Portfolio Manager. Even though the other GCorr outputs (such as default event correlations) are not used in the subsequent simulations, they may be useful to portfolio managers in other contexts.

In GCorr, the correlation of default events for two firms depends on the correlation of the asset values for those firms and their individual probabilities of default. The Moody's KMV documentation suggests that asset correlations range between 0.05 and 0.60 but default correlations are much lower, ranging between 0.002 and 0.15. The correlation of asset values for two firms may be high, but if the EDFs are low, the firms will still be unlikely to jointly default.

Facility Valuation   *Like the preceding subsection, a full description of Moody's–KMV valuation module becomes relatively technical; so we put the technical details in the appendix to this chapter. Readers who do not wish to delve into the technical aspects that deeply can skip that appendix without losing the story line.*

In Portfolio Manager, facility valuation is done in the Loan Valuation Module. Depending on the financial condition of the obligor, an individual facility can have a range of possible values at future dates. What we need to do is find a probability distribution for these values. Exhibit 4.3 provides the logic behind the generation of such a value distribution for a facility in Portfolio Manager.

When we looked at Moody's–KMV Credit Monitor (in Chapter 3), Moody's–KMV assumes that, at some specified time in the future—the horizon—the value of the firm's assets will follow a lognormal distribution. Furthermore, individual value for the firm's assets at the horizon will correspond to values for the facility (loan, bond, etc.). If the value of the firm's assets falls below the default point, the logic of this approach is that the firm will default and the value of the facility will be the recovery value. For values for the firm's assets above the default point, the facility value will in-

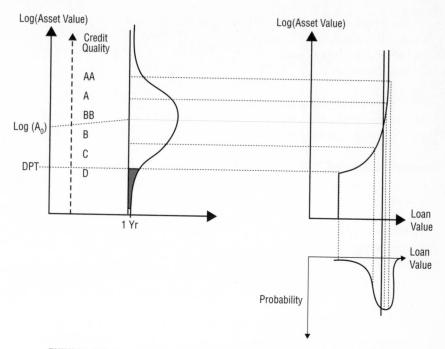

EXHIBIT 4.3 Generating the Loss Distribution in Portfolio Manager

crease steadily with the firm's asset value at, and plateau to, the face value as the asset value increases. Roughly speaking, moving from an implied rating of BB to BBB will have less effect on the facility value than moving from BB to B.

Value Distribution and Loss Distribution In Portfolio Manager, the *portfolio value distribution* is first calculated simply by summing all the facility values. Then, the *loss distribution* is obtained by using the risk-free rate to calculate the future value of the portfolio at the horizon and subtracting the simulated value of the portfolio at the horizon:

Portfolio Loss at Horizon = Expected Future Value of Current Portfolio – Simulated Value of the Portfolio at Horizon

Another way to relate the value distribution to a loss distribution is through the expected value of the value distribution. The probability of a particular loss bin will equal the probability of a bin of portfolio values where the bin has a value equal to the expected value minus the loss.

For example, the probability corresponding to the bin in the value distribution labeled with a value of $133mm, when the expected value is $200mm, will become the bin for a loss of $67mm in the loss distribution.

What we have been saying is that the *portfolio value distribution* and the *loss distribution* are mirror images of each other. Exhibit 4.4 shows how the two distributions are related graphically.

Generating the Portfolio Value Distribution The generation of the simulated portfolio value distribution may be summarized in four steps, as follows.

1. Simulate the asset value. The first step in generating the value distribution is to *simulate* the value of the firm's assets at the horizon (A_H) for each obligor.
2. Value the facilities. The second step is to value each facility at horizon as a function of the simulated value of the obligor's assets at the horizon (A_H).
   If the value of the firm's assets at the horizon is less than the default point for that firm (i.e., if $A_H < DPT$), the model presumes that default has occurred. The value of the facility would be its recovery value. However, Portfolio Manager does not simply use the inputted expected value of *LGD* to calculate the recovery amount (equal to $(1 - LGD)$ times the face amount). Such a procedure would imply that we know the recovery rate precisely. Instead, Portfolio Manager treats *LGD* as a random variable that follows a *beta distribution* with a mean equal to the inputted expected *LGD* value. (More about a beta distribution can be found in the statistical appendix to this book.) For this iteration of the simulation, Portfolio Manager draws an *LGD* value from that distribution. [This use of the beta distribution has proved popular for modeling recovery distributions (we will see that the RiskMetrics Group's CreditManager also uses it) because of its flexibility—it can be made to match the highly nonnormal empirical recovery distributions well.]
   If the value of the firm's assets at the horizon is greater than the default point for that firm (i.e., if $A_H > DPT$), the model presumes that default has not occurred and the value of the facility is the weighted sum of the value of a risk-free bond and the value of a risky bond, as described earlier.
3. Sum to obtain the portfolio value. Once values for each of the facilities at the horizon have been obtained, the third step in generating

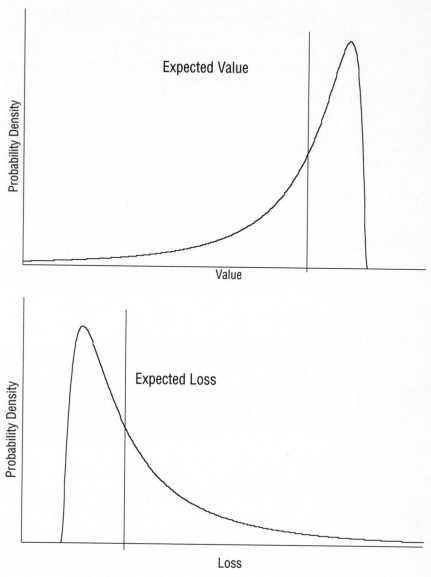

EXHIBIT 4.4   Value Distribution and Loss Distribution

the value distribution is to sum the values of the facilities to obtain the value of the portfolio.

4. Iterate. Steps 1 through 3 provide one simulated value for the portfolio. To get a distribution, it is necessary to obtain additional simulated values. That means repeating steps 1–3 some number of times (e.g., 1,000,000 times).

Outputs   Portfolio Manager outputs various facility level and portfolio level parameters. At the facility level, the important ones are the expected spread and the spread to horizon.

Portfolio Value Distribution   The portfolio level outputs are based on the value distribution. Portfolio Manager can present the value distribution in tabular or graphical format. Exhibit 4.5 illustrates a value distribution, highlighting several reference points from the value distribution:

V_{max}—Maximum possible value of the portfolio at the horizon (assuming there are no defaults and every obligor upgrades to AAA).

V_{TS}—Realized value of the portfolio if there are no defaults and all borrowers migrate to their forward *EDF*.

V_{ES}—Realized value when the portfolio has losses equal to the expected loss (or earns the expected spread over the risk-free rate)—expected value of the portfolio.

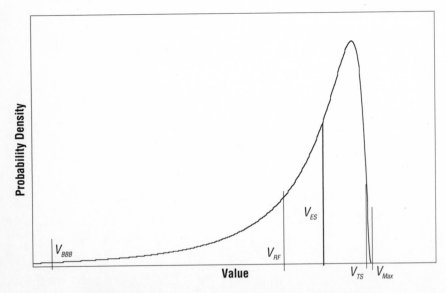

EXHIBIT 4.5   KMV Portfolio Manager Value Distribution

V_{RF}—Realized value when credit losses wipe out all the spread income—zero spread value of the portfolio.

V_{BBB}—Realized value when the losses would consume all the portfolio's capital if it were capitalized to achieve a BBB rating (equivalent to approximately a 15 bp EDF).

Loss Distributions, Expected Loss, and Unexpected Loss   KMV defines two loss distributions. One is based on the expected spread for the portfolio, so the loss is that in excess of the expected loss. The other is based on the total spread to the portfolio, so it is the loss in excess of total spread.

Expected loss is expressed as a fraction of the current portfolio value.

Economic Capital   In Portfolio Manager, economic capital is the difference between unexpected loss and expected loss.

This capital value is calculated at each iteration, and is binned and portrayed graphically as the tail of the *loss* distribution. It answers the question: "Given the risk of the portfolio, what losses should we be prepared to endure?"

RiskMetrics Group CreditManager[3]

The RiskMetrics Group (RMG) released its CreditMetrics® methodology and the CreditManager software package in 1997. CreditManager can be used as a stand-alone system (desktop) or as part of an enterprise-wide risk-management system.

- CreditServer—Java/XML-based credit risk analytics engine that is the core of all RiskMetrics Group's credit risk solutions.
- CreditManager 3.0 web-based client that delivers CreditServer technology with a front-end interface that offers real-time interactive reports and graphs, what-if generation, and interactive drill-down analysis.

Model Type   CreditManager, like the Moody's KMV model, is based on Robert Merton's insight that debt behaves like a short put option on the value of the firm's assets. So default will occur when the value of the firm's assets falls below the value of the firm's debt (or other fixed claims).

Stochastic Variable   Since it is based on Merton's insight that debt behaves like a short put on the value of the firm's assets, the stochastic variable in CreditManager is the value of the firm's assets.

Inputs   Most importantly, CreditManager requires a ratings transition matrix (either created within CreditManager or specified by the user). As the people at the RiskMetrics Group put it: "It all starts with ratings and transition probabilities."

CreditManager requires data regarding the facilities in the portfolio. In the case of obligors, in addition to the name of the obligor, CreditManager needs data on the obligor's total assets, rating, and credit rating system (e.g., S&P eight-state). And in order to incorporate default correlations, CreditManager also requires country and industry weights and obligor-specific volatility percentage. In the case of individual facilities, the user must provide data on the type, amount, coupon, maturity, recovery rates, spread, and seniority class. For commitments, data are also required on the total commitment amount, current drawdown, and expected drawdown.

Exhibit 4.6 provides a sample input screen from CreditManager. The screen shown is the Exposures screen, where the user inputs data on the facility.

CreditManager also requires market data: yield curves, credit spread curves, values of equity indices, and currency exchange rates. However, much of the data are available in the software. As will be described later, CreditManager incorporates or has links to various sources of data:

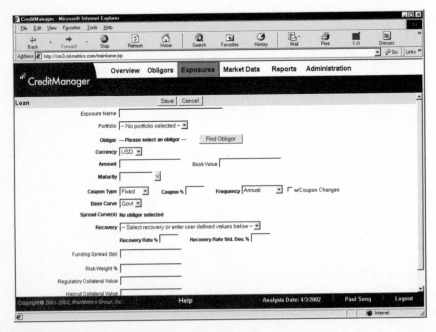

EXHIBIT 4.6   Input Screen for CreditManager
Source: RiskMetrics Group, Inc.

■ Comprehensive database of obligors
■ Probabilities of default
    Moody's RiskCalc for public and private firms
    S&P's CreditModel for public and private firms
    RiskMetrics' CreditGrades

All of these models are described in Chapter 3.

■ MSCI equity indices
■ Market data—automated access to DataMetrics

Probability of Default As noted, CreditManager requires the user to input/specify a ratings transition matrix. This is the key to the workings of CreditManager.

A transition matrix is a distribution of possible credit ratings at a chosen time horizon (e.g., one year hence). The probabilities in each row must sum to 100%. An illustrative transition matrix is illustrated in Exhibit 4.7.

Exhibit 4.7 illustrates some general characteristics of historical transition matrices: An obligor is more likely to stay at the current rating state than to move to other rating states. An obligor is less likely to improve than to decline.

There are a range of sources for the ratings transition matrix. Using applications incorporated in CreditManager, the user could select a transition matrix developed using Moody's RiskCalc or one developed using S&P's CreditModel. The user might use a historical transition matrix. The user might input a transition matrix developed using the Moody's–KMV EDFs. Or if she or he wishes, the user can make up a transition matrix.

EXHIBIT 4.7 Illustrative Ratings Transition Matrix

	Average One-Year Transition Rates							
	Rating at Year End (%)							
Initial Rating	AAA	AA	A	BBB	BB	B	CCC	D
AAA	91.14	8.01	0.70	0.05	0.10	0.00	0.00	0.00
AA	0.70	91.04	7.47	0.57	0.05	0.15	0.02	0.00
A	0.07	2.34	91.55	5.08	0.64	0.26	0.01	0.05
BBB	0.03	0.30	5.65	87.96	4.70	1.05	0.11	0.19
BB	0.02	0.11	0.58	7.76	81.69	7.98	0.87	1.00
B	0.00	0.09	0.28	0.47	6.96	83.05	3.78	5.39
CCC	0.19	0.00	0.37	1.13	2.64	11.52	62.08	22.07

Recovery   As noted earlier, the user must specify loss given default (LGD). The user can employ LGD data that are contained in CreditManager, which have been taken from academic studies by Altman and Edwards (1996) and Carty and Lieberman (1997). Or users can input their own LGD estimates.

Default Correlation   In the CreditManager framework, we need to know the *joint probability* that any two obligors migrate to a given ratings pair (e.g., the probability that Firm 1 migrates from BBB to BB *and* firm 2 migrates from A to BBB). CreditManager deals with this by relating the firm's asset values to ratings states. Exhibit 4.8 shows how this would be accomplished for a single facility.

As was the case with the Moody's–KMV Credit Monitor model, we start with the current market value of the firm's assets, the growth rate of that asset value,[4] and the volatility of the asset value. Since we know the probability of default (from the transition matrix that we input), we can estimate the value of the firm's assets at which default would occur. This is shown as the area shaded with the diagonal lines in Exhibit 4.8. Next, since we know the probability that the rating will decline from B to CCC (again from the transition

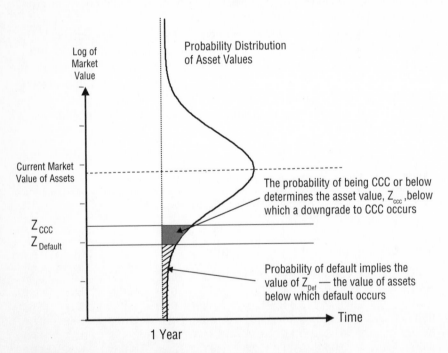

EXHIBIT 4.8   Mapping Ratings to Asset Values in CreditManager
Source: RiskMetrics Group, Inc.

matrix that we input), we can estimate the value of the firm's assets that would correspond to a rating of CCC. This is shown as the solid shaded area in Exhibit 4.8. If we continue this process, we can construct a distribution of asset values that correspond to ratings, as illustrated in Exhibit 4.9.

Extending this framework from one asset to many requires estimating the joint probability that any two obligors migrate to a given ratings pair. With a single obligor and eight ratings states, the probability table contains eight cells. With more than one obligor, the probability table increases in size exponentially.

To see this, let's take a look at an example. Exhibit 4.10 considers two obligors—Obligor 1's initial rating is BBB and Obligor 2's initial rating is AA. Each obligor has eight different probabilities for future state ratings. If these two obligors were independent, the joint probability of these two obligors being in specified rating classes would be obtained by multiplying the obligors' probabilities. For example, the likelihood of both Obligor 1 and Obligor 2 to be rated BB is 0.53% × 5.72% = 0.03%. So calculating

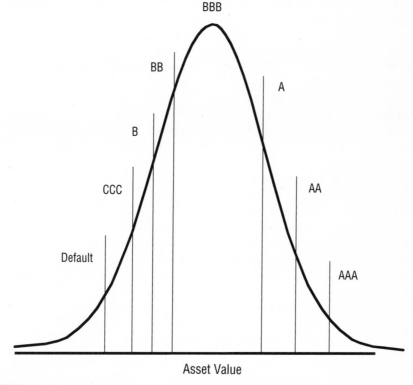

EXHIBIT 4.9 Ratings Map to Asset Values in CreditManager
Source: RiskMetrics Group, Inc.

EXHIBIT 4.10 Two Obligors with Their Rating Transition Probabilities

Obligor 1		Obligor 2	
Year-End Rating	Probability (%)	Year-End Rating	Probability (%)
AAA	0.04	AAA	2.3
AA	0.44	AA	90.54
A	5.65	A	4.5
BBB	86.18	BBB	1.7
BB	5.72	BB	0.53
B	1.42	B	0.42
CCC	0.25	CCC	0.01
Default	0.3	Default	0

the joint probability of a pair of two obligors requires us to build the 64-cell table illustrated in Exhibit 4.11.

Rather than create the joint probability tables for every obligor, Credit Manager uses a factor model. (As we see, the process is similar to that employed in the Moody's–KMV approach described earlier.) The RiskMetrics Group explains that their use of a factor model is prompted by the fact that they need to cover many obligors (a factor model lets you reduce your dimensionality and the amount of data you store) as well as the need to allow users to add in their own obligors (with a factor model, you just provide the mappings rather than a whole new time series).

However, instead of using asset correlation, CreditManager uses equity correlation as a proxy for asset correlation. (Equity correlation would be a perfect proxy if the value of the debt remained fixed. The RiskMetrics Group argues that the approximation is good as long as the firm's volatility is primarily driven by equity fluctuations, and the volatility of the debt level is relatively small in comparison to the equity fluctuations.)

The original CreditMetrics approach was to map obligors to countries and industries, but the RiskMetrics Group determined that this led to a number of arbitrary or ambiguous choices. CreditManager now maps directly to the MSCI indices mentioned previously. According to the RiskMetrics Group, this clarifies some of the ambiguities, eliminates the need to have logic to map when a combination is missing (for example, a user maps to Mexico and Forestry but there is no Mexican Forestry index), and creates a framework within which users can add other indices (e.g., interest rates and commodity prices). This mapping is illustrated in Exhibit 4.12.

The returns for each obligor are expressed as a weighted sum of returns on the indices and a firm-specific component. The firm-specific risk—

EXHIBIT 4.11 Joint Migration Probabilities with Zero Correlation

Obligor 2 (AA)		Obligor 1 (BBB)							
		AAA	AA	A	BBB	BB	B	CCC	Default
		0.04%	0.44%	5.65%	86.18%	5.72%	1.42%	0.25%	0.30%
AAA	2.30%	0.00%	0.01%	0.13%	1.98%	0.13%	0.03%	0.01%	0.01%
AA	90.54%	0.04%	0.40%	5.12%	78.03%	5.18%	1.29%	0.23%	0.27%
A	4.50%	0.00%	0.02%	0.25%	3.88%	0.26%	0.06%	0.01%	0.01%
BBB	1.70%	0.00%	0.01%	0.10%	1.47%	0.10%	0.02%	0.00%	0.01%
BB	0.53%	0.00%	0.00%	0.03%	0.46%	0.03%	0.01%	0.00%	0.00%
B	0.42%	0.00%	0.00%	0.02%	0.36%	0.02%	0.01%	0.00%	0.00%
CCC	0.01%	0.00%	0.00%	0.00%	0.01%	0.00%	0.00%	0.00%	0.00%
Default	0.00%	0.00%	0.00%	0.00%	0.00%	0.00%	0.00%	0.00%	0.00%

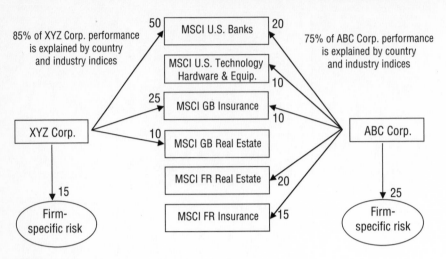

EXHIBIT 4.12   Factor Model Used in CreditManager
Source: RiskMetrics Group, Inc.

R^2—shows how much of an obligor's equity price movements are not explained by country or industry indices. The weights and index correlations are used to compute correlations between obligors.

CreditManager contains the "country/industry" decomposition for approximately 9,000 obligors (50% U.S., 35% Europe, and 15% Asia) based on data from the firm's annual report data. (This is the MSCI index mappings mentioned earlier.) For those same obligors, CreditManager contains a measure of systemic risk for each in the form of the R-squared from the estimation of the factor equation.

For obligors not included in the CreditManager dataset, the decomposition for "country" and "industry" could be accomplished via either *regression* or *fundamental* analysis.

Valuation   CreditManager calculates the market value of the loan or other credit asset for each possible rating state. Using the current forward credit spread curve, CreditManager calculates the mark-to-market (MTM) value of the asset for each possible rating state. Note that this MTM process ignores the possibility of future changes in the level of interest rates (market risk). The valuation methodology used in CreditManager is illustrated in Exhibit 4.13.

In this illustration, the initial rating state for the asset is BBB. The first row lists the eight rating states that are possible one year from today. The second row provides the current values for the assets associated with the different future rating states. That is, using the forward spread curve, the current

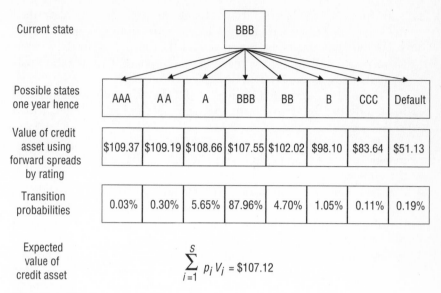

Current state				BBB				
Possible states one year hence	AAA	A A	A	BBB	BB	B	CCC	Default
Value of credit asset using forward spreads by rating	$109.37	$109.19	$108.66	$107.55	$102.02	$98.10	$83.64	$51.13
Transition probabilities	0.03%	0.30%	5.65%	87.96%	4.70%	1.05%	0.11%	0.19%

Expected value of credit asset

$$\sum_{i=1}^{S} p_i V_i = \$107.12$$

EXHIBIT 4.13 Valuation Methodology Used in CreditManager
Source: RiskMetrics Group, Inc.

value of the asset is calculated for each of the eight possible states (e.g., the current value of an asset with a rating of AAA in one year is $109.37). The third row, the likelihood of the asset's future rating state, is taken directly from the transition matrix. In this simple illustration, we could get the expected value of the asset by calculating the probability-weighted sum of the values in the second row.

Generating the Value Distribution

Pre-Processing: Rating-Specific Facility Values In order to reduce the computational burden, CreditManager does not calculate a facility value corresponding to the simulated rating for each iteration in the simulation process. Instead, CreditManager calculates the facility values for all the ratings states using the forward credit spread curve and stores these values. These stored values are called by the software during the simulation.

1. Simulate asset value at horizon. CreditManager simulates the value of the firm's assets at the horizon, using the assumption that asset return is a *correlated standard* normal random variable. The correlation matrix is as described previously. From this correlated standard normal distribution, independent random draws are made to simulate the firm's asset value.

2. Transform asset value to ratings. Using the procedure we described the asset value obtained in step 1 is transformed to a rating.
3. Value the facilities. If the rating obtained in step 2 is not D, Credit-Manager assigns the facility the value corresponding to its rating that was calculated in the Pre-Processing Step.

    If the rating obtained in step 2 is D, the value of the facility will be determined by a stochastic recovery rate, which follows a *beta distribution*.

    The implication of this process is that all values corresponding to default outcomes can be different; but all nondefault outcomes will be the same within a given credit rating.
4. Sum to obtain portfolio value. Once values for each of the facilities at the horizon have been obtained, the fourth step in generating the value distribution is to sum the values of the facilities to obtain the value of the portfolio.
5. Iterate. Steps 1 through 4 provide one simulated value for the portfolio. To get a distribution, it is necessary to obtain additional simulated values. That means repeating steps 1–4 some number of times (e.g., 1,000,000 times).

The RiskMetrics Group is focusing on making their model work to provide more accurate results using fewer iterations. As described in the following they are turning to a statistical technique called *importance sampling*.

Simulation Techniques in CreditManager*

The RiskMetrics Group notes that characteristics of credit portfolios present difficulties in the context of a simulation: *The small default probabilities and concentrations mean that the portfolio distribution smoothes out very slowly.*

Also the typical applications make things even harder: *The portfolios are large and the measures of economic capital require looking at extreme percentiles.*

The biggest issue is that the loss distribution is very sensitive to extreme factor moves and a standard Monte Carlo simulation will not have many iterations in the area of largest changes in the loss.

An obvious solution is to increase the number of iterations in the simulation. However, that would increase the run time.

The RiskMetrics Group has turned to a statistical technique called *importance sampling*. This technique involves cheating and forcing the scenarios where they are most interesting. In the context of credit portfolios, this means that scenarios are shifted into the region where portfolio value is more sensitive.

*See Xiao (2002).

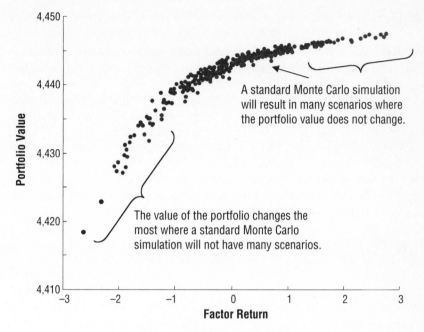

Source: RiskMetrics Group, Inc.

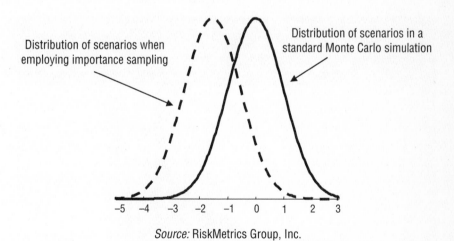

Source: RiskMetrics Group, Inc.

By having more of the scenarios in the sensitive area, this technique provides better estimates of the shape of the loss distribution at extreme levels, or, as the RiskMetrics Group describes it, *importance sampling* provides greater precision with fewer scenarios required, particularly at extreme loss levels.

Outputs

**Portfolio Value Distribution, Expected and Unexpected Loss, and Credit
VaR**   An illustration of a portfolio value distribution from CreditManager
is provided in Exhibit 4.14.

Note that CreditManager also provides value-at-risk (VaR) measures
for this value distribution. The RiskMetrics Group asserts that "VaR or expected shortfall provides better measures of the economic capital required
for a solvency guarantee or insurance premium than the commonly-used
standard deviation" (*RMG Journal*).

"Expected loss" is defined as the difference between the expected horizon value of the portfolio and the current value of the portfolio. Any loss
in excess of expected loss is called unexpected loss.

Economic Capital   The RiskMetrics Group defines economic capital as
"the equity capital banks and other financial institutions hold to guarantee
a pre-defined solvency standard or to insure against potential loss scenarios
over a given time period, typically one year" (*RMG Journal*). Exhibit 4.15
provides an illustration of the manner in which economic capital is displayed in CreditManager.

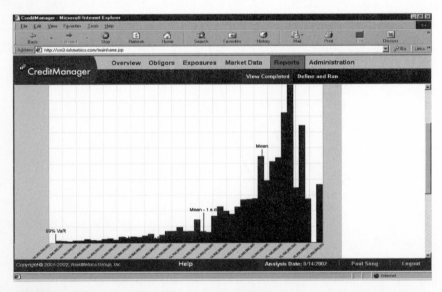

EXHIBIT 4.14   Estimated Portfolio Value Distribution from CreditManager
Source: RiskMetrics Group, Inc.

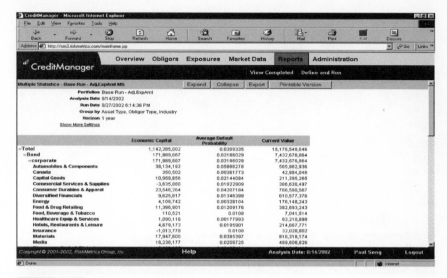

EXHIBIT 4.15 Illustrative Report from CreditManager
Source: RiskMetrics Group, Inc.

Risk Contribution CreditManager provides four different calculation methods for risk contribution:

1. Standard deviation contribution—This measures the contribution of the facility to the dispersion of loss around the expected loss level. This measure is illustrated in Exhibit 4.16.
2. Marginal risk measures—This measures the amount a facility adds to overall portfolio risk by adding or removing that single exposure.
3. VaR contribution—This is a simulation-based risk measure.
4. Expected shortfall contribution (average loss in the worst p percentage scenarios; it captures the tail risk contribution).

(We pick up a discussion of the usefulness of various risk contribution measures in Chapter 8.)

CreditManager provides diagrams of portfolio risk concentrations. Exhibit 4.17 shows a portfolio that contains a concentration in B-rated industrial and commercial services.

CreditManager also provides analyses of risk versus return. Exhibit 4.18 provides an illustrative plot of VaR risk contribution against expected returns.

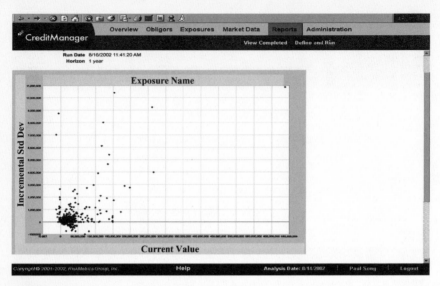

EXHIBIT 4.16 Plot of Risk Contributions from CreditManager
Source: RiskMetrics Group, Inc.

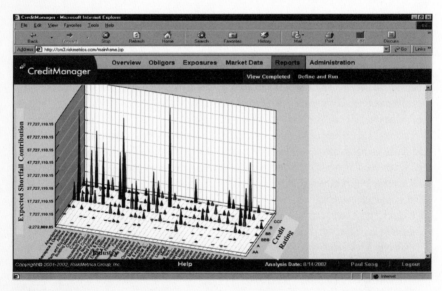

EXHIBIT 4.17 Diagram of Portfolio Risk Contributions from CreditManager
Source: RiskMetrics Group, Inc.

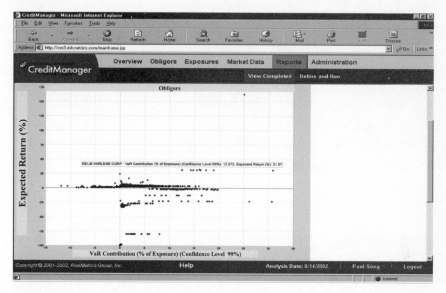

EXHIBIT 4.18 Plot of Expected Return to Risk Contribution from CreditManager
Source: RiskMetrics Group, Inc.

EXPLICIT FACTOR MODELS

Implicitly so far, we have been drawing "defaults" out of a single "urn"—
the "average" urn in Exhibit 4.19. In a Macro Factor Model, defaults depend on the level of economic activity, so we would draw defaults out of
more than one urn. Exhibit 4.19 envisions three urns—one for the "average" level of economic activity, another if the economy is in a "contractionary" state, and a third if the economy is in an "expansionary" state.
Note that the probability of default—the number of black balls in the
urn—changes as the state of the economy changes. (There are fewer black
balls in the "expansionary" urn than in the "contractionary" urn.)

Consequently, the way that a Macro Factor Model works is as follows:

1. *Simulate* the "state" of the economy. (Note that we are simulating a
   future state of the economy, not forecasting a future state.)
2. Adjust the default rate to the simulated state of the economy. (The
   probability of default is higher in contractionary states than in expansionary states.)
3. Assign a probability of default for each obligor, based on the simulated
   state of the economy.

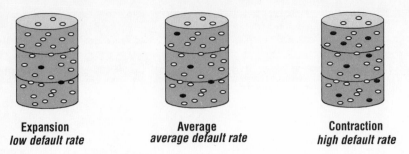

Expansion
low default rate

Average
average default rate

Contraction
high default rate

EXHIBIT 4.19   Logic of a Macro Factor Model

4. Value individual transactions (facilities) depending on the likelihood of default assigned to the obligor in #3.
5. Calculate portfolio loss by summing results for all transactions.
6. Repeat steps 1–6 some number of times to map the loss distribution.

In factor models, correlation in default rates is driven by the coefficients on the various factors. That is, the state of the economy causes all default rates and transition probabilities to change together. A "low" state of economic activity drawn from the simulation of macrovariables produces "high" default/downgrade probabilities, which affect all obligors in the portfolio, thereby producing correlation in default/migration risk. Ignoring risk that is unique to each firm (i.e., risk that is not explained by the factors), any two firms that have the same factor sensitivities will have perfectly correlated default rates. [See Gordy (2000).]

The first widely discussed macrofactor model was introduced by McKinsey & Company and was called CreditPortfolioView. In order to be able to compare a Macro Factor Model with the other credit portfolio models, Rutter Associates produced a Demonstration Model that is similar to the McKinsey model.

McKinsey's CreditPortfolioView

In McKinsey's CreditPortfolioView, historical default rates for industry/country combinations are described as a function of macroeconomic variables specified by the user. For example, the default rate for German automotive firms could be modeled as a function of different macroeconomic "factors."

$$(\text{Prob of Default})_{German\ Auto} = f(\text{GDP, FX, } \ldots \text{,UNEMP})$$

The McKinsey model specifies the functional form $f(\ )$, but not the macroeconomic variables that should be used. Historical data on default rates (and credit migrations) are used to estimate the parameters of the model. Because of this reliance on historical data, default rates are specified at the industry level rather than the obligor level.

In the McKinsey approach, default rates are driven by sensitivity to a set of systematic risk factors and a unique, or firm-specific, factor. Exhibit 4.20 summarizes the key features of the McKinsey factor model.

CreditPortfolioView captures the fundamental intuition that economy-wide defaults rise and fall with macroeconomic conditions. It also captures the concept of serial correlation in default rates over time. Given the data and the specification of the relation between macrovariables and default/transition probabilities, the McKinsey model can calculate time-varying default and transition matrices that are unique to individual industries and/or countries.

Unfortunately, CreditPortfolioView specifies only the functional form of the model. It does not provide guidance on the correct macrovariables or estimated weights for the industry/country segment. Furthermore, given a functional form, it is unlikely that the available data would be sufficient

EXHIBIT 4.20   Key Features of CreditPortfolioView

Unit of analysis	Industry/country segments
Default data	Empirical estimation of segment default rate as a function of unspecified macroeconomic variables, e.g., GDP, unemployment
Correlation structure	Driven by empirical correlation between the chosen macroeconomic variables and the estimated factor sensitivities
Risk engine	Autoregressive Moving Average Model fit to evolution of macrofactors. Shocks to the system determine deviation from mean default rates at the segment level.
Default rate distribution	Logistic (normal)
Horizon	Year by year marginal default rate to maturity

to estimate the needed model parameters except in the most liquid market segments of developed countries.

Rutter Associates Demonstration Model

The Rutter Associates Demonstration Model is, as its name implies, a simplified version of a macrofactor model. In developing the model, we first needed to identify a set of macroeconomic factors that determine the state of the economy. We then fit the resulting factor model to historical data. Once we had that estimated model, we simulated future paths for the macrofactors and used the simulations of the macrofactors to simulate the probability of default in that simulated state of the economy. The following subsections describe how we did that.

Selecting the Macroeconomic Factors (i.e., the Stochastic Variables)   In a macrofactor model, the macroeconomic factors are the stochastic variables. Simulations of the stochastic macrofactors identify the simulated state of the economy.

In the Demonstration Model, we used three macroeconomic factors:

1. GDP
2. Unemployment
3. Durable goods

Developing a Model to Simulate the Possible Future Values of the Macrofactors   We fit a purely statistical model to historical data to generate possible future states of the world. We wanted to capture general characteristics of each variable (e.g., serial correlation and volatility).

We employed an ARIMA time series model in which the current state of each variable depends on its prior path and a random surprise:

Gross domestic product $\quad GDP_t = c_1 + \Phi_1(GDP_{t-1}) + \Psi_1(a_{1t}) + \varepsilon_{1t}$
Unemployment $\quad\quad\quad\quad UMP_t = c_2 + \Phi_2(UMP_{t-1}) + \Psi_2(a_{2t}) + \varepsilon_{2t}$
Durable goods $\quad\quad\quad\quad DUR_t = c_3 + \Phi_3(DUR_{t-1}) + \Psi_3(a_{3t}) + \varepsilon_{3t}$

In the preceding equations, the current state of each variable is related to the previous value and its multiplier Φ_i, the (moving) average value of the variable up to time t (a_{it}) and its multiplier Ψ_i, and a normally distributed (independent) random "surprise" ε_{it}. We use an ARIMA model because that class of models produces good "fits" to the historical patterns in macroeconomic data. Remember, we are not making *predictions*; the purpose of the ARIMA model is to generate realistic simulations of *possible* future states of the economy.

What Is an ARIMA Model?

In empirical finance, you will hear people talk about autoregressive moving average (ARMA) models and autoregressive integrated moving average (ARIMA) models. Both of these are "time series" models, meaning that the current value of the variable in question is determined by past values of that variable.

An ARMA model, like the one employed in CreditPortfolioView, is based on the assumption that each value of the series depends only on a weighted sum of the previous values of the same series (autoregressive component) and on a weighted sum of the present and previous values of a different time series (moving average component) with the addition of a noise factor. For example, the following process would be called an ARMA(2, 1) process.

$$Y_t = \beta_1 Y_{t-1} + \beta_2 Y_{t-2} + \theta_0 Z_t + \theta_1 Z_{t-1} + \varepsilon_t$$

The variable Y is related to (1) its values in time periods $t-1$ and $t-2$, (2) the current and $t-1$ values of variable Z, and (3) a random error term, ε_t.

The ARIMA model extends the ARMA process to include a measure of the stationarity of the process. For example, if the preceding process was an ARIMA(2,0,1), it would be a stationary process.

Exhibit 4.21 provides six illustrative possible future paths for GDP (i.e., six simulations of GDP using an ARIMA model).

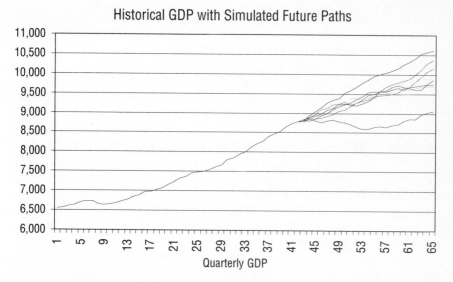

EXHIBIT 4.21 Simulated Future Paths from an ARIMA Model

Relating Observed Defaults to the Macroeconomic Factors

Adjusting the Default Rate to the Simulated State of the Economy   The
default rate for each obligor evolves through time along with the macrofactors. One of the major challenges in this type of model is specifying the relationship between the default rate and the macrovariables.

- The horizon in macromodels typically exceeds one year. The state of
  the economy is simulated out to the average life of the portfolio.
- The serial correlation inherent in macrovariables produces serially correlated default rates (i.e., business cycle effects).

In the Demonstration Model, we fit the default rate to the macrofactors. From S&P's CreditPro, we obtained historical data on the "speculative" default rate (i.e., rating classes from BB to CCC). We used the
speculative default rate because of data limitations (i.e., so few investment
grade defaults occur that there are little data with which to fit a model). We
fit these data on historical defaults to our economic factors via a logit regression (for a reminder about logit regression see Chapter 3).

$$Default\ Rate = \frac{1}{(1 + e^{-y})}$$

$$y = a + \beta_1(GDP) + \beta_2(UMP) + \beta_3(DUR) + \varepsilon$$

The coefficients (the βs) provide the link between the simulated state of
the economy and the default rates used in the model. Note that as y tends
to infinity, the default rate tends to 1 and as y tends to minus infinity, the
default rate goes to zero.

Exhibit 4.22 provides an illustration of the fit obtained. (Note that,
since this is an "in-sample" prediction, the excellent fit we obtained is
not unexpected.)

Modeling all Ratings and Transition Probabilities   To this point in our discussion, the Demonstration Model relates changes in the *speculative default* rate to changes in the state of the economy (as expressed through the
macroeconomic factors). We want to expand this framework to include investment grade obligors. If we assume that the speculative rate is a good indicator for the direction of all credits, we can link the default rates for the
investment grade obligors to the speculative rate.

In addition to expanding our framework to include investment grade
obligors, we also want to model migration probabilities as well as default
probabilities. Consequently, we need a mechanism for creating a State De-

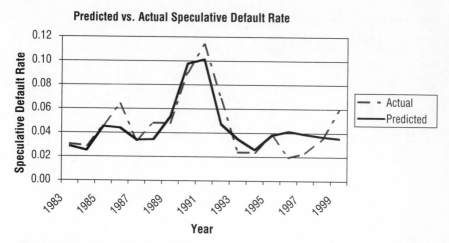

EXHIBIT 4.22 Fitting Default Rates to Macro Factors in Rutter Associates'
Demonstration Model

pendent Transition Matrix (i.e., a transition matrix that evolves as a function of the speculative default rate, which in turn depends on the state of the economy).

In CreditPortfolioView, Tom Wilson defined a "shift operator" that would shift the probabilities in a transition matrix up or down depending on the state of the economy. Hence, this shift operator could be expressed as a function of the speculative default rate. The logic of this shift operator is provided in Exhibit 4.23.

As the economy contracts, the shift operator would move migration probabilities to the right (i.e., as the economy contracts, it is more likely for an obligor to be downgraded than upgraded). Conversely, as the economy expands, migration probabilities would be shifted to the left.

In the Rutter Associates' Demonstration Model, we implemented such a shift parameter, by estimating the parameters of the shift operator from historical upgrade and downgrade data. That is, using historical transition matrices, we estimated a function that would transform the transition matrix based on the state of the economy.

In order to determine how well the model works, we compared our simulations to actual cumulative default rates. Exhibit 4.24 provides an illustration of the results. (Again note that these are "in-sample" predictions.)

Valuation In the Demonstration Model, the valuation module takes the *simulated* rating of the obligor, and facility information, as the inputs to

Contraction causes right shifts

AAA	**92.61**	6.83	0.42	0.10	0.03	0.00	0.00	0.00
AA	0.60	**91.78**	6.78	0.63	0.05	0.12	0.03	0.01
A	0.06	2.40	**91.82**	4.97	0.50	0.22	0.01	0.04
BBB	0.04	0.26	5.38	**88.51**	4.61	0.86	0.13	0.22
BB	0.04	0.11	0.48	7.11	**82.31**	7.87	1.10	1.01
B	0.00	0.12	0.31	0.55	6.04	**83.26**	3.91	5.81
CCC	0.16	0.00	0.33	1.30	1.79	10.59	**61.73**	24.10

Expansion causes left shifts

EXHIBIT 4.23   Logic of "Shift Parameter" in Rutter Associates' Demonstration Model

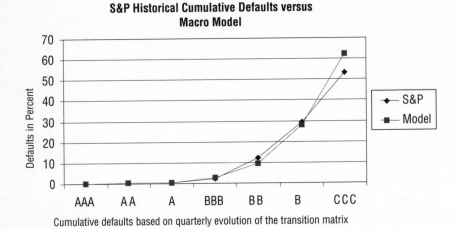

EXHIBIT 4.24   Comparison of Simulations to Actual Cumulative Default Rates in Rutter Associates' Demonstration Model

valuation. Valuation can be accomplished either in a mark-to-market mode or a default-only mode:

- In the mark-to-market mode, valuation can be based on input credit spreads (like CreditManager) for each rating.
- In the default-only mode, the model would consider only losses due to defaults.

Generating the Loss Distribution The generation of the loss distribution can be viewed as a process with seven steps:

1. Simulate the future values for the macroeconomic factors at time t_i.
2. Use the simulated future values of the macroeconomic factors to specify a speculative default rate at time t_i.
3. Use the speculative default rate and the shift operator to specify a transition matrix for time t_i.
4. Value each facility at time t_i using the simulated credit rating of the obligor.
5. Sum across all facilities to obtain a portfolio value.
6. Repeat steps 1 through 5 for time step $t_1, t_2, \ldots, t_H$ where t_H is the specified horizon.
7. Repeat steps 1 through 6 some large number of times (e.g., 1,000,000 times).

ACTUARIAL MODELS

The type of model we refer to as an *actuarial model* could also be called a "reduced form" model of default. Economic causality is ignored—there is no "story" to explain default. Consequently, specific asset values and leverage details for specific firms are irrelevant.

Actuarial models specify a distribution for the default rate and apply statistics to obtain a closed form expression for the joint distribution of loss events. By extension the expected severity can be incorporated to arrive at a distribution of losses.

The best known of the actuarial models is Credit Risk+, introduced by Credit Suisse First Boston.

Credit Risk+

Stochastic Variable As we noted, in an actuarial model, economic causality is ignored. Consequently, in Credit Risk+, the stochastic element is the default event itself. Default just occurs at random points in time and Credit Risk+ makes no attempt to explain the cause of the defaults.

Credit Risk+ does, however, provide some specificity regarding the default events:

- Default is a "low"-frequency event.
- Default losses tend to be correlated. This implies that the loss distribution is fat tailed.

By making distributional assumptions consistent with the above, a closed form solution for the loss function can be obtained.

Modeling the Number of Defaults—The Poisson Distribution   A distribution that fits low-frequency events and would result in a fat-tailed loss distribution is a *Poisson distribution*. Rather than dealing with the probability of default for a single obligor, the Poisson distribution deals with the number of defaults in a portfolio per year, and it is the Poisson distribution that forms the basis for Credit Risk+.

Credit Risk+ specifies that the "arrival rate of defaults" follows a Poisson process. The probability of *n* defaults occurring over some time period in a portfolio is thus given by a Poisson distribution.

What Is a Poisson Distribution and How Does it Relate to Defaults?

The Poisson distribution is one that governs a random variable in which "rare" events are counted, but at a definite average rate. A Poisson Process is one in which discrete events are observable in an area of opportunity—a continuous interval (of time, length, surface area, etc.)—in such a manner that if we shorten the area of opportunity enough, we obtain three conditions: (1) the probability of observing exactly one occurrence in the interval is stable; (2) the probability of observing more than one occurrence in the interval is 0; (3) an occurrence in any one interval is statistically independent of that in any other interval.

Examples of Poisson processes include finding the probability of the number of:

Radioactive decays per second
Deaths per month due to a disease
Imperfections per square meter in rolls of metals
Telephone calls per hour received by an office
Bacteria in a given culture per liter
Cases of a rare disease per year
Stoppages on a production line per week
Accidents at a particular intersection per month
Firms defaulting in a portfolio of loans per year

The distribution was first applied to describing the number of Prussian soldiers killed by being kicked by horses, and is named after the French mathematician Simeon-Denise Poisson (1781–1840). Actuaries use a Poisson distribution to model events like a hurricane striking a specific location on the eastern seaboard of the United States. The Poisson distribution is a limiting form of the binomial distribution, that being when the probability of an event is very small (e.g., default events), and the number of "trials" n (e.g., the number of names in a portfolio) is large.

It turns out that the Poisson distribution, giving the probability of n events occurring in some unit (space or time) interval when there is an *average* of μ events occurring in that interval, is

$$p_\mu(n) = e^{-\mu}\frac{\mu^n}{n!}$$

where the exclamation mark ("!") is the factorial symbol or operation (e.g., 5! = 5·4·3·2·1 = 120, and by definition, 0! = 1).

The Poisson distribution takes only *one* parameter: the mean of the distribution, μ. In a Poisson distribution, the variance is equal to the mean, so the standard deviation is $\sqrt{\mu}$. Both the Poisson distribution and the binomial distribution are described in the statistics appendix at the end of the book.

The Poisson distribution takes only one parameter—the expected number of defaults. Note that the number of exposures does not enter the formula. Also, note that the obligors do not need to have the same default probability.

If we define the expected number of defaults per year in a portfolio of n firms to be μ, and the ith firm has an annual probability of default equal to p_i, then

$$\mu = \sum_{i=1}^{n} p_i$$

and the distribution of default events (i.e., the probability of n defaults occurring in the portfolio in one year) is

$$p_\mu(n) = e^{-\mu}\frac{\mu^n}{n!}$$

Adjusting the Poisson Distribution—Introduction of Default Rate Volatility
Applying the relation between the mean and the variance in a Poisson distribution that was described above:

Std dev of number of defaults = Square root of mean number of defaults

In the case of a portfolio consisting of only one obligor, this implies that the standard deviation of the default probability (or rate) is equal to the square root of the default probability.

It turns out that this implication of the Poisson distribution simply doesn't match the data. Historical data indicate that actual standard deviations are much larger than those that would be implied by the Poisson distribution.

Historical default rate volatilities range from seventy-five percent of the default rate for speculative grade credits to several hundred percent of the default rate for investment grade credits.

To make the model more realistic, Credit Risk+ assumes that the default rate may vary, thus introducing the concept of "default rate volatility" for each obligor. Because this implies an underlying distribution for the average default rate, the developers made the assumption that the *mean* default rate (for each sector) is governed by a *gamma distribution* (see the statistics appendix). Though there is no upper bound for the gamma distribution, this is permissible because the default rate for a sector can be greater than one, as opposed to a default probability.

The impact of including default rate volatility as a parameter is illustrated in Exhibit 4.25. Panel A shows the impact on the number of defaults. Panel B shows the impact on the loss distribution. (The "jagged" lines for the loss distributions—especially when including default rate volatility—are due to the particulars of the exposures in the hypothetical portfolio and the size of the loss bins.) Note that the effect of including default rate volatility is to make the tail of the loss fatter.

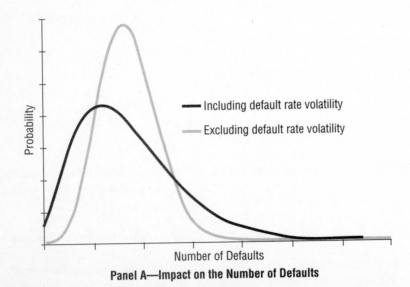

Panel A—Impact on the Number of Defaults

EXHIBIT 4.25   The Effect of Including Default Rate Volatility in Credit Risk+

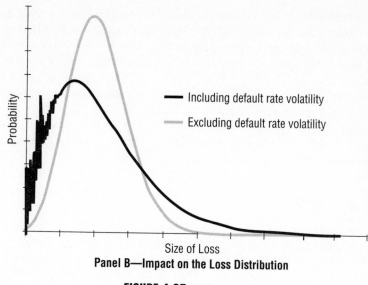

Panel B—Impact on the Loss Distribution

FIGURE 4.25 *(Continued)*

Inputs An attractive feature of Credit Risk+ is that it requires only limited data. There are three required inputs:

1. Mean default rate for the obligor.
2. Volatility of default rate for the obligor—It turns out that the model is very sensitive to this parameter; and this parameter is difficult to accurately measure.
3. Facility exposure (amount at risk net of recovery)—Credit Risk+ takes the loss given default as fixed. The user inputs a net figure taking into account usage at default (for committed lines) and the amount of recovery. Unlike the Moody's–KMV model and the RiskMetrics Group's model, there is no simulation of how much is actually lost when default occurs.

And there is one optional input:

4. Portfolio segments (factors)—The user can specify sector (factor) weightings. This segmentation allows the riskiness of the obligors to be broken down uniquely into components sensitive to common risk factors. Credit Risk+ accommodates two types of sectors: a specific risk sector and systematic sectors (up to nine can be specified). The systematic sectors are commonly used to decompose by industry/country as in the Moody's–KMV model and the RiskMetrics Group's model.

Default Correlation   In Credit Risk+, the *volatility of the default rate for the obligors* (input 2) is a primary determinant of the correlation of defaults.

The optional sector weightings also affect default correlation. Sectors allow users to influence the degree of default correlation between obligors:

- Specific risk sector—Placing some of an obligor's risk in the specific risk sector means that that risk can be fully diversified away.
- Systematic sectors (maximum nine)—Within each sector, the default rates of each obligor are correlated. Across the sectors, the default rates are independent.

Correlation in Credit Risk+

As in the macrofactor models, in Credit Risk+ default correlation between two firms is maximized if the two firms are allocated in the same country or industry sector. Two obligors A and B that have no sector in common will have zero default event correlation. This is because no systematic factor affects them both. In the Credit Risk+ technical document, an approximation for the default event correlation is calculated as:

$$\rho_{AB} = \sqrt{p_A p_B} \sum_{k=1}^{K} w_{Ak} w_{Bk} \left(\frac{\sigma_k}{p_k} \right)^2$$

where

there are K sectors,

p_A (p_B) is the average default probability of Obligor A (B),

w_{Ak} (w_{Bk}) is the weight of Obligor A (B) in sector k and

p_k and σ_k are the average default probability and volatility (standard deviation) of the default probability, respectively, in sector k:

$$p_k = \sum_{i=1}^{N} w_{ik} p_i \text{ and } \sigma_k = \sum_{i=1}^{N} w_{ik} \sigma_i$$

There are N obligors in the portfolio and the weights of each obligor on a sector satisfy

$$\sum_{k=1}^{K} w_{ik} = 1$$

Outputs   The loss distribution and summary table generated by Credit Risk+ is illustrated in Exhibit 4.26.

EXHIBIT 4.26 Loss Distribution and Summary Table from Credit Risk+

Percentile	Credit Loss Amount
Mean	564,507,608
50	359,285,459
75	781,272,140
95	1,799,264,354
97.5	2,241,332,132
99	2,824,856,005
99.5	3,266,316,896
99.85	4,033,167,753
99.9	4,291,418,688

The manner in which Credit Risk+ outputs expected loss and risk contributions for individual facilities is illustrated in Exhibit 4.27. In this, the risk contribution is a "standard-deviation-based" risk contribution.

The actuarial approach has the appearance of precision because results are calculated via mathematical model rather than a simulation; however, just the opposite is true. Actuarial models are closed form approximations to the true distribution of defaults. Credit Risk+ is subject to at least two approximation errors.

1. It is possible for a credit to default more than once.
2. The approximation used to calculate the portfolio distribution from the individual loss distributions relies on default rates being small. This means, for example, that noninvestment grade credits of longer

EXHIBIT 4.27 Expected Loss and Risk Contributions from Credit Risk+

Name	Expected Loss	Risk Contribution
Merrill Lynch & Co.	8,175,453	84,507,098
Frontier Ins. Grp. Inc.	16,098,618	69,179,984
Dynex Capital Inc.	13,333,491	56,562,108
Tenneco Automotive Inc.	12,412,990	55,440,436
Assoc. Fst. Capital CP–CL A	7,646,288	46,183,522
Host Marriott Corp.	8,981,823	42,211,822
Exide Corp.	8,687,461	36,250,480
Nationwide Finl. Svcs.–CL A	6,597,600	36,243,725
AMF Bowling Inc.	8,905,219	33,635,363

maturity have cumulative default rates that violate conditions under which the model was derived.

ANALYTICAL COMPARISON OF THE CREDIT PORTFOLIO MODELS

Comparison of Design

A comparison of the design of the models is summarized in Exhibit 4.28. The remainder of this subsection examines parts of this table.

Types of Exposures Covered   All the models cover loans, bonds, guarantees, and asset-backed securities.   In the case of standard derivatives, Portfolio Manager and CreditManager have input screens for standard derivatives exposures (market driven credit exposures) in which estimated maximum exposures are used to proxy for the replacement cost. However, because the credit risk itself is variable over time and depends on the replacement cost of the contract, neither model does a complete job of modeling the credit risk of standard derivatives. The estimated maximum exposures (at some confidence level) are calculated outside the credit model by modeling the market value of the derivative. For the McKinsey approach, while it is theoretically possible to calculate replacement cost within the model, this element was not implemented and remains only a theoretical possibility.

Both Portfolio Manager and CreditManager explicitly include credit default swaps and total return swaps. Both implement credit default swaps by linking the swap counterparty to the obligor of the credit being hedged.

The data structures of Portfolio Manager and CreditManager make incorporating reinsurance and similar guarantee type exposures easy. Those models allow obligors to be linked at various levels, depending on the firmness of the guarantee (e.g., Parent/Subsidiary with a parent guarantee, Parent/Subsidiary with no parent guarantee, and third-party credit support).

Portfolio Manager, CreditManager, and Credit Risk+ all approach credit support through a decrease in expected severity.

Type of Credit Risk Measured   As summarized in Exhibit 4.28, Credit Risk+ is a "default only" model (i.e., it measures the cumulative risk of default over the remaining average life of the portfolio). This is the appropriate measure for exposures that are not liquid and it is also consistent with the approach traditionally taken by the rating agencies. The other credit portfolio models can view credit risk in either a default mode or a mark-to-market (model) mode.

EXHIBIT 4.28 Comparison of Credit Portfolio Models—Design

	McKinsey CreditPortfolioView	CSFB Credit Risk+	Moody's–KMV Portfolio Manager	RMG CreditManager
Model Classification	Factor Model	Actuarial	Structural	Structural
Types of Exposures				
Loans/Bonds	✓	✓	✓	✓
Guarantees	✓	✓	✓	✓
Asset-backed Sec.	✓	✓	✓	✓
Std. derivatives	✓		✓	✓
Credit derivatives			✓	✓
Contingent exposures	None	None	Parent/Sub—Yes	Parent/Sub—Yes
Credit support		Via Loss Given Def.	Guarantor—Yes ✓	Guarantor—Yes ✓
Risk measured	MTM or Default	Default Risk	MTM or Default	MTM or Default
Return included	No	No	Fees and spreads	All in spread
Losses present valued	Yes	No	Yes	Yes
Calculation Method	Simulation	Analytical	Simulation	Simulation

All the Models Are Factor Models

The first row of Exhibit 4.28 stresses the difference among the models—one is a factor model, one is an actuarial model, and two are structural models. While this difference is important, it can be overstated. Indeed, at one level, all the models are factor models.

ACTUARIAL MODELS AS FACTOR MODELS

Actuarial models like Credit Risk+ are closely related to explicit factor models. Indeed, Credit Risk+ can also be viewed as an *approximation* to a factor model. The approximation is accomplished by making some simplifying assumptions about the nature of defaults and losses. In the Credit Risk+ model, three simplifications are employed:

1. Default events follow a Poisson distribution.
2. The mean default rate is distributed gamma.
3. Loss given default is fixed (and allocated to ranges).

Not surprisingly, Credit Risk+ can be recast as a factor model. (See Gordy, 2000.) In Credit Risk+ multiple factors are represented by segments. Within segments expected default rates are perfectly correlated, while across segments default rates are independent. The allocation of a credit to different sectors is therefore equivalent to the factor model approach, in which an obligor's default rate is related to different (independent) risk factors based on the factor loadings.

FACTOR MODELS EMBEDDED IN STRUCTURAL MODELS

Structural models, like those in Portfolio Manager and CreditManager, attempt to describe the process that drives defaults rather than specify a distribution for the default rate itself. The asset volatility models accomplish this by positing a relation between the market value of a firm's assets and a critical value of debt: If the value of assets falls below this critical level, the firm is assumed to have defaulted. The key variable is the volatility of asset value, since this drives the likelihood of a solvent firm's becoming insolvent.

It should be noted that factor models are embedded in these structural models. Remember that Portfolio Manager uses a factor model to characterize asset returns, which drive default correlation, which in turn is a primary determinant of the loss distribution. CreditManager also uses a factor model to characterize equity returns, which leads to the default correlation and the resulting loss distribution.

Comparison of Economic Structure

Exhibit 4.29 compares the economic structures underlying each of the models. Whether implicitly or explicitly, each framework requires three basic elements:

EXHIBIT 4.29 Comparison of Credit Portfolio Models—Economic Structure

	McKinsey CreditPortfolioView	CSFB Credit Risk+	Moody's-KMV Portfolio Manager	RMG CreditManager
Default rate distribution	Logistic	Poisson for events. Gamma for mean default rate.	Default risk derived from lognormal model of asset values.	Default risk derived from lognormal model of asset values.
Expected default frequency	Derived from historical data	User input	As implied by a Merton-style asset volatility model.	Transition matrix supplied by user.
Default rate volatility	Derived from historical data	User input	Implied by proprietary asset volatility model.	Implied by ratings transition matrix.
Is default rate conditional on the "state" of the economy?	Yes: Expected defaults conditioned on *levels* of user-defined macro-variables and a firm-specific shock.	Yes: The mean of the default distribution is assumed to follow a Gamma distribution. This approximates a single-factor model.	Yes: Asset values are conditioned on equity index factors. Default risk is a function of asset value.	No: Default rates and transition probabilities are static.
Contingent exposures	Not specified	Not available	Changes correlation and/or default rates.	Changes default rates.
Distribution	Beta	Fixed	Beta	Beta
Mean recovery	User defined	User defined	User defined	User defined
Recovery volatility	Not specified	Defined as zero	KMV defined	RiskMetrics defined
Source of correlation	Mean default rates vary with fitted exposure to macrofactors.	Mean default for all obligors is Gamma distributed. Segments mimic a factor model structure.	Asset values linked to a global factor model of equity indices.	Asset values linked to country/industry equity indices.

1. Probability distribution for default.
2. Severity of loss in the event of default.
3. A correlation model.

Probability Distribution for Default   In structural models, like Portfolio Manager and CreditManager, default risk derives from a model of how default occurs (i.e., from the "structure" of the firm). Both Portfolio Manager and CreditManager focus on the change in value of a firm's assets as the primary determinant of default risk.[5]

By specifying the distribution of the default rate directly, reduced form models can be applied to any structure and obligor. The challenge is to choose the distribution and parameters correctly. Credit Risk+ leaves the choice of parameters (e.g. expected default rates and volatility) to the user. Instead of a single distribution for the default rate, Credit Risk+ employs two—a Poisson distribution for the arrival rate of defaults and a gamma distribution for mean default rates.

Furthermore, McKinsey's CreditPortfolioView estimates the parameters of the default distribution via a logistic model (normally distributed factor changes).

Severity of Loss in Event of Default   At times we talk about recovery and at other times we talk about severity. The two are mirror images of each other—Recovery is equal to (1 − Severity).

Recovery Distribution   The beta distribution is the generally accepted model for uncertain recovery in the event of default. As reflected in Exhibit 4.29, Portfolio Manager, CreditManager, and CreditPortfolioView use it.

Mean Recovery and Volatility   In order to model recovery in the event of default, it is necessary to specify the mean recovery and the variability of the mean recovery rate.

In both RiskMetrics and KMV the user can specify loss given default based on characteristics of the exposure.

Correlation Model   In Chapter 3, we described two approaches. One treats correlation as an explicit input. The theoretical models underlying both Portfolio Manager and CreditManager presuppose an explicit correlation input. Both models implement this via a separate factor model that examines asset or equity correlations. The other approach is to treat correlation as an implicit factor. In both CreditPortfolioView and Credit Risk+, the source of the correlation is the model itself.

EMPIRICAL COMPARISON OF
THE CREDIT PORTFOLIO MODELS

Previously Reported Model Comparisons

ISDA/IIF   This ambitious project covered a range of model types. It compared 4 commercially available models (Moody's–KMV Portfolio Manager, RMG's CreditManager, CSFB's Credit Risk+, and McKinsey's CreditPortfolioView), and 11 other proprietary models.

Using what was described as a "very standardized" portfolio, the report indicated that, initially, the capital measures varied substantially across different types of models. But once the parameters were harmonized, the study found that capital measures are fairly consistent within the same type of models and expected losses were very much consistent throughout all models.

While this was a project that added much to knowledge about the models, it was a one-time effort. Moreover, because of the way the project was structured, it is not reproducible.

Academic   Several academic papers examining the portfolio models have appeared. In general, these papers identify the mathematical relation between model types and provide some simulation results using stylized portfolios.

Lopez and Saidenberg (1998)   Jose Lopez and Marc Saidenberg discuss the differences between market risk models and credit risk models that make the validation of credit risk models more difficult. They propose a "cross-sectional simulation" method to evaluate credit risk models.

Gordy (2000)   Michael Gordy demonstrates that CreditManager and Credit Risk+ both have a similar underlying probabilistic structure, despite the surface differences. Gordy shows that both models can be mathematically mapped into each other.

Gordy also shows that the difference between CreditManager and Credit Risk+ is the result of different distributional assumptions that affect the kurtosis of the loss distribution and therefore affect the economic capital measure.

Hickman and Koyluoglu (1998)   Andrew Hickman and Ugar Koyluoglu examined three different portfolio models—CreditManager, Credit Risk+, and CreditPortfolioView. They found that similar inputs yield similar outputs. In their opinion, the real difference in outputs comes from "parameter variance," not the "model variance."

Rutter Associates Comparison

We at Rutter Associates performed these comparisons for a number of reasons. First, we wanted to obtain a working knowledge of a variety of models. The models differ substantially in ways including obligor, exposure, and parameter setup; calculations and simulation; and the definition and interpretation of model output. Second, we wanted to illustrate practical differences across models and help answer important questions like:

- What drives differences?
- How can models be reconciled or parameterized for consistency?
- Is one framework more suitable for certain applications?

Third, we wanted to develop implications for portfolio managers'

- Interpretation of risk measures.
- Techniques for capital attribution, pricing, and RAROC.

We compared four models:

1. Moody's–KMV Portfolio Manager (Version 1.4)
2. RiskMetrics Group's CreditManager (Version 2.5)
3. CSFB's CreditRisk+
4. Rutter Associates' Macro Factor Demonstration Model

To make the comparison as valid as possible, we wanted to input the same probabilities of default into all four models. Consequently, we used the EDFs from Credit Monitor for Portfolio Manager, Credit Risk+, and the Rutter Associates Demonstration Model, as well as using those EDFs to form the transition matrix for CreditManager.

Test Portfolio   We assembled a test portfolio made up of 3,136 facilities with a total exposure of $61 billion. This portfolio was based on 2,903 obligors. As will be described later, we tried to make this portfolio look like the portfolio of a larger commercial bank.

Credit Quality   The distribution of credit quality in the test portfolio is summarized by number of exposures and by exposure amount in Exhibit 4.30. The "implied" S&P ratings are implied from KMV EDFs. We started out with the firms within KMV's database, which was the most logical choice since they had the greatest number of firms in their database. Then we used the following EDF-Rating Map to map firms into ratings.

Rating Map	
Rating	**EDF (%)**
AAA	0
AA	0.019
A	0.0349
BBB	0.099
BB	0.75
B	3.03
CCC	10

Exhibit 4.30 shows the number of firms in each rating group. We did not have any AAA firms because by the time we started this project, most firms' credit had started to decline and therefore, EDFs were already reflecting the downside trend.

Exhibit 4.31 looks at the same data, but this time in terms of percentages of the number and the exposure amount.

Our test portfolio has more below investment grade exposures than investment grade exposures, but the amount exposed to investment grade exceeds that for below investment grade:

	Number of Exposures	Exposure Amount
Investment grade	43%	57%
Below investment grade	57%	43%

Facility Type As shown in Exhibit 4.32, revolvers make up the largest percentage of the exposure amount of the portfolio.

Exhibit 4.32 also shows the care we took to make our test portfolio look like a real portfolio at a large commercial bank. For example, you will

EXHIBIT 4.30 Test Portfolio—Credit Quality by Number of Exposures and Exposure Amount

Implied S&P Rating	Number of Exposures	Exposure Amount
AAA	0	0
AA	69	$ 4,610,564,897
A	203	$ 6,816,507,742
BBB	1,073	$23,731,635,122
BB	959	$17,164,000,067
B	551	$ 6,563,359,945
CCC	281	$ 3,195,884,887
Total	3,136	$62,081,952,659

EXHIBIT 4.31   Test Portfolio—Credit Quality—Percentages

Implied S&P Rating	Percentage: Number of Exposures	Percentage: Exposure Amount
AAA	—	—
AA	2.2%	7.4%
A	6.5%	11.0%
BBB	34.2%	38.2%
BB	30.6%	27.6%
B	17.6%	10.6%
CCC	9.0%	5.1%

EXHIBIT 4.32   Test Portfolio—Distribution by Facility Type and by Implied Rating

	Revolvers 55%	Term Loans 13%	Guarantees 11%	Bonds 20%	
	Revolvers	Term Loans	Guarantees	Bonds	Total
AA	10%	0%	9%	5%	7%
A	12%	0%	17%	13%	11%
BBB	40%	13%	53%	43%	38%
BB	27%	50%	10%	25%	28%
B	8%	25%	8%	10%	11%
CCC	4%	13%	4%	5%	5%

note that more than $3/5$ of the revolvers are to investment grade obligors, while only 13% of the term loans are to investment grade obligors.

Industries   We also tried to select obligors in such a way that the industries represented in the portfolio would be similar to those in the credit portfolio of a large commercial bank. Exhibit 4.33 shows the composition of the portfolio by industry according to KMV's 61 industry codes.

Calibrating the Models   The calibration of the models presented the most difficulty. On the one hand, we wanted to load the data and set the model parameters so as to have the models see the same economic environment. On the other hand, we did not want to force the model parameters to values that would guarantee that the models would produce the same results.

Following is a description of the calibrations we employed.

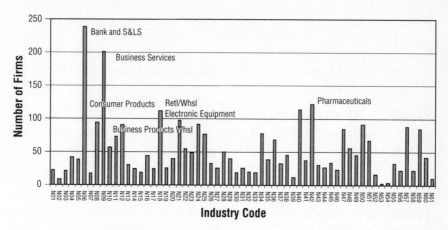

EXHIBIT 4.33   Test Portfolio—Distribution by Industry

Specification of Commitments   For commitments, CreditManager has separate fields for "total commitment," "current drawdown," and "expected drawdown." In contrast, Portfolio Manager users input "net commitment," "usage amount," and "usage given default" for all asset types.

Percentage of "Obligor Specific Risk"   CreditManager requires "obligor specific volatility percentage," while Portfolio Manager requires "R-squared." [One way of converting "obligor specific volatility percentage" into "R-squared" is to take the square root of the term $(1 - R^2)$].

Default Probability   As noted earlier, we used the EDFs from Credit Monitor for the probabilities of default for Portfolio Manager, Credit Risk+, and the Demonstration Model, as well as for generating the transition matrix for CreditManager. However, these default probabilities also had to be calibrated: We calculated the average EDFs for firms in each rating bucket and then applied them to CreditManager's transition matrix.

Default Correlation   This presented the greatest difficulty, because each model uses different methods to calculate correlation. In the case of Credit-Manager and Portfolio Manager, the user has to input industry weights and country weights that will ultimately determine the correlation between the firm's asset/equity values. Although calibrating country weights in Portfolio Manager and Credit Manager is easy, calibrating industry weight is challenging, because the two models use two different industry code systems—Portfolio Manager uses KMV industry codes and CreditManager uses Dow Jones Industry Codes. The problem we face when we use two different industry codes is that, for example, two companies that are in the same industry group in Portfolio Manager might be placed in two different industry groups in CreditManager that will yield more diversification effect in CreditManager. Also the magnitude of industry effects in correlation is different in the two models.

Comparison 1—Economic Capital   Exhibit 4.34 provides a comparison of the four models on the basis of three outputs—expected loss, unexpected loss, and the economic capital necessary to support the portfolio at a confidence level of 99.85%. All of these are expressed as a percentage of the total exposure amount for the portfolio.

Comparison 2—Risk Contributions   In addition to comparing the models on the basis of aggregates (i.e., expected loss, unexpected loss, and capital for the entire portfolio), we also wanted to compare the models on the basis of the risk contributions for individual facilities (transactions). We compared three of the models—Portfolio Manager, CreditManager, and Credit Risk+. (We do not include the Demonstration Model because it does not yet compute risk contributions.) Following are the individual definitions of risk contribution:

- *Portfolio Manager*—Moody's–KMV risk contribution is the addition of an obligor to the total portfolio standard deviation. Note that the Moody's–KMV measure is closely related to the beta risk measure of portfolio theory. The Moody's–KMV risk contributions sum to total portfolio standard deviation.
- *CreditManager*—The RiskMetrics Group defines "risk contribution" as the marginal addition to portfolio risk resulting from an additional unit of exposure. Risk contributions do not sum to total portfolio risk whether measured by standard deviation or the loss at some specified confidence level.

EXHIBIT 4.34   Comparison of the Portfolio Models—Expected Loss, Unexpected Loss, and Capital

	Portfolio Manager	Credit-Manager	Credit Risk+	Demo Model
Expected Loss	0.61%	0.79%	0.73%	0.76%
Unexpected Loss	1.60%	1.04%	1.12%	1.07%
Capital	7.96%	6.25%	7.42%	7.29%

■ *CreditRisk+*—Risk contribution is derived analytically. It is most closely related to the contribution of the obligor to total portfolio standard deviation. Risk contributions approximately sum to total portfolio standard deviation.

To give you an idea how this comparison looked, Exhibit 4.35 lists the 10 largest risk contributions from each of the three models. That is, we ran the same portfolio through Portfolio Manager, CreditManager, and Credit Risk+. Then, based on the risk contributions, we ranked all the facilities in each model, generating three rank lists (which we will refer to as "risk rankings" from here on). In our rankings, a larger rank means a *smaller* risk. Although we had expected to see very similar risk rankings throughout different models (since we inputted the same obligor and exposure information), Exhibit 4.35 shows that our expectation was wrong.

To gain more insight into the comparison, we calculated rank correlation statistics for Portfolio Manager and Credit Risk+ and for Portfolio Manager and CreditManager in the following manner. Using risk rankings as explained, we counted how many firms were in the same range of risk rankings for two models. For example, we counted the number of firms that were in the risk ranking range from 51 to 150 for both Portfolio Manager and CreditManager. We repeated the test for risk rankings

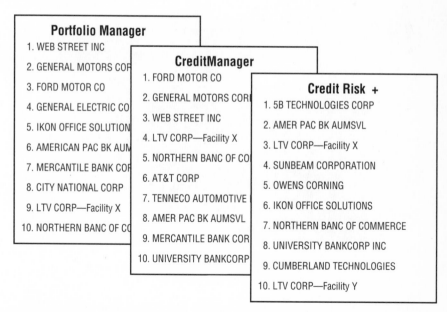

Portfolio Manager
1. WEB STREET INC
2. GENERAL MOTORS COR
3. FORD MOTOR CO
4. GENERAL ELECTRIC CO
5. IKON OFFICE SOLUTION
6. AMERICAN PAC BK AUM
7. MERCANTILE BANK COR
8. CITY NATIONAL CORP
9. LTV CORP—Facility X
10. NORTHERN BANC OF CC

CreditManager
1. FORD MOTOR CO
2. GENERAL MOTORS CORI
3. WEB STREET INC
4. LTV CORP—Facility X
5. NORTHERN BANC OF CO
6. AT&T CORP
7. TENNECO AUTOMOTIVE
8. AMER PAC BK AUMSVL
9. MERCANTILE BANK COR
10. UNIVERSITY BANKCORP

Credit Risk +
1. 5B TECHNOLOGIES CORP
2. AMER PAC BK AUMSVL
3. LTV CORP—Facility X
4. SUNBEAM CORPORATION
5. OWENS CORNING
6. IKON OFFICE SOLUTIONS
7. NORTHERN BANC OF COMMERCE
8. UNIVERSITY BANKCORP INC
9. CUMBERLAND TECHNOLOGIES
10. LTV CORP—Facility Y

EXHIBIT 4.35 Comparison of the Portolio Models—Largest 10 Risk Contributions

between 1,519 and 1,618 and between 2,987 and 3,086. Exhibit 4.36 shows that the models are much more similar for the facilities ranked from 51 to 150 and from 2,987 to 3,086 but that the models are much less similar for the 100 transactions in the middle. Moreover Exhibit 4.36 shows that the risk contribution rankings between Portfolio Manager and CreditManager are much more similar than those between Portfolio Manager and Credit Risk+. (This probably should not come as a great surprise since Portfolio Manager and CreditManager are both the same type of model.)

Exhibit 4.37 takes this one step further by plotting the risk contributions from Portfolio Manager against those from CreditManager. As is in-

EXHIBIT 4.36 Comparison of the Portfolio Models—Rank Correlation Statistics

KMV vs. CR+	
• 16 / 100	(51–150th)
• 5 / 100	(1,519–1,618th)
• 14/ 100	(2,987–3,086th)
KMV vs. RMG	
• 53 / 100	(51–150th)
• 21 / 100	(1,519–1,618th)
• 63 / 100	(2,987–3,086th)

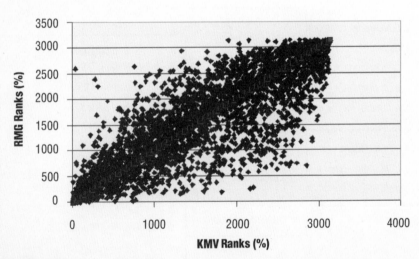

EXHIBIT 4.37 Comparison of the Portfolio Models—Scatter Graph of Risk Contributions: RMG and KMV

dicated by the rank correlation statistics, the risk contributions are much more similar for the facilities that contribute the most and the least to the riskiness of the portfolio. However, the risk contributions are much less similar for facilities in the middle.

WHAT MODELS ARE FINANCIAL INSTITUTIONS USING?

In the *2002 Survey of Credit Portfolio Management Practices* that we describe in Chapter 1, we asked whether the firm was using a credit portfolio model. Eighty-five percent of the respondents indicated that they were using a credit portfolio model.

We then asked those respondents who indicated that they were using a credit portfolio model which model they were using. The results are as follows:

Credit Metrics (RMG's CreditManager)	20%
CSFB's Credit Risk+	0%
KMV's Portfolio Manager	69%
Macro Factor Model (developed internally or by a vendor)	6%
McKinsey's CreditPortfolioView	0%
Internally developed model (other than a macro factor model)	17%

These responses sum to more than 100%, because some respondents checked more than one model.

NOTES

1. Portfolio Manager™ is the trademark of KMV LLC.
2. The discussions concerning the Moody's–KMV Global Correlation Model are based on notes we took in meetings with KMV in 1999.
3. RiskMetrics® is a registered servicemark of JP Morgan Chase & Co. and is used by RiskMetrics Group, Inc. under license. CreditManager™ is a trademark owned by or licensed to RiskMetrics Group, Inc. in the United States and other countries.
4. CreditManager does not make any assumptions about asset growth. As we will see, this approach calibrates the default and migration

threshold to the default and migration probabilities; so, the rate of growth is irrelevant.

5. Portfolio Manager is a pure structural model. CreditManager is a hybrid approach relying on the structural model for some calculations and an implied default distribution for others.

APPENDIX TO CHAPTER 4: Technical Discussion of Moody's–KMV *Portfolio Manager*

Mattia Filiaci

This appendix will cover the technical aspects of four parts of Moody's–KMV Portfolio Manager:[1]

■ The manner in which Portfolio Manager deals with default correlation.
■ The way in which facilities are valued in Portfolio Manager.
■ The way that Portfolio Manager produces the value distribution.
■ Calculation of the outputs from Portfolio Manager.

DEFAULT CORRELATION

In Portfolio Manager, default correlation is computed in the Global Correlation Model,[2] which *implements* the asset-correlation approach via a factor model that generates *correlated* asset returns. Denoting the return on firm A's assets at time t by $r_A(t)$, the factor model starts with the equation

$$r_A(t) = \beta_A r_{CI,A}(t) \tag{4.1}$$

where $r_{CI,A}(t)$ is the return on a *unique* "custom composite index"[3] for firm A in period t and β_A is the sensitivity of firm A's assets on the custom index and is calculated in a linear OLS regression.

The custom index for each firm in equation (4.1) is made up of 45 country indices (labeled r_c) and 61 industry indices (labeled r_i). The custom index may generally be written as:

$$r_{CI,A} = \sum_{c=1}^{45} w_{Ac} r_c + \sum_{i=1}^{61} w_{Ai} r_i \tag{4.2}$$

where

$$r_c = \sum_{G=1}^{2} \beta_{cG} r_G + \sum_{R=1}^{5} \beta_{cR} r_R + \sum_{S=1}^{7} \beta_{cS} r_S + \varepsilon_c \qquad (4.3)$$

and

$$r_i = \sum_{G=1}^{2} \beta_{iG} r_G + \sum_{R=1}^{5} \beta_{iR} r_R + \sum_{S=1}^{7} \beta_{iS} r_S + \varepsilon_i \qquad (4.4)$$

Note that we have dropped the explicit time dependence symbols. In the preceding, w_{Ac} is the fractional allocation of the firm in country c (based on reported sales and assets), w_{Ai} is the fractional allocation of the firm in industry i, and the β regression coefficients are the appropriate regression coefficients of each country index (r_c) and industry index (r_i) on the 14 orthogonal factors (Global (G), Regional (R), and Sector (S)).

Once the composite indices are computed, the Global Correlation Model uses ordinary least-squares regression to estimate the equation

$$r_A(t) = \beta_A r_{CI,A}(t) + \varepsilon_A(t) \qquad (4.5)$$

The information regarding asset correlation with other obligors is contained in the regression coefficients β_A and R^2 of this estimated equation, as well as the weights w_{Ac} and w_{Ai} from the reported sales and assets, the 28 beta coefficients from the country and industry regressions on the orthogonal factors, the standard deviations of the global, regional, and sector factors, and the country and industry specific standard deviations.[4] In a regression, the R^2 tells how much of the variation in the dependent variable—$r_A(t)$—is explained by variation in the independent variable—$r_{CI,A}(t)$. One important relation to keep in mind is that if σ_ε is the standard deviation of the errors $(\varepsilon_A(t))$ and σ is the standard deviation of the returns, the two are related through the R^2:

$$\sigma_\varepsilon = \sigma \sqrt{1 - R^2} \qquad (4.6)$$

FACILITY VALUATION[5]

The value of each facility in the portfolio must be calculated at both the horizon and the "as-of" date (e.g., the current date).

Current (Initial) Value

The user is given four choices for valuation at the as-of date:

1. User supplied value
2. Book value
3. Matrix spread value
4. Risk comparable value (RCV)

The first two are self-explanatory, so the following discussion pertains to options 3 and 4.

It is important to note that the fourth choice, risk comparable value (RCV), is *always* used for valuations in the Monte Carlo simulation at the as-of date and the horizon. The first three options are used only for calculating spreads or expected values (see section on facility-level outputs below).

The value of a credit-risky asset in Portfolio Manager for options 3 and 4 is given by

$$V_{Facility} = (1 - LGD)V_{RiskFreeBond} + (LGD)V_{RiskyBond} \qquad (4.7)$$

where

$$V_{RiskFreeBond} = \sum_{i=1}^{n} C_i \exp(-r_i t_i) \qquad (4.8)$$

and

$$V_{RiskyBond} = \sum_{i=1}^{n} C_i \exp[-(r_i + q_i)t_i] \qquad (4.9)$$

Here n is the number of cash flows from the initial date to maturity, C_i is the cash flow at time t_i, and r_i is the zero-rate at time t_i, and q_i is the credit spread due to a bond that has an LGD equal to 100%: $V_{RiskyBond}$ is the value of a bond presumed to have no recovery in the event of default. The value for q_i in the right-hand side of equation 4.9 depends first of all on the valuation method chosen.

Matrix Spread Valuation   In the case of matrix spread value, the value of q_i is determined by rating-mapped default probabilities and LGD values. The term structure for both of these must be entered as well as credit spread data of bond prices for each rating by year. Since the market's credit spread data include information about the LGD, and since q_i does not, the LGD must be divided out, as we see in a bit.

We can derive equations 4.7–4.9 by first considering a risky (e.g., corporate) zero-coupon bond with a face value of one. The following diagram shows the current value of the bond (V_0) and the two possible future values after some time t:

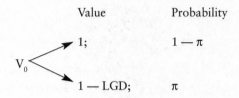

	Value	Probability
	1;	$1 - \pi$
V_0		
	$1 - LGD;$	π

In no-arbitrage asset pricing theory, the present value of an asset is the expected value of the payoffs using the risk-neutral probabilities, discounted at the risk-free rate. The risk-neutral probabilities reflect the risk value the market places on each possible state (final payoff). From the diagram, we see that

$$V_0 = e^{-rt}[1 \times (1 - \pi_t) + (1 - LGD) \times \pi_t]$$

where π_t is the *cumulative* risk-neutral default probability from time zero to time t and r is the continuously compounded risk-free zero-rate to time t. Simplifying,

$$V_0 = e^{-rt}[1 - \pi_t(LGD)] \qquad (4.10)$$

Now we define the continuously compounded risk-neutral probability q_i such that

$$q_i = -\frac{1}{t_i}\ln[1 - \pi_t] \qquad (4.11)$$

Solving for π_t,

$$\pi_t = 1 - \exp[-q_i t_i]$$

so that using this expression for π_t in equation 4.10, we get

$$V_0 = e^{-r_i t_i}[1 - (1 - e^{-q_i t_i})(LGD)]$$
$$= e^{-r_i t_i}[1 - LGD + (LGD)e^{-q_i t_i}]$$
$$= e^{-r_i t_i}[1 - LGD] + e^{-r_i t_i}(LGD)e^{-q_i t_i}$$

and so we have

$$V_{0,i} = e^{-r_i t_i}(1 - LGD) + e^{-(r_i + q_i)t_i}(LGD) \tag{4.12}$$

where we add the subscript i to denote this is a zero-coupon bond paying at time t_i. One can decompose a facility into zero coupon bonds that pay a face value C_i at time t_i, so we have that

$$V_{Facility} = \sum_{i=1}^{n} C_i V_{0,i} \tag{4.13}$$

One can see that combining equations 4.12 and 4.13 yields equations 4.7–4.9.

How is q_i related to the market's credit spreads? If we let the continuous zero-coupon (risky) bond yield be y_i, then $V_{0,i} = \exp(-y_i t_i)$. This means we can rewrite equation 4.12:

$$V_{0,i} \equiv e^{-y_i t_i} = e^{-r_i t_i}[(1 - LGD) + e^{-q_i t_i}(LGD)]$$

so defining a continuous credit spread $s_i \equiv y_i - r_i$, we have

$$e^{-s_i t_i} = 1 - LGD + e^{-q_i t_i}(LGD)$$

and after some simple algebra to solve for q_i we get

$$q_i = -\frac{1}{t_i}\ln\left(1 + \frac{e^{-s_i t_i} - 1}{LGD}\right) \tag{4.14}$$

Note the similarity to equation 4.11. Comparing 4.14 to 4.11 implies that

$$\pi_i = \frac{1 - e^{-s_i t_i}}{LGD}$$

If we define an *annualized* credit spread S_i compounded annually such that

$$s_i = -\frac{1}{t_i}\ln(1 - S_i)$$

then we have that the cumulative risk-neutral probability to time t_i (π_i) is related to the cumulative (annually compounded) market credit spread:

$$\pi_i = \frac{1}{LGD}[1 - \exp(-s_i t_i)]$$

$$= \frac{1}{LGD}\left[1 - \exp\left(\frac{t_i}{t_i}\ln[1 - S_i]\right)\right]$$

$$= \frac{1}{LGD}[1 - (1 - S_i)]$$

so

$$\pi_i = \frac{S_i}{LGD} \qquad (4.15)$$

Equation 4.15 is how q_i is evaluated when we are using the matrix spread calculation (through equation 4.11). The S_i are market observables: If Y_i is the annually compounded yield on a risky zero-coupon bond and R_i is the annually compounded risk-free rate, then

$$S_i = Y_i - R_i$$

The average S_i for each general rating (i.e., AAA, AA, . . . , BBB, CCC) is entered, for maturities ranging from one to five years.

To calculate q_i for a particular internal-rating mapped EDF, the interpolated cumulative probability of default π_i is calculated from

$$\pi_i = \frac{S_i^-}{LGD^-} + \left(\frac{EDF_i - EDF_i^-}{EDF_i^+ - EDF_i^-}\right)\left(\frac{S_i^+}{LGD^+} - \frac{S_i^-}{LGD^-}\right)$$

where EDF is the internal rating-mapped one-year EDF of the facility, and $S_i^{+(-)}$, $EDF_i^{+(-)}$ and $LGD_i^{+(-)}$ denote the spread, EDF, and LGD, respectively of the rating grade with the closest EDF that is greater (smaller) than the rating-mapped value for the facility.

Risk Comparable Valuation (RCV) Under RCV, the value of q_i is determined by what KMV calls the "quasi-risk neutral probability," or QDF. We can understand this concept by reviewing how EDFs are related to obligor asset values. Letting A_t be the asset value of an obligor at time t, then in the Merton model (KMV), the assumed stochastic process for A_t is given by

$$\frac{dA_t}{A_t} = \mu dt + \sigma dW_t$$

where μ is the expected (continuously compounded) return on the firm's assets, σ is the volatility (the standard deviation of the log of the asset values), and W_t is a Brownian motion ($W_t \sim N[0,1]$). The solution to this stochastic differential equation is

$$A_t = A_0 \exp\left[\left(\mu - \frac{1}{2}\sigma^2\right)t + \sigma\sqrt{t}W_t\right] \tag{4.16}$$

We can calculate the probability of default by starting with its definition:

$$
\begin{aligned}
p_t &= \Pr[A_t < DPT_t] \\
&= \Pr\left[A_0 \exp\left[\left(\mu - \frac{1}{2}\sigma^2\right)t + \sigma\sqrt{t}W_t\right] < DPT_t\right] \\
&= \Pr\left[\exp\left[\left(\mu - \frac{1}{2}\sigma^2\right)t + \sigma\sqrt{t}W_t\right] < \frac{DPT_t}{A_0}\right] \\
&= \Pr\left[\ln\left\{\exp\left[\left(\mu - \frac{1}{2}\sigma^2\right)t + \sigma\sqrt{t}W_t\right]\right\} < \ln\left(\frac{DPT_t}{A_0}\right)\right] \\
&= \Pr\left[\left(\mu - \frac{1}{2}\sigma^2\right)t + \sigma\sqrt{t}W_t < \ln\left(\frac{DPT_t}{A_0}\right)\right] \\
&= \Pr\left[\sigma\sqrt{t}W_t < \ln\left(\frac{DPT_t}{A_0}\right) - \left(\mu - \frac{1}{2}\sigma^2\right)t\right] \\
&= \Pr\left[W_t < \frac{\ln\left(\dfrac{DPT_t}{A_0}\right) - \left(\mu - \dfrac{1}{2}\sigma^2\right)t}{\sigma\sqrt{t}}\right]
\end{aligned}
$$

where DPT_t is the default point at time t and so

$$p_t = N\left[-d_2^*\right] \tag{4.17}$$

where $N[\ldots]$ is the cumulative standard normal distribution function and

$$d_2^* \equiv \frac{\ln\left(\dfrac{A_0}{DPT_t}\right) + \left(\mu - \dfrac{1}{2}\sigma^2\right)t}{\sigma\sqrt{t}} \tag{4.18}$$

$$\equiv \text{Distance to Default}$$

KMV calls p_t the Expected Default Frequency (*EDF*), and it is derived from the natural probability distribution. For valuation, the so-called "risk-neutral" measure (distribution) is used, so that

$$\frac{dA_t}{A_t} = r\,dt + \sigma d\hat{W}_t$$

where the "^" over the W_t signifies that it is a Brownian motion in the risk-neutral measure. The value of the firm's assets is

$$A_t = A_0 \exp\left[\left(r - \frac{1}{2}\sigma^2\right)t + \sigma\sqrt{t}\hat{W}_t\right]$$

and so following the same steps as taken to arrive at equations 4.17 and 4.18, the cumulative risk-neutral default probability π_t is given by

$$\pi_t = N[-d_2] \tag{4.19}$$

where

$$d_2 \equiv \frac{\ln\left(\dfrac{A_0}{DPT_t}\right) + \left(r - \dfrac{1}{2}\sigma^2\right)t}{\sigma\sqrt{t}} \tag{4.20}$$

In theory, one could calculate the risk-neutral probability merely from these two equations. However, for the as-of date valuation, in KMV the risk-neutral probability is calculated from a model that allows for calibration to real-market bond prices. This is described as follows. One can express the risk-neutral default probability in terms of the EDF by noting that

$$d_2^* - d_2 \equiv \frac{\mu - r}{\sigma}\sqrt{t}$$

Inserting this into equation (4.19) yields

$$\pi_t = N[-d_2]$$

$$\equiv N\left[-d_2^* + \frac{\mu - r}{\sigma}\sqrt{t}\right]$$

$$\equiv N\left[N^{-1}[EDF_t] + \frac{\mu - r}{\sigma}\sqrt{t}\right]$$

where we used $EDF_t = N[-d_2{}^*]$ and $N^{-1}[\ldots]$ is the inverse of the cumulative standard normal distribution. One can interpret the second term in the right-hand side by invoking the capital asset pricing model:

$$\mu - r = \beta(\mu_M - r)$$

where μ_M is the expected rate of return of the market portfolio, $\beta = \rho\,\sigma / \sigma_M$ is the beta (sensitivity) coefficient, ρ is the correlation coefficient between the return on the firm's assets and the market portfolio, and σ_M is the volatility of the rate of return on the market portfolio. Using the definition for the beta coefficient, we have

$$\mu - r = \frac{\rho\sigma}{\sigma_M}(\mu_M - r)$$

so

$$\frac{\mu - r}{\sigma} = \frac{\rho}{\sigma_M}(\mu_M - r)$$

Recalling that the market Sharpe Ratio S_r is defined to be the excess return over the volatility we have that

$$\frac{\mu - r}{\sigma} = \rho S_r$$

so we obtain an expression for the risk-neutral default probability π_t using the market Sharpe Ratio, where now we call this a quasi-risk-neutral default probability (QDF_t):

$$QDF_t = N\left[N^{-1}(EDF_t) + \rho S_r \sqrt{t}\right] \tag{4.21}$$

Since generally there is positive correlation between the returns of the firm and the market, equation 4.21 implies that

$$QDF > EDF$$

Note that now we have switched to the label QDF. This is because KMV calibrates EDFs to QDFs through a least-squares analysis of a variant of equation 4.21:

$$QDF_t = N\left[N^{-1}(EDF_t) + \rho S_r t^{\Omega}\right] \tag{4.22}$$

Theoretically, equation 4.21 tells us that $\Omega = \frac{1}{2}$, but the observed *QDF*s from prices of bonds issued by the firm (the observed dependent data are obtained through equation 4.15 using observed credit spreads and LGD) are calibrated to observed (historical) EDFs by estimating both Ω and S_r in a least-squares analysis of equation 4.22. KMV says that S_r has been close to 0.4 and Ω has been generally near 0.5 or 0.6.

The following figure provides a little more insight into the *Quasi EDF (QDF)*.

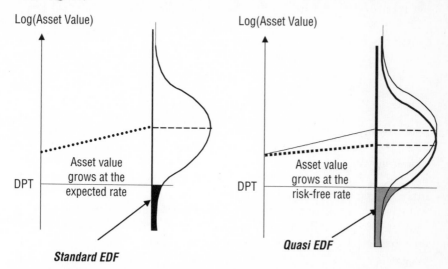

Standard EDF   *Quasi EDF*

The left-hand figure is the now familiar illustration for the calculation of *EDF*s, where the assumption is that the value of the assets rises at an expected rate. In the right-hand figure, the shaded area illustrates the graphical calculation of the *QDF*. Note that for the calculation of the *QDF*, the assumption is that the value of the assets rises at the risk-free rate. Because of this, the area below the default point is larger for the area under the risk-neutral probability distribution, and therefore *QDF* > *EDF*.

To summarize, the RCV at the as-of date is done using the estimated equation 4.22 (note that here is where the inputted term structure of the *EDF*s are required and so the default points (DPT_t) are not required), equation 4.11 (where QDF_t is substituted in for π_t), equations 4.8 and 4.9, and finally equation 4.7.

Valuation at Horizon

For the facility-level outputs (e.g., spread to horizon), the user is given three choices: (1) RCV, (2) linear amortization, and (3) exponential amortization. Note that there is no matrix spread calculation for valuation at horizon and that for the Monte Carlo simulation of the portfolio loss distribution, RCV is always used for facility valuation.

In the case of RCV at the horizon, the value of a facility is still determined by equations 4.7–4.9, but equations 4.8 and 4.9 are slightly modified to reflect the different valuation time:

$$V_{RiskFreeBond,\ H} = \sum_{i\ni t_i > t_H} C_i \exp(-_H r_{iH} t_i) \qquad (4.23)$$

and

$$V_{RiskFreeBond,\ H} = \sum_{i\ni t_i > t_H} C_i \exp\left[-(_H r_i +_H q_i)\ _H t_i\right] \qquad (4.24)$$

where by definition $_H t_i = t_i - t_H$, $_H r_i$ is the risk-free forward rate from $t_i - t_H$, and $_H q_i$ is the annualized risk-neutral forward default probability. Note that as viewed from the as-of date, the cumulative default probability from horizon to time $t_i > t_H$, $_H EDF_i$, *conditional on no default*, is random. In other words, it will depend on the stochastic asset value return at horizon. But *given* the simulated asset value at the horizon time A_H (we see how it is simulated in just a bit), the forward risk-neutral default probability is given by equations 4.11 and 4.22 modified appropriately:

$$_H q_i = -\frac{1}{t_i - t_H} \ln[1 -_H QDF_i] \qquad (4.25)$$

$$_H QDF_i = N[N^{-1}(_H \tilde{EDF}_i) + \rho S_r (t_i - t_H)^\Omega] \qquad (4.26)$$

where we put a tilde ("~")over the obligor's forward conditional *EDF* to remind us that this will depend on the simulated asset value at horizon, as discussed later. In contrast to RCV at the as-of date, RCV at the horizon would theoretically require the default point at *maturity* or the cash-flow date t_i: DPT_M or DPT_i. These future *DPT*s will not necessarily be the same as the default point at the horizon date (DPT_H), used for the as-of date valuation. As with the valuation at the as-of date, Portfolio Manager does not need to specify the default point at maturity (DPT_M), but uses the mapping of distance to default to the inputted *EDF*s (the *EDF* term structure) and the calculation of forward *QDF*s from forward *EDF*s using equation 4.26. In versions of *PM* prior to v. 2.0, there was no relation between default point at maturity and the asset value realization at horizon. In reality, firms will change their liability structure according to their asset values, so that in general the higher the asset values, the larger the liabilities. One of the major developments introduced in *PM* v. 2.0 after the previous version (*PM* v. 1.4) was the incorporation of this concept based on empirical distance to default distribution dynamics.

Default Point Dynamics

In Portfolio Manager v. 2.0, the interplay between asset values at horizon and the liability structures of firms is brought about by the empirical conditional (on no default) distance to default distributions. Default point dynamics are implied by equating the probability of a particular asset value realization to the probability of a particular distance to default *change*. For *PM* 2.0, KMV analyzed approximately 12,000 North American companies from January 1990 to February 1999. Conditional distance to default (*DD*) distributions (i.e., companies that defaulted were not counted) were created for different time horizons for 32 different initial *DD*s. Each initial *DD* "bucket" results in an empirical *DD* distribution at some time in the future. This now provides the link between the stochastic asset value realization in the simulation and the forward *QDF* needed for the RCV valuation. First, forward default probability is the probability that the firm defaults between two points in time in the future given that the firm is not in default at the first point:

$$CEDF_t = CEDF_H + (1 - CEDF_H)_H EDF_t$$

where now we use the prefix "C" to denote cumulative probability starting at time zero. We thus have

$$_H EDF_t = (CEDF_t - CEDF_H)/(1 - CEDF_H)$$

Since $_H EDF_t$ is random, this implies that $CEDF_t$ is random, and is calculated from the realization of the *standard normal* random variable in the simulation, W_t (see next section). If we define G to be the mapping using the empirical distance to default distribution over time from the current distance to default[6] to the conditional forward default probability $_H EDF_t$, the *forward* distance to default is given by

$$_t DD_H{}^* = G^{-1}[(N[W_t] - CEDF_H)/(1 - CEDF_H)] \qquad (4.27)$$

The asterisk is there because the forward *DD* here needs to be adjusted to reflect the exposure's individual term structure of *CEDF*s. This is because the empirical *DD* dynamics based on the 12,000-firm study are averages of firm ensembles, and need to be calibrated to individual exposures through a time dependent multiplier, $a(t)$:

$$_tDD_H = {}_tDD_H{}^*(1 + a(t))$$

After determining $a(t)$,[7] *PM* again uses KMV's proprietary mapping from distance to default to *EDF* and determines the *forward* default probability ${}_HEDF_t$ from the obtained forward distance to default $({}_tDD_H)$. The forward default probability ${}_HEDF_t$ is now inserted in equation 4.26 to obtain the forward quasi-risk-neutral default probability, ${}_HQDF_t$, and the RCV calculation at horizon can be completed using equations 4.23 to 4.25.

GENERATING THE PORTFOLIO VALUE DISTRIBUTION[8]

In Portfolio Manager, the portfolio *value* distribution is calculated from the sum of all the facility values.

The first step in generating the value distribution is to *simulate* the value of the firm's assets at the horizon (A_H) for each obligor using equation 4.16:[9]

$$\ln(A_H) = \ln(A_0) + \left(\mu - \frac{1}{2}\sigma^2\right)t_H + \sqrt{t_H}\tilde{f} \tag{4.28}$$

where A_0 is the current value of the firm's assets, t_H is the time to horizon, μ is the expected value of the firm's assets, σ is the volatility of the firm's assets (the standard deviation of the log of the asset value), and $\tilde{f}$ is a normally distributed *correlated* (that is, to $\tilde{f}$s of other firms) random variable with mean zero and standard deviation equal to σ, the asset value volatility (i.e., $\tilde{f} \sim N[0,\sigma_2]$). Note that $\ln(A_H/A_0)$ is just the continuously compounded rate of return of the asset value. The random variable $\tilde{f}$ is simulated from independent standard normal random variables, the market factor weights (b_j), market factor variances (σ_j) and R^2 obtained from the linear regression of the firm's asset returns on its custom index, calculated in the Global Correlation Model (see equations 4.2– 4.4):

$$\tilde{f} = \sum_{j=1}^{120} b_j\sigma_j\tilde{\lambda}_j + \sigma\sqrt{1-R^2}\tilde{v} \tag{4.29}$$

Note that in this expression the 120 regression coefficients (b_j) are linear combinations of the βs from the regression on the custom index for firm A ($r_{CI, A}$), the allocations to the countries and industries (from reported sales and assets), and the regression coefficients of the country and industry indices on the 14 orthogonal factors (i.e., the two global, five regional, and seven sector indices), as described. The variables $\tilde{v}$ and $\tilde{\lambda}_j$ are independently drawn, standard normal random variables (i.e., $\tilde{v} \sim N[0,1]$ and $\tilde{\lambda}_j \sim N[0,1]$). The first component of equation 4.29 for $\tilde{f}$ (or rather the sum of all the components containing the λs) is the *systematic risk*, which is proportional to the correlation of the asset returns to the returns on the firm's composite factor (that is, proportional to R), while the second component $\left(\sigma \sqrt{1 - R^2} \, \tilde{v} \right)$ is called the *firm-specific (idiosyncratic) risk*.

One can see that equation 4.28 for the continuously compounded asset return is identical to equations 4.2–4.5 for the factor model of the continuously compounded returns, by recalling equation 4.6 relating the standard deviation of the errors to the asset return standard deviation, and letting $t_H = 1$.

The second step is to value each facility at horizon as a function of the simulated value of the obligor's assets at the horizon (A_H):

■ *If the value of the firm's assets at the horizon is less than the default point for that firm (i.e., if $A_H < DPT$)*, the model presumes that default has occurred. Portfolio Manager treats *LGD* to be a random variable that follows a *beta distribution* with a mean equal to the inputted expected LGD value and LGD standard deviation determined by a portfolio-wide parameter, and draws an LGD value for this iteration of the simulation from that distribution.

In this step, the value of the default point is critical as it is compared with the simulated asset value. In the Portfolio Manager Monte Carlo simulation (as opposed to Credit Monitor, in which the *DPT* is equal to the current liabilities plus one-half the long-term debt), the default point is essentially given by equations 4.17 and 4.18, which are solved for the *DPT*:

$$DPT = A_0 \exp\left\{ \left(\mu - \frac{1}{2}\sigma^2 \right) t_H + \sigma\sqrt{t_H}\, N^{-1}[EDF_H] \right\}$$

■ *If the value of the firm's assets at the horizon is greater than the default point for that firm (i.e., if $A_H > DPT$)*, the model presumes that default has not occurred and the value of the facility is the weighted sum of the value of a risk-free bond and the value of a risky bond, as described earlier.

OUTPUTS

Facility Level Outputs

At the facility level, Portfolio Manager outputs the expected spread (*ES*) and the spread to horizon (*STH*):

$$ES = \frac{E[V_H] - V_0}{V_0} - r$$

and

$$STH = \frac{E[V_H \mid ND] - V_0}{V_0} - r$$

where $E[V_H \mid ND]$ is the expected value of the facility at horizon *given no default*. From this definition, it is clear that $STH > ES$ and is the promised spread over the risk-free rate.

Loss Distributions, Expected Loss, and Unexpected Loss

The loss distribution is related to the value distribution by taking the future value of the current value of the portfolio using the risk-free rate to horizon and subtracting the simulated value of the portfolio at the horizon given some confidence interval α (i.e., $V_{P,H}$ is a function of α):

$$L_{P,H} = V_{P,0} e^{r_H t_H} - V_{P,H} \qquad (4.30)$$

Note that $V_{P,H}$ and therefore $L_{P,H}$ are simulated portfolio values at the horizon.

The expected loss of the portfolio in Portfolio Manager is calculated from the portfolio *TS* and *ES* mentioned earlier. Since these output spreads are annualized,

$$EL_P = \left[V_0 (1 + r + TS)^H - V_0 (1 + r + ES)^H \right]^{\frac{1}{H}}$$

We see that when $H = 1$, this expression becomes

$$EL_P = V_0 (TS - ES) \equiv V_0 EL$$

where EL is the expected loss (EL_p) as a fraction of the current portfolio value. KMV defines two loss distributions—one based on the portfolio ES (the loss after the expected loss, or L_{EL}) and one based on the portfolio TS (the loss in excess of total spread or L_{TS}):

$$L_{EL} = V_{ES} - \tilde{V}_H = V_0(1 + r + ES)^H - \tilde{V}_H$$

and

$$L_{TS} = V_{RF} - \tilde{V}_H = V_0(1 + r)^H - \tilde{V}_H$$

where $\tilde{V}_H$ is the simulated value of the portfolio at the horizon.

Economic Capital

In Portfolio Manager, economic capital is the difference between unexpected loss and expected loss, and is calculated using the discounted value of the loss calculated in equation 4.30 divided by the current value of the portfolio:

$$Capital = \frac{e^{-r_H t_H} L_{P,H}}{V_{P,0}} = \frac{V_{P,0} - V_{P,H} e^{-r_H t_H}}{V_{P,0}}$$

This capital value is calculated at each iteration, binned, and portrayed graphically as the tail of the *loss* distribution. It answers the question: "Given the risk of the portfolio, what losses should we be prepared to endure?"

Tail Risk Contribution

One important development in Portfolio Manager v. 2.0 is the addition of a capital allocation measure based on frequency and severity of extreme losses due to an exposure, also called tail risk contribution. KMV defines a facility's tail risk contribution (TRC_f) to be the marginal increase in portfolio capital (C_p) associated with an increase in the current exposure size of the facility (V_0):

$$TRC = \frac{\partial C_P}{\partial V_0}$$

It is calculated as the expected value of the difference between the facility value loss point and the facility value at horizon present valued, conditional on the present value of the portfolio loss value being equal to some target portfolio capital amount. In *PM* v. 2.0, there are two methods to calculate this: one where loss is in excess of expected loss (*EL*) and one where loss is in excess of total spread (*TS*). In general, the weighted sum of the tail risk contributions will equal the portfolio capital.

In its implementation of tail risk contribution, Portfolio Manager v. 2.0 requires the user to specify a capital interval upon which to perform the calculations. If we define C_{LB} to be the lower bound and C_{UB} to be the upper bound of this interval, then the tail risk contribution is given by

$$TRC = \frac{\partial C_P}{\partial V_0} = E\left[\frac{V_{LP} - \tilde{V}_H}{V_0(1 + r_H)^H} \middle| C_{LB} < \frac{\tilde{L}_P}{(1 + r_H)^H} < C_{UB} \right]$$

where V_{LP} is the facility value at horizon from which loss starts to accrue, V_H is the facility value at horizon from the *simulation*, r_H is the risk-free rate to horizon, L_P is the portfolio loss amount from the simulation, and C_P is the portfolio capital for the target probability α.

Importance Sampling

As of this writing, Moody's–KMV is working on adding importance sampling to Portfolio Manager to increase the speed of the simulator. KMV asserts that this should offset increases in computation time that were created due to the addition of the distance-to-default dynamics in the valuation section discussed earlier.

NOTES

1. Version 2.0 of Portfolio Manager, released in November 2001, includes significant developments over its predecessor, version 1.4, regarding "risk comparable valuation" and capital allocation based on tail risk.
2. The sections concerning the Global Correlation Model are adapted from notes on KMV, [1999].
3. Originally KMV called this index the "composite" index for the firm.
4. As of this writing, Moody's–KMV last updated the Global Correlation Model's regression coefficients in April 2002 and plans to update them annually.
5. The sections concerning facility valuation are based on notes from KMV (1998, 1) and the KMV Portfolio Engineering Course attended September 25 to 27, 2002, regarding PM 2.0.

6. Determined by KMV's proprietary mapping between *EDF* and distance to default (*DD*).

7. KMV uses a fitting technique based on conditional (forward) survival probabilities.

8. The section pertaining to calculation of the portfolio loss distribution is adapted from notes on KMV, 1998 [2] and the KMV Portfolio Engineering Course attended September 25 to 27, 2002.

9. Equation 4.28 is obtained by simply taking the logarithm of both sides of equation 4.16 and setting $\tilde{f} = \sigma W_t$.

Tools to Manage a Portfolio of Credit Assets

In the *2002 Survey of Credit Portfolio Management Practices* that we described in Chapter 1, we asked the respondents to tell us which tools were most important in managing a credit portfolio:

> *Please rank the following tools in order of their importance to the management of your credit portfolio. (Use 1 to denote the most important and 4 to denote the least important.)*

The responses to this question are summarized below in terms of the average importance scores for each of the tools and the percent of respondents who provided a response for each of the tools.

	Average Importance Score	Percent of Respondents Who Provided Response
Approval/disapproval of new business and renewal/nonrenewal of existing business	1.10	100%
Loan sales and trading	2.74	93%
Credit derivatives	2.97	95%
Securitizations	3.15	95%

While there is little that we can add on the approval/disapproval of new business or the decision to renew existing business, we can say something about the other tools. Loan sales and trading are covered in Chapter 5. Chapter 6 deals with Credit Derivatives, and Chapter 7 covers securitization.

Loan Sales and Trading[1]

The corporate loan market has grown dramatically in size and in the diversity of its investors. A market that began as a bank market has developed to include institutional investors and the rating agencies that monitor them. Moreover, the growth of retail mutual funds, some of which are subject to the rules of the U.S. Securities and Exchange Commission, has changed the way the loan market does business.

As a rule, the loans that are traded are syndicated loans. (If the loan being sold is not syndicated, it is a bilateral transfer.) Syndicated loans are also called leveraged loans. Barnish, Miller, and Rushmore (1997) define leveraged loans as LIBOR plus 150 bp or more.

PRIMARY SYNDICATION MARKET

In essence, a syndicated credit facility involves the combined activities of a number of banks to provide a relatively large loan to a single borrower under the direction of one or several banks serving as lead managers. Syndicated loan facilities represent a cross between debt underwriting and traditional commercial bank lending.

Syndicated loans carry interest rates that reset periodically (typically on a quarterly basis) based on a fixed spread over LIBOR or a similar reference rate.

Borrowers can reduce their administrative burden and costs. (This comes at a cost of relinquishing some control over their bank group.)

Mechanics of a Syndication*

A prospective *lead bank* will draw up a proposal to arrange the loan, thereby seeking a *syndication mandate*. The proposal will specify pricing, terms, fees, and other pertinent aspects

---

*This discussion was adapted from Roy Smith and Ingo Walter, "International Commercial Lending" in *Global Banking*. Oxford University Press, 1997, pp. 24–27.

of the loan. The proposed syndication could be (1) a *fully committed syndication* (in which case the prospective lead bank will undertake to provide the full amount of the loan to the borrower according to the terms of the mandate, whether or not it is successful in its efforts to interest others in participating in the loan), (2) a *partially committed syndication* (in which case the prospective lead bank will guarantee to deliver part of the loan, with the remainder contingent on market reaction to the loan), or (3) a *best-efforts syndication* (in which case the borrower will obtain the funds needed only if sufficient interest and participation can be generated among potential participating lenders by the good-faith efforts of the bank seeking the mandate).

The prospective lead bank may have solicited one or more co-lead managers to help with the syndication and share in the underwriting commitment. For larger loans, the management group may include several *lead managers, managers,* and *co-managers,* each group accepting a different share of the underwriting responsibility, and several "brackets" of *participants*, whose role is usually confined to supplying funds.

The management group will produce an *information memorandum*, in which the borrower discloses financial and economic—and sometimes historical and political—facts pertinent to current and projected creditworthiness. The management group will also produce a *term sheet* restating the conditions of the loan.

If things go well, the loan will be fully subscribed. If it is oversubscribed, participants will either be *prorated* among the interested banks, or occasionally the total amount of the loan will be increased at the option of the borrower.

The servicing of a syndicated loan falls on the *agent bank* (usually the lead bank or one of the lead managers). The functions of the agent bank include:

- Seeing that the terms of the loan agreement (drawdown, rollover, interest payments, grace period, and repayment of principal) are complied with.
- Collecting funds from participants according to the drawdown provisions and disbursing the funds to the borrower.
- Fixing the interest rate periodically against the floating-rate base.
- Computing interest and principal due, collecting from the borrower, and distributing to the lenders.
- Monitoring loan supports (e.g., collateral valuation and guarantees).
- Evaluating and ensuring compliance with covenants in the loan agreement.
- Collecting periodic reports from the borrower, independent auditors, or other information and distributing them to participants.

Evolution of the Syndicated Loan Market

The precursor to syndication was "participations." There had been a longstanding practice of multibank term lending to corporate customers in the United States, with the facilities priced at or above the domestic prime lending rate.

The syndication of medium-term credit facilities began in the late 1960s. In this period, changes in interest rate levels and volatilities made floating-rate financing attractive, relative to fixed-rate bond issues. The resultant demand for loans outstripped the lending capabilities of individual banks.

During the 1970s and 1980s, more than half of all medium-term and long-term borrowings in international capital markets were in the form of syndicated loans, with the percentage rising to 80% for borrowings by developing countries and essentially 100% for borrowings by centrally planned economies. Lending to emerging countries and project financings took up the bulk of syndications in the 1970s. Mergers and acquisitions and leveraged buyout syndications dominated in the latter part of the 1980s.

Pro Rata and Investor Tranches

Syndicated loans generally have two types of tranches—a *pro rata tranche* and an *institutional tranche.*

The pro rata tranche is composed of a revolving loan and a term loan referred to as the "term loan A." The term loan A generally has the same maturity as the revolver and is fully amortizing. Historically, the pro rata tranche was dominated by banks.

The institutional tranche is composed of one (or more) term loan(s) referred to as the "term loan B" (and "term loan C"). These term loans have maturities six months to one year longer than the term loan A and have minimal amortization with a bullet payment required at maturity (called "backend amortization").

Exhibit 5.1 traces primary leveraged loan volumes from 1997 to the first quarter of 2002.

To date, the revolvers have been recognized to be the least valuable of the credit assets involved in a securitization. Consequently, in new deals, banks have tried to minimize the size of the revolver and increase the size of the institutional tranche. This shift in the relative size of the institutional tranche is reflected in Exhibit 5.1. That is, the percentage of the total syndicated loan represented by the institutional tranche has risen from the low- to mid-teens to the mid- to high-twenties.

Investors in Syndicated Loans

In the 1970s and 1980s, non-U.S. banks—especially Japanese banks—were the primary purchasers of the syndicated loans. Syndicators began to establish relationships with insurance companies and mutual funds in the 1980s. In 1989, institutional investors accounted for only 10% of the primary market for highly leveraged loans. But, as portrayed in Exhibit 5.2, the relative levels of participation by banks and non-banks changed

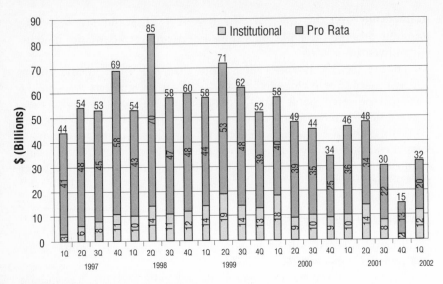

EXHIBIT 5.1 Leveraged Loan Volumes
Source: Standard & Poor's.

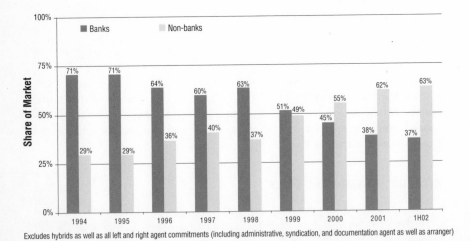

Excludes hybrids as well as all left and right agent commitments (including administrative, syndication, and documentation agent as well as arranger)

EXHIBIT 5.2 Primary Market for Leveraged Loans: Banks versus Non-Banks
Source: Standard & Poor's.

dramatically over the next 13 years. (In Exhibit 5.2, non-banks include institutional investors, insurance companies, finance companies, and securities firms.)

Non-Bank Investors   Exhibit 5.3 permits us to drill down to see that, among the non-bank investors, it is institutional investors that are the primary investors in leveraged loans. Indeed, by 2001, institutional investors represented more than 50% of the primary market for leveraged loans.

In 1997, Barnish, Miller, and Rushmore estimated that institutional investors held $25–$30 billion in leveraged loans, and in 2002, the Loan Syndication and Trading Association (LSTA) reported that market insiders were estimating that institutional investors held as much as 80% of all leveraged loans.

Exhibit 5.4 permits us to drill down even further to see that loan and hybrid funds (i.e., funds that invest in both loans and corporate bonds) have become the dominant investors in leveraged loans, rising from 17.2% in 1994 to 54.7% in the first half of 2002.

Investing in loans by funds is not only getting larger in aggregate but also getting widespread. Exhibit 5.5 indicates that the number of portfolios that invest in loans rose from 14 in 1993 to 253 in the first half of 2002.

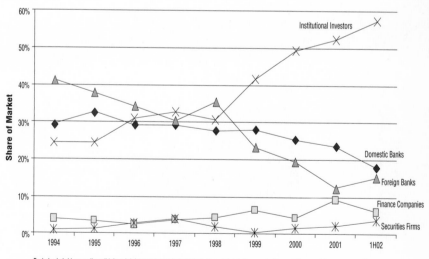

Excludes hybrids as well as all left and right agent commitments (including administrative, syndication, and documentation agent as well as arranger)

EXHIBIT 5.3   Primary Market for Leveraged Loans by Broad Investor Type
Source: Standard & Poor's.

1994

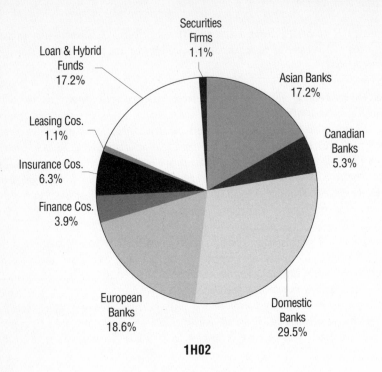

Securities Firms 1.1%

Loan & Hybrid Funds 17.2%

Asian Banks 17.2%

Leasing Cos. 1.1%

Canadian Banks 5.3%

Insurance Cos. 6.3%

Finance Cos. 3.9%

European Banks 18.6%

Domestic Banks 29.5%

1H02

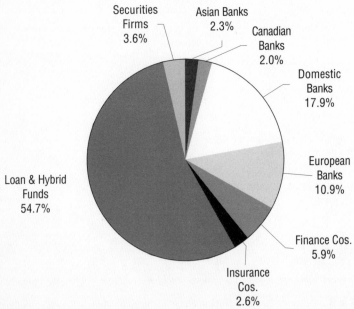

Securities Firms 3.6%

Asian Banks 2.3%

Canadian Banks 2.0%

Domestic Banks 17.9%

European Banks 10.9%

Loan & Hybrid Funds 54.7%

Finance Cos. 5.9%

Insurance Cos. 2.6%

EXHIBIT 5.4 Primary Market for Leveraged Loans by Investor Type
Source: Standard & Poor's.

188

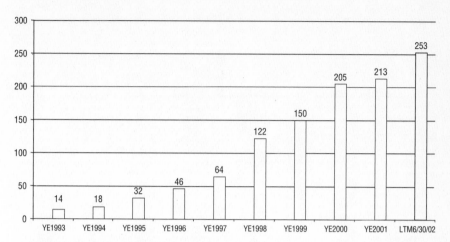

EXHIBIT 5.5 Institutional Loan Investor Portfolios
Source: Standard & Poor's.

There are a number of reasons for the investor interest in syndicated loans. First, risk-adjusted returns for syndicated loans can be higher than those for comparable securities. Second, since the correlation of bank loans with other fixed income securities is low [see White and Lenarcic (1999)], syndicated loans provide a means of portfolio diversification for investors. Finally, syndicated loans have acceptable credit characteristics. Because of their collateral provisions and their secured status, syndicated loans experience higher average recovery rates than unsecured issues. Their senior status affords the lender in a syndicated loan preferential treatment over general creditors in a bankruptcy claim. Lenders in syndicated loans benefit from bank loan documentation, which can provide control should credit conditions degenerate.

Banks Foreign banks used this market to expand their lending activities in the United States and to gain access to client relationships that the U.S. commercial banks had developed.

As institutional investors have become more active in investing in loans, banks have become less active—not only on a relative basis, but also on an absolute basis. Exhibit 5.6 shows that the number of banks that made 10 or more commitments in the primary syndication market declined dramatically in 2000.

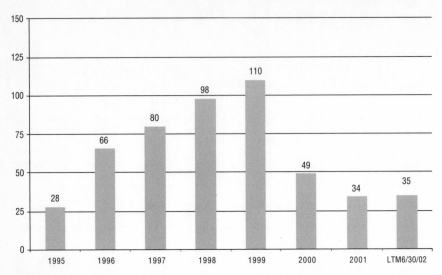

EXHIBIT 5.6   Number of Pro Rata Investors (Lenders) That Made 10 or More Primary Commitments
Source: Standard & Poor's.

GOLD SHEETS

The "gold" in the title of the weekly publication *Gold Sheets* refers to the color of the paper they are printed on, not the market that they cover. The product of Loan Pricing Corporation (a subsidiary of Reuters Group PLC), *Gold Sheets* provides weekly analyses of market trends in the global syndicated loan and high-yield bond markets, including coverage of pricing, structure, tenor, and industry segments. A monthly *Gold Sheets Middle Market* for middle market professionals is also available.

Loan Pricing Corporation also offers a web-delivered product called LoanConnector that provides real-time coverage of the global loan and high-yield bond markets through Gold Sheets Real-Time news, data, and analytics (e.g., pricing structure, what is trading in the secondary market and for how much, relative value analysis, and pricing grids).

DealScan®, LPC's historical database, contains detailed deal terms and conditions for more than 100,000 loans, high-yield bonds, and private placements worldwide.

SECONDARY LOAN MARKET

The secondary market in syndicated loans refers to any sale by assignment after the primary syndication document is closed and signed. As is illustrated in Exhibit 5.7, the secondary loan market has been growing steadily over the past decade.

In Exhibit 5.7, Loan Pricing Corporation has defined a "distressed loan" as one trading at 90 or less. However, the definition of a "distressed loan" is not yet hard and fast. Market participants will refer to a loan trading from the low 90s up as a "par" loan. Loans trading from the mid-80s to the low 90s are referred to as "crossover," and those trading below that as "distressed."

The current syndicated loan environment is in large part the result of the M&A and LBO syndications. Chase, Bank of America, and a few other banks that were active in highly leveraged transactions experienced concentration risk in names like Federated Department Stores, Macy's, Stone Container, Black & Decker, HCA, Time Warner, and RJR Nabisco. The banks responded by establishing loan syndication desks that arranged, underwrote, and distributed the burgeoning volume of activity at that time.

Loan trading desks ultimately broadened distribution capabilities beyond a core syndicate of banks, advancing the development of a viable secondary market. Barnish, Miller, and Rushmore (1997) reported that, by the end of the 1990s, more than 30 loan trading desks had been established and that these were split approximately equally between commercial banks and investment banks.

Spreads for the pro rata and institutional tranches in the secondary loan market are provided in Exhibit 5.8.

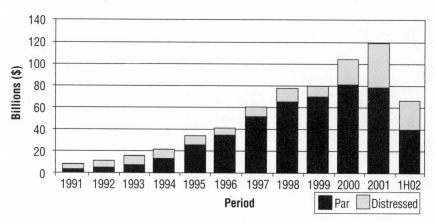

EXHIBIT 5.7 Secondary Loan Volumes
Source: Loan Pricing Corporation, *Gold Sheets.*

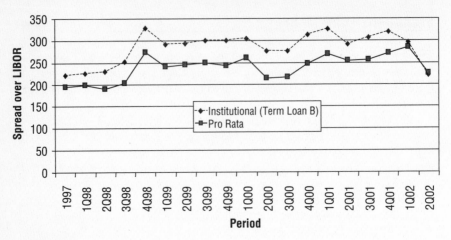

EXHIBIT 5.8 Spreads in the Secondary Loan Market (BB-Rated)
Source: Loan Pricing Corporation, *Gold Sheets*.

LSTA/LPC Mark-to-Market Pricing Service

Bank loan investors and dealers want and need to know the market value for individual loan tranches and loan portfolios.

In 1999, the Loan Syndications and Trading Association (LSTA) licensed Loan Pricing Corporation (LPC) to implement a subscription service for the distribution of daily mark-to-market prices from bank loan dealers to investors. These indicative values provided price discovery to institutional investors, as well as benchmarks for valuing nontraded loans in a bank's portfolio. (Note that independence is provided by the fact that neither LPC nor the LSTA makes a market in or trades bank loans.)

Prices are available for almost 2,000 bank loan tranches on a daily, weekly, or monthly basis. (This covers almost 100% of the loans currently held by fund managers.) The prices are obtained from loan traders that specialize in trading particular loan facilities. Price data are provided daily by dealers and traders from more than 25 institutions. LPC employs a data verification and audit process to ensure data integrity, with outliers identified and corrected including price verification with dealers.

LSTA/LPC Mark-to-Market Pricing service subscribers receive mark-to-market alerts via e-mail notifying them of significant changes to secondary market loan prices on a daily basis.

NOTE

1. This chapter relies on Barnish, Miller, and Rushmore (1997), Smith and Walter (1997), and Cilia (2000).

CHAPTER 6

Credit Derivatives[1]

with Gregory Hayt

While "credit derivatives" is still a new term for many of us, derivative contracts on credit have been around a long time. Bond insurance, which has existed for more than 20 years, is essentially an option that pays in the event of default on a particular bond. In addition, many traditional banking products could be thought of as credit derivatives, even though they are not generally labeled as such. For example, a letter of credit is an option on the creditworthiness of a borrower, and a revolving credit facility includes an option on the borrower's credit spread.

Notwithstanding the fact that traditional credit products have derivative elements, the term "credit derivative" generally relates to the over-the-counter markets for total return swaps, credit default swaps, and credit-linked notes, a market that dates from approximately 1991.

TAXONOMY OF CREDIT DERIVATIVES

Credit derivatives transfer credit risk from one counterparty to another. This simple statement requires us to consider the *source of the risk* and the *method of transfer*. Both of these are summarized in Exhibit 6.1.

As seen in the bottom half of Exhibit 6.1, the source of the transferred credit risk can be a single asset—a specific corporate bond, loan, sovereign debt, or derivative (for example, an interest rate swap)—or a pool of assets. If the pool is small and the assets are specifically listed in the contract, then the pool is referred to as a basket. Larger portfolios can be identified through characteristics of the underlying pool of loans or receivables.

Once the underlying source of credit exposure is identified, there must be a mechanism for transferring the credit exposure. The top half of

EXHIBIT 6.1 Taxonomy of Credit Derivatives

Primary Cashflow Driver		
Asset Return	Credit Event	Credit Spread
• Total return swap • Default contingent forward	• Credit default swap • Credit linked note • First default basket	• Spread forward • Spread option

Potential Underlying Assets	
Individual Assets	"Basket" Assets
• Corporate loans • Corporate bonds • Sovereign bonds/loans	• Specified loans or bonds • Porfolio of loans or bonds

Exhibit 6.1 shows the transfer methods grouped by the type of risk being transferred.

Total Return Swap

Exhibit 6.2 provides a graphical exposition of a total return swap. Since the *purchaser* of the total return swap (i.e., the total return receiver) receives all the cash flows and benefits (losses) if the value of the reference asset rises (falls), the *purchaser* is *synthetically* "long" the underlying reference asset during the life of the swap. Total return swaps have similarities to traditional bond financing transactions. In a typical transaction, a bank or other financial institution will carry the underlying asset on its balance sheet and will pay the total return to the swap purchaser. The purchaser in turn pays the banks financing costs plus a spread.

At origination, the parties agree on a reference asset, typically a bond or a loan that trades in the secondary market, and a reference rate. During the life of the swap the *purchaser* (total return receiver) receives all the cash flows on the reference asset from the seller. In exchange the purchaser pays

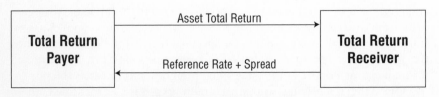

EXHIBIT 6.2 Total Return Swap

the reference rate (typically LIBOR) plus or minus an agreed spread to the seller. At maturity of the swap, the counterparties revalue the reference asset. If it has appreciated, the *seller* of the total return swap pays the appreciation to the purchaser; if it has depreciated, the purchaser pays the depreciation to the seller.

Exhibit 6.3 provides a term sheet for a total return swap on a Sinclair Broadcast Group bond.[2]

- The first section of the term sheet identifies the key characteristics of the transaction. A specific reference bond is identified and a notional amount and initial price of the reference bond are defined. At maturity of the swap the final price of the reference asset will be determined by actually selling the reference bond.
- The purchaser of the swap (the swap receiver) will pay a spread of 0.85% over 6 month LIBOR. The term sheet also indicates that the swap receiver will post collateral. The initial collateral is set at 10% of the funded amount of the swap (i.e., 10% of $10 million times 102%)

EXHIBIT 6.3 Stylized Term Sheet for a Total Return Swap

Reference Asset Details

Reference Party:	Sinclair Broadcast Group	
Facility Type:	Bond	
Notional Amount:	$10,000,000	
Facility Maturity Date:	7/15/07	
Coupon Rate:	9%	

SWAP Details

Initial Price of Reference Asset:	102%	◄——— Agreed to by
Swap Counterparty:	Bank ABC	Counterparties
Trade Date:	8/5/2002	
Swap Termination Date:	8/8/2005	
Swap Amount:	$10,000,000	
Settlements:	Semiannual	
Reference Rate:	6-Month LIBOR	
Deal Spread:	.85%	◄——— Negotiated
Initial Collateral:	An amount of cash equal to 10% of the swap funded amt	
Marginal Collateral:	Cash collateral by the Swap Receiver to the Swap Payer Greater of Ref. Asset Initial Price minus the Market Price, and zero	

with margin collateral required to the extent the market price of the collateral declines. In practice, margin might be required on a two-way basis and will be asked for only if the amount becomes material to one of the counterparties.

■ The procedures for determining the payments under the swap are defined for both the receiver and the payer. The periodic payments are based on LIBOR plus the spread for the swap receiver and the actual nonprincipal cash flows on the reference asset for the swap payer. The change in principal is paid only at the maturity of the swap, or if one of the defined credit events occurs, in which case the reference asset is sold or marked-to-market and a final payment determined.

A key element of the total return swap is that both market risk and credit risk are transferred. It does not matter whether the asset depreciates in value because the borrower's credit quality declines, credit spreads widen, or underlying interest rates increase. If there is a default on the underlying asset during the life of the total return swap, the parties will terminate the swap and make a final payment. Either the total return swap will be cash settled, in which case the asset is marked-to-market, or physically settled, in which case the seller delivers the defaulted asset to the purchaser against receipt of the reference asset's price at origination of the swap.

Credit Default Swap

The buyer of a credit default swap (CDS) is purchasing credit risk protection on a "reference asset." If a "credit event" occurs during the credit default swap's term, the seller makes a "payment" to the buyer. (All the terms in quotation marks are defined later.) In contrast to total return swaps, credit default swaps provide pure credit risk transfer.

Exhibit 6.4 provides a diagram of a credit default swap. The buyer of a credit default swap—the protection buyer—pays a premium (either lump sum or periodic) to the seller.

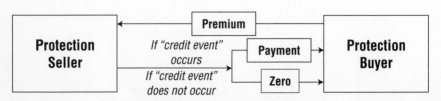

EXHIBIT 6.4   Credit Default Swap

The buyer and seller of the credit default swap must agree on three critical terms of the transaction: (1) the reference asset, (2) the credit event, and (3) the structure of the payment if a credit event occurs.

Reference Asset   The reference asset could be a specific obligation, an enumerated group of obligations, or all obligations in a specified class (e.g., "foreign currency bonds") as mutually agreed by the parties.

Credit Event   The ISDA Credit Derivatives Confirm (1999) gives the parties to a credit default swap a great deal of latitude in defining the credit event. (1) The parties could limit the credit event to default on the reference asset, or, (2) the parties could restrict the definition of a credit event to be a formal bankruptcy filing by the obligor, or (3) the parties could broaden the definition to include downgrade, failure to pay, repudiation or moratorium, acceleration, or restructuring.

Since restructuring typically extends the maturity and eases the repayment terms on existing loans or bonds, most credit portfolio managers want restructuring included as a credit event. As we discuss in a display later, many dealers and sellers of protection have argued that restructuring should be excluded. Their concern is that restructuring is hard to define, and coupled with the delivery option in most CDSs, puts dealers at a disadvantage.

The parties will typically specify materiality conditions in the form of a minimum amount of money involved in a default or failure to pay. Specific obligations may be *excluded* from the list of obligations that would trigger a credit event. Also, there are a number of limitations that can be placed on the assets that could be delivered in a physically settled swap.

Default Payment   The parties to a credit default swap must specify how it will be settled, if the credit event occurs.

- If the credit default swap is to be cash-settled, the counterparties will obtain a market price for the defaulted reference asset and the swap seller will pay the difference between the current price and the strike price specified in the contract—typically par.
- If the credit default swap is to be physically settled, the protection buyer will deliver the reference asset, or another asset that satisfies the conditions of the Deliverable Obligations, to the seller in exchange for a cash payment of the strike price.
- If the transaction is a "digital" credit default swap, the protection seller will make a predetermined payment to the protection buyer if the credit event occurs.

The Restructuring Debate

During the financial crisis in Asia in 1997, numerous credit default swaps were triggered. In some cases, protection buyers with physically settled swaps who did not own the specific reference asset were unable to deliver into the swap, or had to pay relatively high prices to obtain deliverable assets from others. This and other problems led to calls for a new credit default swap confirmation.

A new ISDA confirm (1999) dealt with the immediate problem . . .

In June 1999 ISDA released a new credit default swap confirmation and a set of definitions. This new confirm dealt with the meaning of "restructuring" as a credit event: The old requirement of "materially less favorable" changes was replaced with a definition of restructuring that includes a payment default and objective criteria, such as a reduction in coupon, deferral of principal or interest, or a change in priority.

The 1999 definitions also provide more flexibility about specifying default. The Russian default highlighted the uncertainty that can arise when one class of securities is treated differently from another (e.g., domestic vs. foreign debt) and when tight cross-default provisions do not link an issuer's debt instruments. The new confirm uses a "matrix" allowing the parties to be as general or specific as they desire about the instruments or missed payments that could trigger a default. For example, the parties can choose to use anything from a missed payment on any owed money, to default on a particular class of securities (e.g., domestic currency debt, or bonds rather than loans). Alternatively, the parties can reference a specific obligation. Going further, the parties can specify particular issues or classes of obligations that will not be considered in determining if a credit event occurred.

Furthermore, it provided physical settlement enhancements. The defaults in Indonesia and South Korea stemming from the 1997 financial crisis illustrated that credit swaps outstanding can exceed the supply of deliverable collateral. Protection buyers with physically settled swaps that did not already own the reference asset were forced to compete for the limited supply of reference obligations, forcing up prices. The new confirm provides for a broader specification of deliverable obligations for physically settled contracts. It also contains a cash settlement fallback when physical delivery is impossible or illegal.

. . . but the 1999 Definitions created another problem.

The revised documentation had the effect of giving protection buyers a "delivery option" on physical settlement by expanding the acceptable range of deliverable assets to include both bonds and loans and giving the protection buyer wide latitude over the maturity.

This delivery option led to a restructuring controversy.

In September 2000, Bank of America and Chase granted an extension to Conseco on approximately $2.8 billion of short-term loans. The extension, which prevented an immediate Conseco bankruptcy, resulted in some of their longer-term public bonds trading higher. It also triggered a credit event on as much as $2 billion of credit default swaps.

The owners of CDS played a "cheapest to deliver" game with the dealers: They did not deliver the restructured loans, which were relatively short-term obligations. Instead, they delivered the lower-priced, long-term bonds, expecting to receive par.

Not surprisingly, the credit protection sellers were not happy. Some argued that such bank restructurings, although technically a credit event, were never intended as such. Others argued that delivering long-term obligations was, for lack of a better term, bad faith. Almost immediately credit derivative dealers in the United States announced their intention to eliminate the restructuring event. Bank portfolio managers objected to the proposed change and ISDA convened a series of meetings to hammer out a resolution.

The controversy appeared to be resolved . . .

On May 11, 2001, ISDA released a "restructuring supplement." Three main elements of the new restructuring definition are:

1. Limit instances in which restructuring triggers a credit event—*A restructuring is considered a trigger event if the debt matures in less than 30 months.*
2. Impose a maturity limitation on deliverables—*Protection buyer can deliver securities with a maturity of less than 30 months following the restructuring date or to the extended maturity of the restructured loan.*
3. Require deliverables to be fully transferable.

. . . but the resolution appears to be coming unstuck.

While participants in the credit default swap market in North America generally accepted the compromise embodied in the May 2001 restructuring supplement, participants in Europe did not.

In the early summer of 2002, signs were positive. It appeared that agreement on a new definition for restructuring for the European market was close.

Then, in July 2002 a group of 10 large insurance companies (ACE Capital Re, Ambac Credit Products, CIFG, Chubb Financial Solutions, Financial Security Assurance, MBIA Insurance Corporation, MSI Financial Solutions, Pacific Life Insurance Company, Radian Asset Assurance, and XL Capital Assurance) sent an open letter to ISDA and the committees working on the restructuring issue in which they stated that "the current definition of Restructuring is clearly not workable." In essence, this group of insurance companies asked for the discussion to be started again.

Early in August 2002, the end providers of credit protection issued a position paper in which they stated: "Ultimately Restructuring should be removed as a Credit Event, and in the interim the definition of Restructuring should be revised."

Late in August 2002, in a memo to the ISDA committees working on the restructuring issue and to U.S. bank portfolio managers, JP Morgan Chase announced that: "JP Morgan, acting in its capacity as an end user, will drop Restructuring from its required credit events in our 'standard' contract for non-sovereign credit derivatives."

So, as this book went press, the future of restructuring is in doubt.

Credit-Linked Note

A credit-linked note is a combination of straight debt and a credit default swap. As is illustrated in Exhibit 6.5, the purchaser of the note effectively sells a credit default swap in return for an above-market coupon.

The payment default by Ecuador in 1999 highlights how credit-linked note structures work: Credit-linked notes had been issued in which the principal repayment was tied to Ecuadorian credit performance. If Ecuador did not default, the issuer would repay the principal at maturity as in an ordinary debt issue. But if Ecuador missed a payment (as was the case on

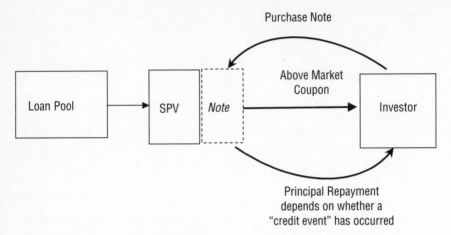

EXHIBIT 6.5   Credit Linked Note

its Brady bond debt in August)[3], issuers exercised the embedded credit default swap; the issuer had the right to call the debt from investors and return principal according to the post-default market value of specified Ecuador bonds. Since those bonds were trading at very steep discounts after Ecuador missed the debt payment, the investors suffered substantial loss of principal.

First-to-Default Basket

First-to-default baskets (also called "basket credit default swaps") extend the concept of the credit default swap to a portfolio of assets. In a typical structure 3 to as many as 10 individual credits will be listed as reference assets. The basket protection buyer agrees to pay a fixed spread to the seller in return for protection against the first default among the reference assets.

In Exhibit 6.6, three bonds are listed as reference assets. The liability of the protection seller is limited to the loss on the first company to default only. If any one of the three bonds defaults, the protection buyer will deliver up to $10 mm face value of the defaulted asset to the seller in return for the agreed-upon payment, usually par. The basket CDS terminates upon the first default event. The structure is interesting to investors for several reasons, but the most notable aspect is the inherent leverage. First, an investor can take this exposure to the three underlying credits without funding the position in the cash market. Second, the CDS seller is liable for only $10 mm of notional (i.e., no more than the purchase of a single one of the underlying assets), yet the spread on the structure is considerably higher

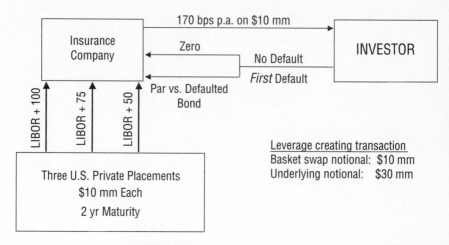

EXHIBIT 6.6   First-to-Default Basket

than the spread available on any single bond in the basket were the investor to buy the position outright. Of course the investor must determine if the higher spread is adequate compensation for the greater risk of default on the structure with three reference assets versus a single exposure.

THE CREDIT DERIVATIVES MARKET

Evolution of the Market

Although credit derivatives are very new instruments, they are already in their third "incarnation."

The first incarnation could be regarded as defensive, in the sense that they evolved from financial institutions' need to manage their own illiquid credit concentrations. Dealers had some success using default puts to hedge their credit exposures, but interest in these structures was limited elsewhere because counterparties were unfamiliar with them.

Efforts to turn this one-sided market into a two-sided market spawned the second incarnation of credit derivatives. Existing derivatives techniques were applied to emerging market debt and to corporate bonds and syndicated bank loans. In this phase of investor-driven trades, the credit derivatives market was still a "cash-and-carry" market. Dealers would hold the underlying instruments—corporate bonds or syndicated loans—on their balance sheets and sell customized exposures to investors via total return swaps and structured notes. Investors were attracted to these new structures for a number of reasons:

■ Credit derivatives gave investors access to new asset classes. For example, investors are not capable of providing the servicing that goes with bank loans; therefore, they have been precluded from investing directly in loans. Credit derivatives overcome this obstacle by passing the return on a loan to the investor while the back office processing is handled by a bank. In a similar vein, by selling the total return on a loan or bond, an investor can effectively "go short" in a market where physical short sales are difficult if not impossible.

■ Like derivatives on interest rates, currencies, equities, or commodities, credit derivatives can reduce transaction costs.

■ Credit derivatives permit some investors to leverage positions on bonds or loans.

■ The pricing of credit derivative structures was often attractive due to disparities in the way credit was priced in the bond, loan, and equity markets. (As the credit derivatives markets develop, these disparities can be expected to disappear and credit risk will be priced uniformly across an issuer's obligations.)

■ Credit derivatives allowed bond investors to express specific views about credit without necessarily having to accept the interest rate risk associated with holding a firm's debt. Although bond managers are trained to evaluate credit risk, the primary source of volatility in the bond market is interest rate risk. (In Chapter 59 of his *Handbook of Fixed-Income Securities*, Frank Fabozzi notes that interest rate fluctuations account for about 90% of the risk of corporate bonds in the United States.) Since credit derivatives allow credit exposure to be isolated from interest rate exposure, bond managers can express the views they are trained to express.

■ Credit derivatives made it possible to create synthetic assets that meet a specific set of investment criteria.

As credit derivatives have moved into their third incarnation, several factors coincided to make this market look more like other derivatives markets. As a result of efforts to educate counterparties and develop investor interest in these products, there is active two-way business. Dealers warehouse trades and cross-hedge, managing risk on a portfolio basis in the same way that an interest rate derivatives book is managed. Brokers, including electronic exchanges, have entered the market and the International Swaps and Derivatives Association (ISDA) has continued to evolve documentation as new issues have appeared.

Size and Composition of the Credit Derivatives Market

The credit derivatives market has grown rapidly since its inception in the early 1990s. In Exhibit 6.7, the diamonds show survey estimates of global

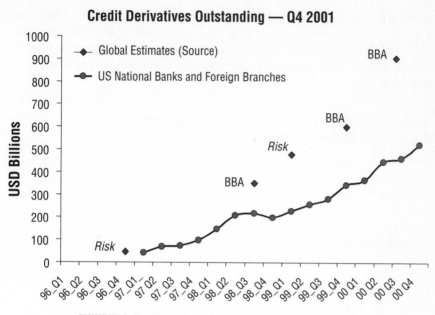

EXHIBIT 6.7 Growth of the Credit Derivatives Market

credit derivatives outstanding, while the line is data obtained from the Office of the Comptroller of the Currency (OCC) based on the Call Reports filed by U.S.-insured banks and foreign branches and agencies in the United States. The Call Report data, while objective, is a limited segment of the U.S. market since it does not include investment banks, insurance companies, or investors.

The 1998 Prebon Yamane and *Derivatives Week* survey of credit derivatives dealers provided more insight about the underlying issuer: Asian issuers were almost exclusively sovereigns (93%). In contrast, the majority of U.S. issuers were corporates (60%), with the remainder split between banks (30%) and sovereigns (10%). European issuers were more evenly split—sovereigns 45%, banks 29%, and corporates 26%.

USING CREDIT DERIVATIVES TO MANAGE A PORTFOLIO OF CREDIT ASSETS

Credit derivatives provide portfolio managers with new ways of shaping a portfolio and managing conflicting objectives. On a microlevel, credit derivatives can be used to reduce the portfolio's exposure to specific obligors

or to diversify the portfolio by synthetically accepting credit risk from industries or geographic regions that were underweighted in the portfolio.
On a macrolevel, credit derivatives can be used to create "synthetic" securitizations that alter the risk and return characteristics of a large number of
exposures at once.

Using Credit Derivatives to Reduce the Portfolio's Exposure to Specific Obligors

Exhibits 6.8 and 6.9 provide simple illustrations of the use of credit derivatives by the credit portfolio manager of a bank. The portfolio manager has
determined that the bank's exposure to XYZ Inc. should be reduced by
$20 million. The source of the $20 million exposure could be a $20 million
loan to XYZ Inc., but it could also be the result of any number of other
transactions, including a standby facility, a guarantee, and the credit risk
generated by a derivatives transaction.

In Exhibit 6.8, we treat the source of the credit exposure as a $20 mil-
lion loan to XYZ Inc. and have illustrated the use of a total return swap to
transfer that risk to another party. In the 1990s the purchaser of the total
return swap was often a hedge fund. The initial interest in the transaction
came as a result of the hedge fund's finding the pricing of the XYZ Inc.
loan attractive in comparison with XYZ Inc.'s traded debt. The primary
reason that the hedge fund elected to take on the loan exposure via a total
return swap (rather than purchasing the loans in the secondary market)

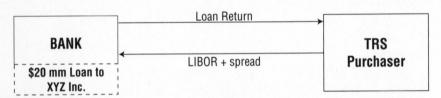

EXHIBIT 6.8 Reducing the Portfolio's Exposure to a Specific Obligor with a Total
Return Swap

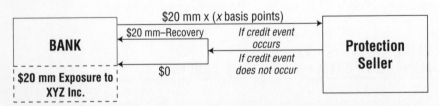

EXHIBIT 6.9 Reducing the Portfolio's Exposure to a Specific Obligor with a Credit
Default Swap

was because the derivative strategy permitted them to leverage their credit view. That is, by using a derivative, the hedge fund did not need to fund the position; it effectively rented the bank's balance sheet. However, it should be noted that, by using the credit derivative, the hedge fund also avoided the cost of servicing the loans, a cost it would have had to bear had it purchased the loans.

Exhibit 6.8 illustrates a risk-reducing transaction originating from the bank's desire to shed exposure in its loan book. As the market has evolved, banks have also developed active total return swap businesses in which they or their customers actively identify bonds for the bank to purchase and then swap back to the investor. These transactions serve multiple purposes for investors, but in their most basic form, are simply a vehicle for investors to rent the balance sheet of their bank counterparties by paying the bank's cost of financing plus an appropriate spread based on the investor's creditworthiness.

In Exhibit 6.9, we have not specified the source of the $20 million exposure. As we noted, it could be the result of a drawn loan (as was the case in Exhibit 6.8), a standby facility, a guarantee, or the credit risk generated by a derivatives transaction. The bank transfers the exposure using a credit default swap. If XYZ Inc. defaults, the bank will receive from the dealer the difference between par and the post-default market value of a specific XYZ Inc. reference asset. (In addition to transferring the economic exposure to XYZ Inc., the bank may also reduce the regulatory capital required on the XYZ Inc. loan. With the Basle I rules, it would calculate capital as if the $20 million exposure were to the dealer instead of XYZ. With a 100% risk weight for XYZ Inc. and a 20% risk weight for the dealer, capital falls from $1.6 million to $320,000.)

The credit derivative transactions would not require the approval or knowledge of the borrower, lessening the liquidity constraint imposed by client relationships. Other factors to consider are basis risk, which is introduced when the terms of the credit swap don't exactly match the terms of the bank's exposure to XYZ, and the creditworthiness of the dealer selling the protection.

Credit derivatives also provide information about the price of pure credit risk, which can be used in pricing originations and setting internal transfer prices. Many banks, for example, require loans entering the portfolio to be priced at market, with the originating business unit making up any shortfall. This requires business units that use lending as a lever to gain other types of relationship business to put a transfer price on that activity. Credit derivatives provide an external benchmark for making these pricing decisions.

Moreover, credit derivatives offer the portfolio manager a number of advantages. In addition to the ability to hedge risk and gain pricing information, credit derivatives give the portfolio manager control over timing. With credit derivatives, the portfolio manager can hedge an existing exposure or even synthetically create a new one at his or her discretion. Credit derivative structures are also very flexible. For example, the first loss on a group of loans could be hedged in a single transaction or the exposure on a five-year asset could be hedged for, say, two years.

The primary disadvantage is the cost of establishing the infrastructure to access the market. In addition, managers should be aware that hedging a loan may result in the recognition of income or loss as the result of the loan's being marked-to-market, and credit derivatives are not available for many market segments.

Using Credit Derivatives to Diversify the Portfolio by Synthetically Accepting Credit Risk

Credit derivatives permit the portfolio manager to create new, diversifying exposures quickly and anonymously. For example, by selling protection via a credit default swap, a portfolio manager can create an exposure that is equivalent to purchasing the asset outright. (The regulatory capital—in the banking book—for the swap would also be the same as an outright purchase.)

The credit derivative is an attractive way to accept credit exposures, because credit derivatives do not require funding. (In essence, the credit protection seller is accessing the funding advantage of the bank that originated the credit.)

Furthermore, credit derivatives can be tailored. Panels A, B, and C of Exhibit 6.10 illustrate this tailoring. Suppose Financial Institution Z wants to acquire a $20 million credit exposure to XYZ Inc. Suppose further, that the only XYZ Inc. bond available in the public debt market matures on February 15, 2007.

Financial Institution Z could establish a $20 million exposure to XYZ Inc. in the cash market by purchasing $20 million of the XYZ Inc. bonds. However, Financial Institution Z could establish this position in the derivative market by selling protection on $20 million of the same XYZ Inc. bonds. (As we noted previously, Financial Institution Z might choose the derivative solution over the cash solution, because it would not have to fund the derivative position.) Let's specify physical delivery, so if XYZ Inc. defaults, Financial Institution Z would pay the financial institution purchasing the protection $20 million and accept delivery of the defaulted bonds.

■ Panel A of Exhibit 6.10 illustrates the situation in which the credit default swap has the same maturity as the reference bonds. For the case being illustrated, Financial Institution Z would receive 165 basis points per annum on the $20 million notional (i.e., $330,000 per year).

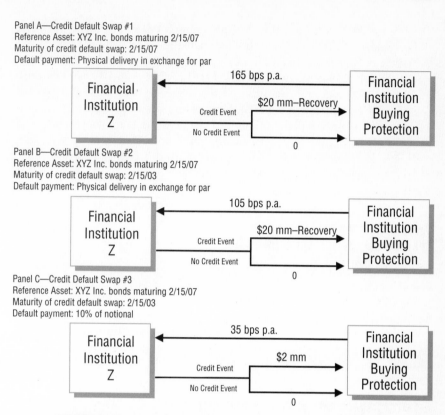

Panel A—Credit Default Swap #1
Reference Asset: XYZ Inc. bonds maturing 2/15/07
Maturity of credit default swap: 2/15/07
Default payment: Physical delivery in exchange for par

Panel B—Credit Default Swap #2
Reference Asset: XYZ Inc. bonds maturing 2/15/07
Maturity of credit default swap: 2/15/03
Default payment: Physical delivery in exchange for par

Panel C—Credit Default Swap #3
Reference Asset: XYZ Inc. bonds maturing 2/15/07
Maturity of credit default swap: 2/15/03
Default payment: 10% of notional

EXHIBIT 6.10 Tailoring an Exposure with a Credit Default Swap

- If, however, Financial Institution Z is unwilling or unable to accept XYZ Inc.'s credit for that long, the maturity of the credit default swap could be shortened—something that would not be possible in the cash market. Panel B of Exhibit 6.10 illustrates the situation in which the credit default swap has a maturity that is four years less than that of the reference bonds. Financial Institution Z's premium income would fall from 165 basis points per annum to 105 basis points per annum on the $20 million notional (i.e., from $330,000 per year to $210,000 per year).

- While Financial Institution Z has accepted XYZ Inc.'s credit for a shorter period of time, the amount at risk has not changed. If XYZ Inc. defaults, Financial Institution Z will have to pay $20 million and accept the defaulted bonds. In Chapter 3, we noted that the recovery rate for senior unsecured bonds is in the neighborhood of 50%, so Financial Institution

Z stands to lose as much as $10 million if XYZ Inc. defaults. Financial Institution Z could reduce this by changing the payment form of the credit default swap from physical settlement to a digital payment. The credit default swap illustrated in Panel C of Exhibit 6.10 has a maturity that is four years less than that of the reference bonds (as was the case with the transaction in Panel B), but this time the default payment is simply 10% of the notional amount of the credit default swap. That is, if XYZ Inc. defaults, Financial Institution Z will make a lump-sum payment of $2 million to its counterparty. With this change in structure Financial Institution Z's premium income would fall to 35 basis points per annum on the $20 million notional (i.e., $70,000 per year).

Using Credit Derivatives to Create "Synthetic" Securitizations

As we see in Chapter 7, in a traditional securitization of bank assets, the loans, bonds, or other credit assets are physically transferred from the bank to the special-purpose vehicle. Such a structure is limiting, because the transfer of ownership requires the knowledge, if not the approval, of the borrower.

A "synthetic" securitization can be accomplished by transferring the credit risk from the bank to the SPV by way of a credit derivative. We describe this in Chapter 7.

Relative Importance of Credit Derivatives to Portfolio Management

The results from the 2002 *Survey of Credit Portfolio Management Practices* that we described in Chapter 1 indicate that credit default swaps are the most important of the credit derivatives to portfolio managers, followed by credit linked notes and total return swaps.

2002 SURVEY OF CREDIT PORTFOLIO MANAGEMENT PRACTICES

Rank the credit derivative structures with respect to their importance to credit portfolio management (using "1" to denote the most important and "3" for the least important).

	Average Ranking
Total return swaps	2.7
Credit default swaps	1.1
Credit linked notes	2.3

PRICING CREDIT DERIVATIVES

We have some good news and some bad news.

The good news is that pricing credit derivatives—and credit risk in general—is quite similar in technique to pricing traditional derivatives, such as interest rate swaps or stock options. At the risk of oversimplifying, credit derivatives and traditional derivatives can all be valued as the present value of their risk-adjusted expected future cash flows. Anyone familiar with the concepts behind the Black–Scholes–Merton option pricing framework, or who can price an interest rate swap using a LIBOR yield curve, is well equipped to understand the models for pricing credit and derivatives on credit.

The bad news is that credit models are considerably more difficult to implement. The difficulty arises in three main areas.

1. The definition of default. Default is an imprecise concept subject to various legal and economic definitions. A pricing model will necessarily have to simplify the economics of default or very carefully define the precise conditions being modeled.
2. Loss given default. Credit risk contains two sources of uncertainty: the likelihood of default and the severity of loss. Pricing models for credit must address this second source of uncertainty or assume that the loss given default is known.
3. Available data. Pricing models require data to estimate parameters. Data on credit-related losses are notoriously limited (although this is beginning to change), and credit spread data (that is, the market price of credit risk) are available for only the largest and most liquid markets.

"Family Tree" of Pricing Models for Default Risky Claims

The past three decades have witnessed the evolution of two general frameworks for valuing default risky claims, and by extension, credit derivatives. The "family tree" of the models is provided in Exhibit 6.11. Both families have their roots in the no-arbitrage analysis of Black–Scholes–Merton, but they differ substantially in form.

The left branch of the family tree in Exhibit 6.11 contains models that analyze the economic basis of default at the firm level. Notable among these models is the Merton model we have used several times in this text. In the Merton model and the others of this line, default is caused by a decline in the value of a firm's assets, such that it can no longer pay its fixed claims. The point at which the value of assets is deemed insufficient for the firm to continue is known as the "default point" or "default threshold."

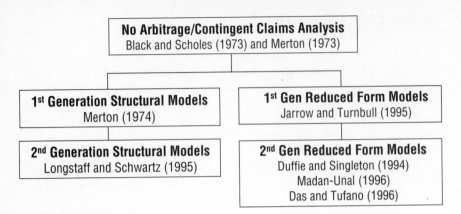

EXHIBIT 6.11   Family Tree of Pricing Models for Default Risky Claims

One distinguishing characteristic of the models on this branch of the tree is the approach to determining the default point. These models have been labeled "structural models" because they require data on the assets and liabilities of individual firms and because they hypothesize a triggering event that causes default.

The right branch of the "family tree" contains models that abstract from the economics of default. In these models, default "pops out" of an underlying statistical process (for example, a Poisson process). These models, labeled "reduced form," estimate the risk-neutral, that is, market based, probability of default from prevailing credit spreads. Reduced form models ignore the specific economic circumstances that trigger default, deriving their parameters from the prices of similar securities.

Structural Models of Default Risky Claims

In the context of a structural model, a credit default swap that pays the difference between par and the post-default value of the underlying bond is an option. In the structural models, the underlying source of uncertainty both for the underlying bond and for the credit default swap is the value of the firm's assets. In the jargon of the options market, the credit default swap is an "option on an option," or a "compound option." The structural models approach this by using standard option-valuation tools to value the "default option."

First-Generation Structural Models   Exhibit 6.12 is the now-familiar illustration of the Merton model for a simple firm with a single zero coupon

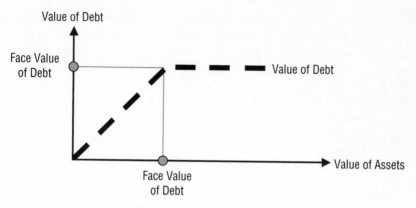

EXHIBIT 6.12 The Merton Model

debt issue. If the value of the assets, at maturity of the debt issue, is greater than the face value of the debt (the "exercise price"), then the owners of the firm will pay the debt holders and keep the remaining value. However, if assets are insufficient to pay the debt, the owners of the equity will exercise their "default option" and put the remaining assets to the debt holders.

In this simple framework, the post-default value of the debt is equal to the value of the firm's remaining assets. This implies that, at maturity of the debt (i.e., at "expiration" of the "default option"), the value of the default-risky debt is

$$D(T) = F - \begin{cases} 0; & \text{If } V(T) > F \\ F - V(T); & \text{If } V(T) \le F \end{cases}$$

where F is the face value of the (zero coupon) debt issue and $V(T)$ is the value of the firm's assets at maturity.

As we discussed in Chapter 3, in a structural model, the value of the default-risky debt is equivalent to the value of a risk-free zero coupon of equal maturity minus the value of the "default option."

$$D(t) = \text{Value of Risk-Free Debt} - \text{Value of Default Option}$$
$$= F \times DF_t - f[V(t), T, r, F, \sigma_v]$$

So it follows that pricing credit risk is an exercise in valuing the default option. As implied in the preceding equation, this valuation could be accomplished using standard option-valuation techniques where the price of the underlying asset is replaced by the value of the firm's assets and the strike price of the "default option" is equal to the face value of the zero-coupon debt. Specifically, the inputs in such an option valuation would be

■ Market value of the firm's assets.
■ Volatility of the market value of the firm's assets.
■ Risk-free interest rate of the same maturity as the maturity of the zero-coupon debt.
■ Face value of the zero-coupon debt.
■ Maturity of the single, zero-coupon debt issue.

This listing of the data requirements for valuing a "default option" points out the problems with the structural models in general and with the first-generation models specifically:

■ The market value of the firm's asset value and the volatility of that number are unobservable.
■ The assumption of a constant interest rate is counterintuitive.
■ Assuming a single zero-coupon debt issue is too simplistic; implementing a first-generation model for a firm with multiple debt issues, junior and senior structures, bond covenants, coupons, or dividends would be extremely difficult.

Second-Generation Structural Models   The second-generation models addressed one of the limitations of the first-generation models—the assumption of a single, zero-coupon debt issue. For example, the approach suggested by Francis Longstaff and Eduardo Schwartz does not specifically consider the debt structure of the firm and instead specifies an exogenous *default threshold*. When that threshold (boundary) is reached, all debt is assumed to default and pay a prespecified percentage of its face value (i.e., the recovery rate). An interesting application of this concept is calculating an "implied default point" in terms of the actual liabilities and asset values of the firm given market observed values for CDS protection and, say, equity volatility as a proxy for asset volatility.

As we noted in Chapter 3, the Moody's–KMV default model (Credit Monitor and CreditEdge) actually implement such a second-generation structural model.

Reduced Form Models of Default Risky Claims

Reduced form models abstract from firm-specific explanations of default, focusing on the information embedded in the prices of traded securities. Traders generally favor reduced form models because they produce "arbitrage-free" prices relative to the current term structure, and because all the inputs are (theoretically) observable.

First-Generation Reduced Form Models Notwithstanding publication dates, we regard the model proposed by Robert Jarrow and Stuart Turnbull (1995) as the first-generation model.

The reduced form model relies on a simple economic argument: *The price of any security—a bond, an interest rate swap, a credit default swap—can be expressed as the expected value of its future cash flows. To calculate the expected value, each possible future cash flow is multiplied by the probability of its occurrence. The probability used is a risk-adjusted (also known as "risk-neutral") probability, obtained from the prices of other traded securities. Risk-adjusted probabilities simply reflect the price of risk in the market. Once calculated, the risk-adjusted expected cash flows are discounted to the present using risk-free interest rates to obtain the security's price.

Risk-Neutral Probabilities Financial engineers have developed the concept of a risk-neutral probability to facilitate the pricing of a wide range of derivative securities, including credit derivatives. A risk-neutral probability is derived from the prices of traded securities rather than measured from historical outcomes. For example, historically the probability that an AAA corporation in the United States defaults within one year is less than 0.0002 based on Moody's or S&P data on defaults. In fact, in some historical time periods the observed probability is zero. Yet traded securities issued by AAA companies have significant credit spreads associated with them on the order of 20 to 60 bps per year. If we ignore other factors such as liquidity, the existence of a positive credit spread of this size implies that investors trade these securities as if the probability of default were higher than history suggests. One way to get at pricing, therefore, is to use the prices of traded assets to compute an implied default probability. If we know the market implied probability of default on, say, IBM, we can use this to calculate the price of a credit derivative on IBM bonds or loans. As illustrated, the market implied probability of default is the "risk neutral" default probability.

A probability obtained from observed market prices is therefore consistent with the prices of other traded securities; thus it is "arbitrage free."

Let's express interest rates in continuously compounded form. If we assume that the spread over Treasuries, s, is compensation for the risk of default only, then, in a risk-neutral world, investors must be indifferent between e^r dollars with certainty and $e^{(r+s)}$ dollars received with probability $(1 - \pi)$, where π is the risk-neutral probability of default. That is

$$e^r = (1 - \pi)e^{(r + s)}$$

or

$$e^{-s} = (1 - \pi)$$

which is approximately

$$(1 - s) \cong (1 - \pi)$$

implying $\pi = s$.

The implication of the preceding is that the risk-neutral probability of default is determined by the spread on a default risky bond, given our assumption that the spread is only compensating for default risk (and not, say, for the liquidity of the bond).

To see how risk-neutral probabilities of default are actually obtained, consider the following relation:

$$CORP_1 = BENCH_1 \times [(1 - \pi) \times 1 + \pi \times RR]$$

$CORP_1$ is the price today of a zero coupon bond issued by Company X that will mature in one period. This price can be interpreted as the present value (using risk-free discount rates) of the risk-adjusted expected cash flows on the bond. The discounting is accomplished with $BENCH_1$, the price today of a zero coupon Treasury that also matures in one period. The expected value is calculated from the cash flows on Company X bonds and the risk-adjusted probability of default, π. Thus, either Company X defaults, paying a known percentage of the face value, RR, with probability π, or it does not default, and pays 100% of the face value with probability $(1 - \pi)$.

Mathematically this pricing model is an equation with four variables: $CORP_1$, $BENCH_1$, π, and RR. Given any three of the variables, we can solve for the fourth. Assuming the recovery rate is known (this can be relaxed later), and with market prices for $CORP_1$ and $BENCH_1$, we can solve for π—the "market's" assessment of the default probability.

Expressing interest rates in continuously compounded form and assuming the risk-free interest rate is r, we can express the price today of the one-year, risk-free zero-coupon bond as

$$BENCH_1 = e^{-rt}$$

The price of the risky one-year, zero coupon bond is

$$CORP_1 = e^{-(r+s)t}$$

where s is the *credit spread*. Incorporating these values into the equation for the value of the risky bond,[4]

$$e^{-(r+s)t} = e^{-rt}\left[(1 - \pi_t) + \pi_t \times RR\right]$$

so the risk-neutral one-period probability of default for Company X is

$$\pi_t = \frac{1 - e^{-st}}{1 - RR}$$

EXAMPLE: IMPLYING A RISK-NEUTRAL PROBABILITY OF DEFAULT

Suppose we observe that the one-year (continuously compounded) zero coupon rate for a credit-risky bond is 5.766% and the risk-free (continuously compounded) one-year zero coupon rate is 5.523%. The continuously compounded spread is 0.243%. Let's assume the recovery rate to be 50%.

The risk-neutral probability of default is 0.486% (48.6 basis points):

$$\pi_{1yr} = \frac{1 - e^{-s}}{1 - RR} = \frac{1 - e^{-0.00243}}{1 - 0.5} = 0.4855\%$$

The preceding example illustrates the relation between recovery rates and the implied risk-neutral probabilities of default. When we assumed a 50% recovery rate, the observed 24 basis point zero rate spread corresponds to a 48.6 basis point default probability. Had we assumed that the recovery rate was 0, that same 24 basis point spread would have corresponded to a one-year probability of default of 24.3 basis points.

Also note that, in order to obtain estimates of the risk-neutral probability of default for a particular company, we must have a precise yield curve specific to Company X debt (or a precise yield curve for debt of other companies that are deemed to be of similar credit risk). Thus it will be difficult to apply reduced form models to middle market companies or illiquid markets.

Pricing a Single-Period Credit Default Swap with a Risk-Free Counterparty
Having obtained π, the risk-neutral probability of default, it is now possible to price a credit swap on Company X bonds. Following the reduced form model, the credit swap price is the discounted value of its expected cash flows. For the swap, the cash flow is either zero (no default by Company X) or *RR* (the assumed recovery in the event of default).

To price a one-period credit default swap, all we need to know is the appropriate value of π and the discount rate.

$$\text{Price of credit default swap on Company X bonds} = BENCH_1 \times [(1 - \pi) \times 0 + \pi \times RR]$$

EXAMPLE: PRICING A SINGLE-PERIOD CDS WITH A RISK-FREE COUNTERPARTY

In the previous example, we used the observed risk-free one-year zero coupon rate of 5.523%. This translates into a current value for the risk-free one-year zero coupon bond of 0.9463.

We assumed the recovery rate to be 50%, and we solved for the one-period risk-neutral probability of default of 0.486%.

Using that, the price of a one-year credit default swap on Company X's bonds is the risk-neutral present value of the expected cash flows

$$0.9463 \times [(1 - 0.00486) \times 0 + 0.00486 \times 0.50] = 0.0023$$

That is, the price of the one-year credit default swap would be 23 basis points.

Pricing a Multiperiod Credit Default Swap with a Risk-Free Counterparty
To move to a multiperiod model requires more data and a little technique. We will have to accomplish five steps:

1. Construct a yield curve for the reference credit.
2. Construct a risk-free or other "base" curve.
3. "Bootstrap" the *forward* credit spreads.
4. Extract forward probabilities of default for Company X.
5. Calculate expected cash flows and discount to present (utilize marginal and cumulative probability of default).

It is probably easiest to explain this by way of an example.

Example: Pricing a Multi-Period CDS with a Risk-Free Counterparty

Let's price the following credit default swap:

Reference Credit:	Company X
Swap Tenor:	3 years
Event Payment:	Par-Post Default Market Value

The first step is to construct yield curves for the risk-free asset and the reference credit.

Maturity (Years)	U.S. Treasury Par Yields	Company X Par Yields	Par Credit Spread
1	5.60%	5.85%	.25
2	5.99%	6.34%	.35
3	6.15%	6.60%	.45
4	6.27%	6.87%	.60
5	6.34%	7.04%	.70
6	6.42%	7.22%	.80
7	6.48%	7.38%	.90

Semiannual 30/360 yields.

The next step is to "bootstrap" the *forward* credit spreads. We calculate the forward rates for the Treasuries and for Company X, and the forward spread is the difference between those forward rates.

Maturity (Years)	U.S. Treasuries Zeros	U.S. Treasuries One-Year Forwards	Company X Zeros	Company X One-Year Forwards	One-Year Forward Credit Spreads *N* Years Forward
1	5.61%	5.61%	5.86%	5.86%	.25
2	6.01%	6.41%	6.36%	6.87%	.46
3	6.17%	6.50%	6.63%	7.18%	.68
4	6.30%	6.68%	6.93%	7.81%	1.13
5	6.37%	6.67%	7.11%	7.86%	1.19
6	6.46%	6.91%	7.32%	8.36%	1.45
7	6.53%	6.94%	7.51%	8.66%	1.72

Semiannual 30/360 zero coupon rates.

The resulting term structures of Company X's credit spread—par and forward spreads—is illustrated next.

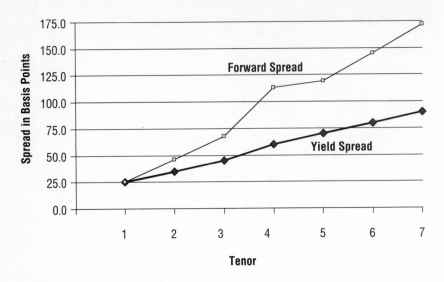

After converting the semiannual zero rates to continuously compounded rates, the risk-neutral default probability between time t_a and time $t_b > t_a$ *conditional* on no default prior to t_a is then given by

$$_a\pi_b = \frac{1 - \exp[-_aS_b(t_b - t_b)]}{1 - RR}$$

where $_aS_b$ is the forward-rate credit spread. Assuming the recovery rate to be 50%, the resulting conditional marginal default probabilities are:

Year	Conditional Marginal Default Probability
0	
	0.4855%
1	
	0.8700%
2	
	1.312%
3	

However, to price the credit default swap, we need *unconditional* marginal default probabilities:

Year	Conditional Marginal Default Probability		Prob. of No Default in Prior Periods		Unconditional Marginal Default Probability
0					
1	0.4855%	×	100.0000%	=	0.4855%
2	0.8700%	×	99.5145%	=	0.8658%
3	1.312%	×	98.6487%	=	1.2943%

The final calculations to price the credit default swap are shown next.

Year	Unconditional Marginal Default Probability	Loss Given Default	Single Period Price	Risk Free Discount Factor	Present Value of Price
1	0.4855%	50%	0.2428%	0.9462	0.2297%
2	0.8658%	50%	0.4329%	0.8884	0.3846%
3	1.2944%	50%	0.6472%	0.8333	0.5393%
Total of Present Values					1.15%

The final calculation uses the unconditional marginal default probability, that is, the probability of actually making a payment on the swap in each period, times the assumed amount of the payment, to arrive at the expected payment in each of the swap periods. Summing all of these payments gives a total price of 1.15%, which would then be expressed as an equivalent annual payment of 43 bp.

How does the recovery rate assumption affect the price? Exhibit 6.13 shows that the price is relatively insensitive to the recovery rate for a wide range of values.

Pricing a Multi-Period Credit Default Swap with a Risky Counterparty
So far, we have been looking at the price of credit default swaps, assuming that the counterparty is risk free. However, in the real world, the protection seller might not pay in the event that the reference entity in the credit default swap defaults. When the counterparty is subject to default risk, determination of the price for a credit default swap requires additional data:

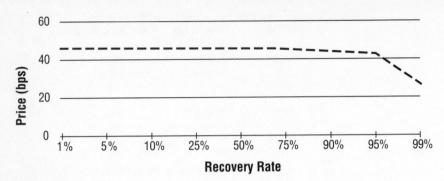

FIGURE 6.13 Effect of the Recovery Rate Assumption on the Price of a Credit Default Swap

■ Yield curve for the risky swap counterparty.
■ Correlation of default by the reference credit and default by the credit default swap counterparty.
■ Recovery rate for the counterparty.

We will need to calculate the forward credit spreads for the counterparty to obtain marginal default probability estimates. Using this we will need to calculate the joint probability of default by the counterparty *and* the reference credit.

It appears that the primary determinants of the price of a credit default swap with a risky counterparty will be sensitive to at least the following factors:

■ The market-implied probability of default by the reference entity.
■ The expected loss severity in event of default.
■ The market-implied probability of default for the protection seller (the counterparty in the credit default swap).
■ The correlation of default for the reference entity and the protection seller.

The last point—the correlation of default between the reference entity and the protection seller—highlights the usefulness of choosing protection sellers intelligently. A credit default swap purchased from an Indonesian bank to protect an Indonesian corporate exposure would be worth less than the same swap purchased from a North American counterparty. Exhibit 6.14, from David Li (at the time, with us at CIBC World Markets, now at Salomon Smith Barney), provided an overview of the significance of the correlation effect on the pricing of credit default swaps. And the following example offers some insight into the size of the effect.

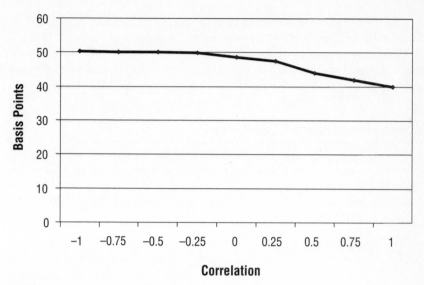

EXHIBIT 6.14 Effect of Default Correlation on the Price of a Credit Default Swap with a Risky Counterparty

Example: Pricing a Multi-Period CDS with a Risky Counterparty

Let's look again at the three-year credit default swap on Company X's bond. Previously, we found that if the counterparty (i.e., protection seller) is risk free, the price would be 43 basis points per annum.

Let's now suppose that the protection seller is subject to default risk. Indeed, let's think about two potential sellers of protection on Company X: The "lower-risk protection seller" has a credit spread (over Treasuries) of 45 basis points; and the "higher-risk protection seller" has a credit spread of 65 basis points.

Clearly, the buyer of the credit protection will pay less for the three-year protection to the "higher-risk seller" than they would to the "lower-risk seller." The question is how much and the answer to this question depends on the correlation of default between Company X and the protection seller. The following table provides the prices for credit default swaps for both of the protection sellers, considering different correlations of default between Company X and the protection seller.

Default Correlation	Lower Risk Protection Seller	Higher Risk Protection Seller
0.10	42 bps	39 bps
0.20	40 bps	37 bps
0.30	38 bps	35 bps

So far, we have been talking about a single stochastic variable—the default—and at least implicitly, assuming interest rates to be fixed. In truth, the model proposed by Robert Jarrow and Stuart Turnbull made both of these elements stochastic. The following illustration provides an introduction to the way that stochastic interest rates were included.

Stochastic Interest Rates in Jarrow/Turnbull

As illustrated below, the interest rate process is modeled as a binomial tree. $B(0,1)$ is the value of a one-period risk-free bond and $B(0,2)$ is the value of a two-period risk-free bond. The risk-neutral probability of an "up" move in rates is q_0 and $r(0)$ is the risk-free rate between time 0 and 1, and $r(1)_{u(d)}$ is the risk-free rate between time 1 and 2 after an "up" ("down") move in rates.

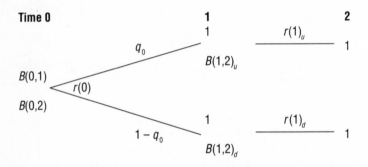

Default is modeled using a discrete-time binomial process. In the following diagram, π_0 and π_1 are the first and second period conditional risk-neutral probabilities of default and δ is the recovery given default.

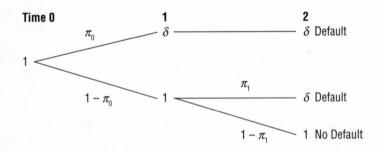

The combination of the risk-free interest rate process with the default process to price a one-period risky bond ($v(0,1)$) or a two-period risky bond ($v(0,2)$), assuming that defaults are *uncorrelated* with interest rates, can be illustrated as:

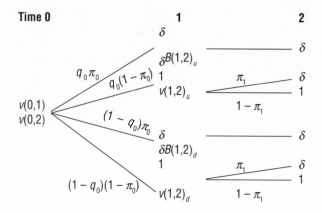

With this assumption, the joint probabilities for the various interest rate and default states can be obtained simply by multiplying the probability of default or no default (π and $1 - \pi$) by the probability of an up or down rate move (q and $1 - q$). For the two-period risky bond ($v(0,2)$), we assume that the recovery δ is not received until $t = 2$ even if default occurs between $t = 0$ and $t = 1$.

To illustrate the use of the binomial tree, the value of the two-period risky bond is

$$v(0,2) = q_0 \pi_0 \delta e^{-r(0)} B(1,2)_u + q_0 (1 - \pi_0) v(1,2)_u$$
$$+ (1 - q_0) \pi_0 \delta e^{-r(0)} B(1,2)_d + (1 - q_0)(1 - \pi_0) v(1,2)_d$$

where

$$B(1,2)_u = \exp[-r(1)_u]$$
$$B(1,2)_d = \exp[-r(1)_d]$$
$$v(1,2)_u = \exp[-r(1)_u](\pi_1 \delta + 1 - \pi_1)$$
$$v(1,2)_d = \exp[-r(1)_d](\pi_1 \delta + 1 - \pi_1)$$

If we assume $q_0 = 0.6$, $\pi_0 = 0.04$, $\pi_1 = 0.05$, $r(0) = 3\%$, $r(1)_u = 3.2\%$, $r(1)_d = 2.8\%$, and $\delta = 0.4$, then

$$v(0,2) = 0.6(0.04)(0.4)e^{-0.03})(e^{-0.032}) + 0.6(0.96)(e^{-0.032})(0.05(0.4) + 0.95)$$
$$+ (0.4)(0.04)(0.4)(e^{-0.03})(e^{-0.028}) + (0.4)(0.96)(e^{-0.028})(0.05(0.4) + 0.95)$$

so

$$v(0,2) = 0.91625$$

Second-Generation Reduced Form Models   The second-generation reduced form models listed in Exhibit 6.11 all build on the basic framework of the first-generation models with extensions in various directions. One extension is in the modeling of recovery as a random variable. The Duffie and Singleton (1994) model was an early modification that produces a variable recovery amount, while Madan and Unal (1996) developed a framework for basing recovery estimates on the relative prices of bonds with different seniority. Another extension is the modeling of a firm's credit rating state, first presented in Das and Tufano (1996). This is a logical extension of modeling default/no default, but requires a risk-neutral framework for modeling transition probabilities.

NOTES

1. Greg Hayt is a senior risk officer at Paloma Partners in Greenwich, Connecticut. Prior to joining Paloma, Greg served as head of CDO Products at the RiskMetrics Group and as Principal at Rutter Associates where he focused on credit portfolio modeling. He has also held positions at CIBC and the Chase Manhattan Bank, where he specialized in risk management and derivatives markets.

   This chapter is based on two articles that we published in the *RMA Journal*: "Credit Derivatives: The Basics" (Feb 2000), "Credit Derivatives: Implications for Bank Portfolio Management" (Apr 2000), and "How the Market Values Credit Derivatives" (March 2000).

2. Our thanks to John Rozario (CIBC World Markets) for permitting us to use this term sheet.

3. Ecuador failed to make an August 1999 coupon payment; however, they did not officially say they would not make the payment within the 30-day grace period until the end of September.

4. We add the subscript "t" to the risk-neutral probability of default to remind us that this is a *cumulative* probability (from $t = 0$ to t).

CHAPTER 7

Securitization

*C*ollateralized debt obligations (CDOs) encompass the two main sources of underlying assets (collateral) in credit asset securitization—*collateralized loan obligations* (CLOs) and *collateralized bond obligations* (CBOs).

CDOs represent another step in the process of debt securitization. The first pass-through mortgage-backed securities were issued in 1968 by Ginnie Mae (Government National Mortgage Association). In 1983, Freddie Mac (the Federal Home Loan Mortgage Corporation) issued the first *collateralized mortgage obligation* (CMO). This was followed by the securitization of auto loans (started in 1985), and credit cards and other consumer loans (started in 1987). The first CLO appeared in 1990 and the first CBO appeared in 1998 (See Exhibit 7.1).

While these structures are built upon each other, they also have some very important differences. The mortgage-backed securities were developed as a way of dealing with interest rate risk. The securitization of auto loans was a result of the weak credit ratings of sellers. The securitization of credit card receivables and other consumer debt was a response to bank capital requirements. In contrast, the CLOs and CBOs appeared as a way of dealing with the credit risk of the borrowers.

Exhibit 7.2 provides an indication of the size of the CDO market in terms of volume.

Exhibit 7.3 looks at the size of the market from the perspective of the number of issuances. Note, however, that Exhibit 7.3 is for CLOs only, rather than both CLOs and CBOs.

Exhibit 7.4 provides some perspective on the way that the market is distributed geographically.

ELEMENTS OF A CDO

A CDO can be thought of as a diversified, actively managed pool of loans or bonds supporting rated securities and a residual claim ("equity"). As

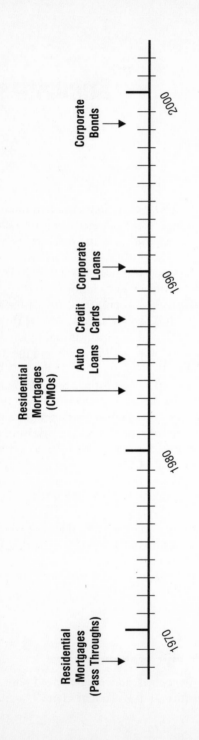

EXHIBIT 7.1 Asset-Backed Securitization: From CMOs to CBOs

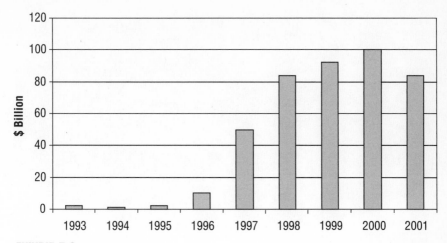

EXHIBIT 7.2   CDO Issuance
Source: Ellen Leander, "CDO Industry at a Crossroad," *Risk*, May 2002.

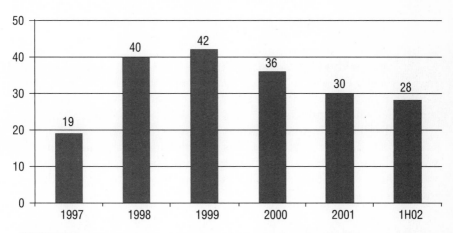

EXHIBIT 7.3   CDO Issuance—Number of New CLOs Introduced
Source: Standard & Poor's.

such, a CDO is a balance sheet with a legal structure—a special-purpose vehicle (SPV).

Assets and Liabilities

The asset side of the balance sheet can include bonds (a CBO) or loans (a CLO). In the case of loans, a CLO can contain a wide range of types of

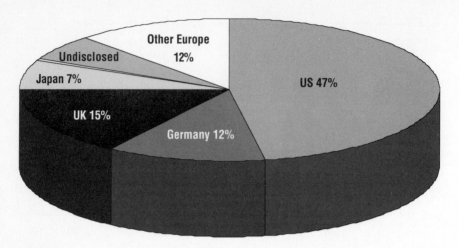

EXHIBIT 7.4   Outstanding Bank CLOs by Domicile of Obligor—2000
Source: Alexander Batchvarov, Ganesh Rajendra, and Brian McManus (Merrill Lynch), "Synthetic Structures Drive Innovation," *Risk*, June 2000.

loans. CLOs can contain term and revolving loans, secured and unsecured loans, syndicated and bilateral loans, and distressed or nonperforming loans. A CDO can also include unfunded commitments and the credit exposures associated with interest rate, foreign exchange rate, equity, or commodity derivative contracts.

The liabilities are structured to appeal to specific investor classes, and may include straight debt of various credit ratings with senior/subordinated structures, commercial paper, and equity. The latter is a very volatile part of the structure that provides the cushion necessary to obtain high ratings on more senior tranches.

Parties Involved in Doing a CDO

The most important parties for a CDO are the investors—conduits, banks, insurance companies, hedge funds, and mutual funds. But there are a lot of other people at the table, each of whom has a role to perform. The issuer (most likely a bank) structures the transaction, places the notes, provides hedging, and may warehouse the collateral. The lawyers handle issues dealing with documentation, taxes, and securities law. The collateral manager selects the collateral and monitors its credit quality, monitors compliance with covenants, and is the one who directs the trustee to buy or sell. The trustee handles all the cash, processes all trading of collateral, and monitors compliance with all covenants. The auditor reconciles all modeled values and audits the trustee. The rating agencies provide the initial rating for the securities and provide ongoing monitoring.

"TRADITIONAL" AND "SYNTHETIC" CDO STRUCTURES

Exhibit 7.5 traces the evolution of the CDO structures.

Traditional CDOs

Exhibit 7.6 illustrates a "traditional" (or "cash-funded") CDO structure. In a traditional CDO, the ownership of the assets is legally transferred

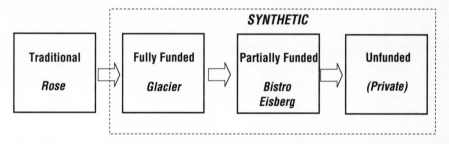

EXHIBIT 7.5   Evolution of CDO Structures

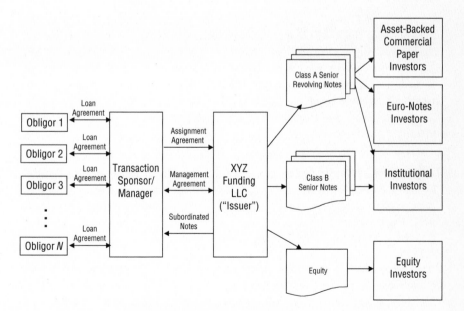

EXHIBIT 7.6   Traditional CDO Structure

ROSE FUNDING

Notwithstanding the fact that CLOs had existed as early as 1990, National Westminster Bank PLC's 1996 Rose Funding transaction is usually regarded as the "first," because this $5 billion transaction was unusual for its size (200 high quality corporate loans—15%–20% of Nat West's loan book) and its structure (i.e., it included revolving and undrawn facilities from 17 countries).

---

from the transaction sponsor (e.g., the bank that owns the loans or other credit assets) to a bankruptcy-remote trust or special-purpose vehicle (SPV). The SPV issues securities backed by these credit assets and distributes those securities to investors. In a traditional CDO, the credit assets are fully cash funded with the proceeds of debt and equity issued by the SPV, with repayment of the obligations directly tied to the cash flow of the assets.

Synthetic CDOs

A synthetic CDO effects the risk transfer without a legal change in the ownership of the credit assets. This is accomplished by a credit derivative. The sponsoring institution transfers the credit risk of a portfolio of credit assets to the SPV by means of a total return swap, credit default swap, or credit-linked note, while the assets themselves remain on the sponsoring institution's balance sheet.

As was illustrated in Exhibit 7.5, synthetic CDOs can be subdivided into three categories.

Fully Funded Synthetic CDOs   A fully funded CDO is illustrated in Exhibit 7.7. It is called "fully funded," because all the credit risk in the pool of credit assets is transferred to the SPV and this credit risk is fully cash funded with the proceeds of the securities issued by the SPV.

The steps involved in Exhibit 7.7 are as follows:

1. The credit risk is transferred to the SPV by means of the SPV's selling credit protection to the bank via a credit default swap. (This means that the SPV will be receiving premium income on the credit default swap.)

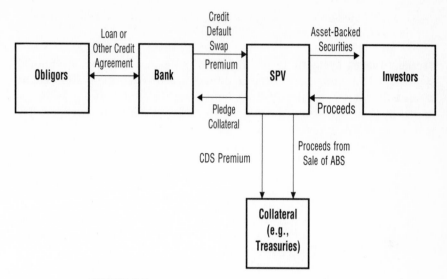

EXHIBIT 7.7 Synthetic CDO Structure—Fully Funded

2. The SPV issues one or more tranches of securities with repayment contingent upon the actual loss experience relative to expectations.
3. The SPV invests the proceeds from the sale of the securities and the premium income from the credit default swap in highly rated, liquid collateral.

GLACIER FINANCE

Perhaps the most widely discussed fully funded CLO was Swiss Bank's Glacier Finance (1997). This structure was collateralized by a pool of 130 credit-linked notes, where each credit-linked note was tied to the performance of a Swiss Bank obligor. While 95% of the obligors were investment grade, the identities of the specific obligors were not revealed (because of Swiss banking law). Swiss Bank retained the right to actively manage the pool of credit-linked notes within preset guidelines to reflect its evolving exposure.

Because the obligor identities were not revealed and because Swiss Bank could actively manage the pool of credit-linked notes, credit enhancement was critical. It was provided by a series of privately placed B tranches, a subordinated equity piece retained by Swiss Bank, and an excess spread of 10 basis points.

4. The SPV pledges the collateral to the bank (to make the SPV an acceptable counterparty in the credit default swap).

Partially Funded Synthetic CDOs   Exhibit 7.8 illustrates a partially funded synthetic CDO. Only part of the credit risk arising from the pool of credit assets is transferred to the SPV; the balance of the credit risk might be retained by the originating bank or transferred to a third party in the OTC market (via a credit derivative).

BISTRO

The most familiar structure of this type is JP Morgan's Bistro. The first Bistro, done in 1997, was based on a pool of 300 corporate and public finance credits located in Canada, the United States, and Europe. In contrast to Glacier Finance, the identities of all the obligors underlying the structure were disclosed.

JP Morgan guaranteed that the composition of the portfolio would remain static over the transaction life. Defaults would be realized by the investors at the final maturity, rather than when they occurred.

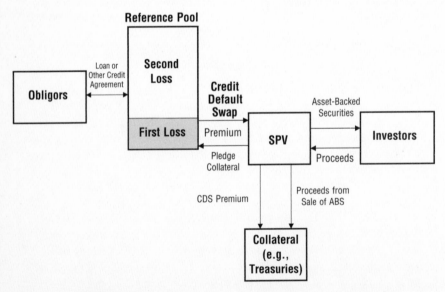

EXHIBIT 7.8   Synthetic CDO Structure—Partially Funded

Unfunded Synthetic CDOs Exhibit 7.9 illustrates an unfunded synthetic CDO. None of the credit risk in the pool of credit assets is transferred to an SPV and funded by investors. Instead, the credit risk is transferred to an OTC counterparty via a credit derivative transaction.

APPLICATIONS OF CDOs

Exhibit 7.10 summarizes the various ways in which CDOs are being used.

Balance Sheet CDOs

Balance sheet CDOs are used primarily by banks for managing economic and regulatory capital.

Until recently, banks issued CLOs to reduce regulatory capital. As we noted in Chapter 1, since banks must hold an 8% regulatory capital posi-

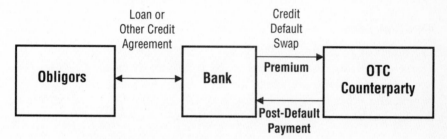

EXHIBIT 7.9 Synthetic CDO Structure—Unfunded

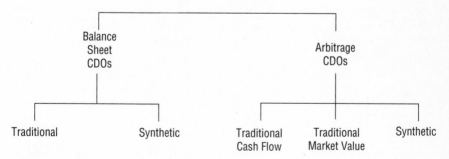

EXHIBIT 7.10 Segmentation of CDO Market
Source: Adapted from Fitch Ratings Special Report, "Synthetic CDOs: A Growing Market for Credit Derivatives," February 6, 2001.

tion against all corporate loans and bonds, the returns for loans to highly rated obligors will generate small returns to regulatory capital.

Nat West's 1996 Rose Funding, which we described earlier, was in large part motivated by a desire to reduce regulatory capital. It reportedly released $400 million of regulatory capital.

Under the Basle I rules, synthetic securitizations would allow banks to retain loans on their balance sheets while reducing regulatory capital from 8% to 2%–3%.

Merritt, Gerity, Irving, and Lench (2001) argue that banks—especially European banks—are increasingly relying on synthetic structures to execute balance sheet CDOs. The reason given for the particular interest by European banks is the ability of a synthetic structure to reference exposures across multiple legal and regulatory regimes. They point to ABN AMRO's Amstel 2000-1 and 2000-2, a EUR8.5 billion synthetic CDO issued in December 2000, as an example of a typical, albeit large, synthetic structure that transfers the credit risk of a portfolio of large European corporates.

Arbitrage CDOs

The intent of an arbitrage CDO is to exploit the spread between the yield on the underlying assets and the lower cost of servicing the CDO securities. Arbitrage CDOs are widely used by asset managers, insurance companies, and other investment firms; and arbitrage CDOs are increasingly used by banks.

Cash Flow and Market Value CDOs   Of the traditional CDOs, cash flow structures are more common than market value structures. This is illustrated in Exhibit 7.11.

The majority of bank-issued CDOs are structured and rated based on the *cash flow* generated by the collateral. The rating agencies focus on the likelihood of various default scenarios and assign ratings to the different tranches based on the probability that the investor will receive all the promised cash flows.

In a cash flow deal, principal is collected as the collateral matures. For an initial period (five to seven years), collections are reinvested in new collateral. After this point the senior securities are amortized.

Most cash flow deals incorporate a call that belongs to the subordinated investor, who can call the structure if and only if they can make the senior investor whole. (The subordinated investor will exercise the call if the market value of the structure is sufficiently large.)

Alternatively, CDOs are structured and rated on the basis of the *market value* of the collateral. If, for example, the market value of the assets

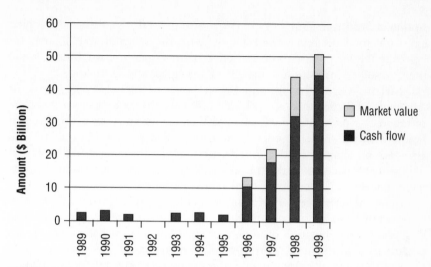

EXHIBIT 7.11 Cash Flow vs. Market Value CDO Issuance (1989–1999)
Source: Alexander Batchvarov, Ganesh Rajendra, and Brian McManus (Merrill Lynch), "Synthetic Structures Drive Innovation," *Risk*, June 2000.

falls below a given level, the structure will be unwound and investors paid from the proceeds. Market value transactions are typically executed to take advantage of an "arbitrage" between the value of the collateral and the price at which the liabilities can be sold.

In a market value deal, all the collateral will be sold at the end of the transaction and the proceeds will be used to pay investors.

The differences between cash flow and market value CDOs are summarized in Exhibit 7.12.

EXHIBIT 7.12 Market Values vs. Cash Flow CDOs

Market Value Deals	Cash Flow Deals
• Performance (repayment) linked to the market value of the collateral	• Performance based strictly on cash flow of the collateral
• Ratings based on overcollateralization tests	• Ratings based on cash flow and expected losses
• Collateral must be liquid	• Collateral can be illiquid (up to 100% can be bank loans)
• More special situation debt, i.e., distressed debt	• Longer term; smaller equity; more conservative
• More active management of the pool; higher management fees	• Less active management (lower management fees)

Synthetic Arbitrage CDOs[1]   Synthetic arbitrage CDOs replicate a leveraged exposure to a reference portfolio of assets (e.g., syndicated loans). Investors have the potential for attractive returns on a leveraged basis, while the sponsoring institution (typically a bank) generates fee income.

Merritt, Gerity, Irving, and Lench point to Chase's CSLT, Bank of America's SERVES, and Citibank's ECLIPSE as illustrations of synthetic arbitrage CDO programs in which an SPV enters into a series of total return swaps with the sponsoring bank on a diversified portfolio of credits. The reference portfolio is funded on-balance-sheet by the sponsoring bank and is actively managed over the transaction's life, subject to established investment guidelines. Through the total return swap, the SPV receives the total return on the reference portfolio and pays the sponsoring bank LIBOR plus a spread (to match the bank's funding costs for the reference portfolio). The SPV issues a combination of notes and equity, which fund the first loss exposure to the reference portfolio. The total return swap is normally marked-to-market resulting in one or more market value triggers.

TO WHAT EXTENT AND WHY ARE FINANCIAL INSTITUTIONS USING SECURITIZATIONS?

In the 2002 *Survey of Credit Portfolio Management Practices* that we described in Chapter 1, we asked the respondents to tell us about their use of CLOs.

The survey indicates that the preponderance of the large, sophisticated financial institutions that responded to this survey are using CLOs to transfer credit risk out of their institution, and both traditional and synthetic structures are being used:

In order to transfer loans from the institution, has your institution issued a CLO—either cash or synthetic?

No	27%
Yes, traditional CLOs	20%
Yes, synthetic CLOs	24%
Yes—both cash and synthetic CLOs	29%

The survey results were surprising in that the financial institutions' use of CLOs is motivated more by reducing regulatory capital and freeing up lines than by economic capital considerations:

If your institution has issued a CLO, rank these motivations by order of importance. (Use 1 to denote the most important and 3 to denote the least important.)

	Average Ranking
Regulatory capital	*1.68*
Economic capital	*2.21*
Exposure management (freeing lines)	*2.07*

While the majority is using CLOs to transfer credit risk out of their institution, a minority is using CLOs to diversify the portfolio by transferring in exposures:

Has your institution used a CLO structure as a way of transferring loan exposures into the institution? That is, have you purchased the equity or subordinated tranches of someone else's CLO or have you set up a CLO structure using assets from other originators as a way of importing credit risk into your portfolio?

No	*59%*
Yes, traditional CLOs	*10%*
Yes, synthetic CLOs	*13%*
Yes—both cash and synthetic CLOs	*18%*

REGULATORY TREATMENT

At the time this book went to print, the regulatory treatment for securitizations was still uncertain. Following is a brief description of the proposed treatment of securitizations from the January 2001 consultative document.

Regulatory Treatment of Explicit Risks Associated with Traditional Securitization

The Basle Committee recognized the value of securitizations, noting that banks that securitize assets are able to reduce their regulatory capital requirements, obtain an additional source of funding, generally at a lower cost, enhance financial ratios, and manage their portfolio risk (e.g., reduce large exposures or sectoral concentrations). However, the Basle Committee expressed concerns.

. . . securitisation activities . . . have the potential of increasing the overall risk profile of the bank . . . . Generally, the risk exposures that banks encounter in securitisation are identical to those that they face in traditional lending. . . . However, since securitisation unbun-

dles the traditional lending function into several limited roles, such as originator, servicer, sponsor, credit enhancer, liquidity provider, swap counterparty, underwriter, trustee, and investor, these types of risks may be less obvious and more complex than when encountered in the traditional lending process.

In the January 2001 Consultative Document, the Basle Committee proposed treatment for the originating and sponsoring banks' traditional securitizations. The Basle Committee also laid out the outline of a treatment of traditional securitizations under the internal ratings-based (IRB) approach, which follows the same economic logic used for the standardized approach.

Standardized Approach—Proposed Treatment for Originating Banks   In order for an originating bank to remove a pool of securitized assets from its balance sheet for purposes of calculating risk-based capital, the bank must transfer the assets legally or economically via a true sale (e.g., novation, assignment, declaration of trust, or subparticipation). More specifically, a "clean break" has occurred only if:

- The transferred assets have been legally isolated from the transferor, that is, the assets are put beyond the reach of the transferor and its creditors, even in bankruptcy or receivership. This must be supported by a legal opinion.
- The transferee is a qualifying special-purpose vehicle (SPV) and the holders of the beneficial interests in that entity have the right to pledge or exchange those interests.
- The transferor does not maintain effective or indirect control over the transferred assets.

Credit enhancement may be provided only at the outset of the securitization and the full amount of the enhancement must be deducted from capital, using the risk-based capital charge as though the asset were held on the balance sheet.

Liquidity facilities are permitted only to the extent that they smooth payment flows, subject to conditions, to provide short-term liquidity.

Early amortization clauses in revolving securitizations will be subject to a minimum 10% conversion factor applied to the securitized asset pool.

Standardized Approach—Proposed Treatment for Sponsoring Banks   A first-loss credit enhancement provided by a sponsor must be deducted from capital. Second-loss enhancements should be risk-weighted based on their external ratings. If they are not externally rated or if the assets are in multiple buckets, they should be risk-weighted according to the highest weighting of the underlying assets for which they are providing loss protection. Other commitments (i.e., liquidity facilities) usually are short term and, therefore, effectively are currently not assessed a capital charge since they are converted at 0% to an on-balance-sheet credit equivalent amount as required by the 1988 Basle Accord. Under certain conditions, liquidity facilities provided by the sponsor may be converted at 20% and risk-weighted at 100%. Otherwise these facilities will be treated as credit exposures.

IRB Approach—Treatment for Issuing Banks   For banks issuing securitization tranches, the Basle Committee proposed that the full amount of retained first-loss positions would be deducted from capital, regardless of the IRB capital requirement that would otherwise be assessed against the underlying pool of securitized assets.

The Basle Committee indicated that it is considering whether issuing banks that retain tranches with an explicit rating from a recognized external credit assessment institution could apply an IRB capital requirement tied to that rating by mapping this assessment into the PD/LGD framework. However, the Basle Committee indicated that internal ratings will not be acceptable.

IRB Approach—Treatment for Investing Banks   The Basle Committee proposed to rely primarily on ratings for such tranches provided by external credit assessment institutions. Specifically, the bank would treat the tranche as a single credit exposure like other exposures, and apply a capital requirement on the basis of the PD and LGD appropriate to the tranche. The appropriate PD would be that associated with the external rating on the tranche in question.

Treatment of Explicit Risks Associated with Synthetic Securitization

Reacting to the fact that banks had used synthetic CDOs to reduce regulatory capital, the Basle Committee stated that the new rules will reduce the incentive for banks to engage in a synthetic securitization in order to minimize their capital requirements.

The Basle Committee indicated that a number of issues need to be resolved in order to develop a consistent and comprehensive treatment of synthetic securitizations (both standardized and IRB approaches). A key issue the committee raised is the amount of credit risk that is transferred to third parties and whether a large degree of risk transference is necessary in order to obtain regulatory capital relief.

NOTE

1. This subsection relies heavily on Merritt, Gerity, Irving, and Lench (2001).

Capital Attribution and Allocation

Capital Attribution and Allocation

Attribution is a measurement problem. Given the current portfolio and the corresponding amount of economic capital needed to support that portfolio, how would the capital be assigned currently to individual business units or to individual transactions? It has implications for how the institution prices its services internally and externally, how it compensates employees, and how much it would pay to acquire a business (or how much it would accept from a buyer for one of its businesses).

Allocation is the optimization problem. The allocation decision requires me to determine if some rearrangement of my capital would result in a higher value for the firm.

However, before we can deal with either of these, we need to consider how the total economic capital for the firm—not just economic capital for credit risk—would be measured.

MEASURING TOTAL ECONOMIC CAPITAL

So far, we have been looking at one slice of economic capital—that associated with credit risk. We now need to broaden our scope and think about the capital associated with all risks (i.e., including market risk and operational risk, as well as credit risk).

Economic capital is associated with the volatility of the economic value of the bank or its business units. Unfortunately, this volatility in value frequently cannot be observed, so it is calculated via proxy measures, such as the volatility of earnings or of the value of individual transactions. Banks may measure volatility (unexpected losses) with a "top-down" measure, a "bottom-up" measure, or more likely, a combination of the two.

Top-Down Approach

The top-down measures employ earnings (or cash flow) volatility to estimate the volatility of the unit's asset value. These models use historical data on earnings, or a model, to project volatility into the foreseeable future. The volatility of market value can easily be implied from these proxy measures. [See Matten (2000) for a full discussion of this approach.] Top-down measures are most appropriate for high volume businesses (e.g., consumer lending), where transaction level detail is unavailable and the allocation of capital to specific transactions is not required.

In the top-down approach, we consider the whole firm and examine earnings volatility. We collect data on period-to-period earnings and then create a distribution of historical profit volatility.

This kind of approach is applicable to firms in which the businesses remain stable over time (i.e., when we look at one period to the next, the business hasn't changed). Furthermore, it requires a lot of data—hopefully high frequency data. (I would like daily observations of earnings, but it's likely that monthly or quarterly is the best I can get.) In the stylized example in Exhibit 8.1, we've collected the data and used them to create a histogram.

In order to obtain a measure of economic capital, we must specify the confidence level. Note that this confidence level is in terms of earnings (a flow), rather than in terms of value. If we want a 99% confidence level, we need to select the value of earnings that will isolate 1%, the area of the distribution in the left-hand tail. (Note that we look at the left-hand tail, because we are looking at a distribution of earnings, rather than a distribution of losses.)

Suppose that the board has specified the target insolvency rate to be $1/10$ of 1% (i.e., a 99.9% confidence level). We would use a histogram like

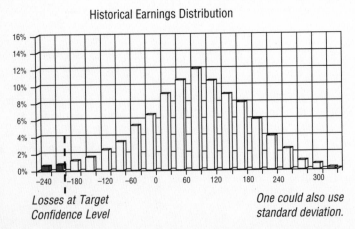

EXHIBIT 8.1 Top-Down Approach to Measuring Total Economic Capital—
Earnings at Risk

that in Exhibit 8.1 to find the earnings number that will put $^1/_{10}$ of 1% of the area of the histogram in this left-hand tail. We call this number "earnings at risk" (EAR).

Given that we have identified a critical earnings number, how do we convert that earnings number into a capital number? We need to convert this flow number into a stock—into a capital number. The question is: "How much capital is needed to provide the necessary support to earnings?" That is, how much capital is needed to ensure that earnings will be at least the specified level (EAR) per period? And since we need that amount every period, we solve for the required capital by treating this as a perpetual annuity:

$$\text{Capital} = \frac{\text{EAR}}{r}$$

The advantage of a top-down approach is that it provides an estimate of total economic capital. By looking at earnings for the business unit or for the entire firm, we are picking up credit risk, market risk, and operational risk.

The problem is that there are very few businesses for which you could do a top-down approach. Again, you need the business to be stable and you need to have high frequency data in order to do this.

Bottom-Up Approach

The "bottom-up" designation derives from the fact that individual transactions are modeled and then aggregated to arrive at portfolio or business unit capital. The financial institutions that use this approach obtain separate measures of credit risk capital, market risk capital, and operational risk capital:

- The financial institution could use one of the credit portfolio models we described in Chapter 4 to determine credit risk capital.
- A Value at Risk (VaR) model could be used to estimate market risk capital. For an overview of VaR, I would point you first to Chapter 19 in my book on market risk management, *Managing Financial Risk* (McGraw-Hill, 1998).
- In the case of operational risk capital, there is no generally accepted model. We have provided an overview of the various approaches to measuring operational risk capital in the appendix to this chapter.

As illustrated in Exhibit 8.2, to date, most firms are simply summing credit risk capital, market risk capital, and operational risk capital to get

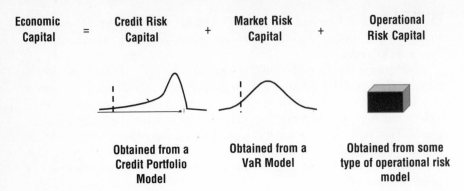

| Economic Capital | = | Credit Risk Capital | + | Market Risk Capital | + | Operational Risk Capital |

Obtained from a Credit Portfolio Model   Obtained from a VaR Model   Obtained from some type of operational risk model

EXHIBIT 8.2   Bottom-Up Approach to Measuring Total Economic Capital—Sum Credit, Market, and Operational Risk Capital

their estimate of total economic capital. By summing them, the firm is making a conservative estimate (i.e., the estimate of total economic capital will be too big). By summing the three risk capital numbers, we have assumed that the risks are perfectly positively correlated. If the risks are less than perfectly positively correlated, total economic capital will be less than the sum.

While the more common approach is simply to sum the risk capital numbers, some firms are beginning to devote research to identifying the degree of correlation. The following excerpt from JP Morgan Chase's *2001 Annual Report* indicates that they have measured the correlations between credit risk, market risk, operating risk, and private equity risk:

Credit Risk	13.6
Market Risk	3.9
Operating Risk	6.8
Private Equity Risk	5.3
Goodwill	8.8
Asset Capital Tax	3.7
Diversification Effect	(9.0)
Total Economic Capital	$33.1

Comparison of Top-Down and Bottom-Up Approaches

Exhibit 8.3 provides a comparison of top-down and bottom-up approaches to measuring economic capital.

EXHIBIT 8.3 Comparison of Top-Down and Bottom-Up Approaches to Measuring Total Economic Capital

Top Down	Bottom Up

• Historical earnings data are available.
  It is "clean."
  It reflects current business.
• Better suited to evaluating business unit than transaction level returns.
  Does not give a capital figure for individual transactions.
	• Models intensive
	  Credit VARs are still relatively new concepts.
	  Operational VARs pose a challenge.
	• Suited to both business unit and transactional capital calculations.
	  May be used in pricing of transactions, e.g., loans.

ATTRIBUTING CAPITAL TO BUSINESS UNITS

Without question, banks and other financial institutions are interested in measuring the capital consumed by various activities. The conundrum of capital attribution is that there is no *single* way to accomplish it. In fact, Nobel laureate Robert Merton and his colleague at the Harvard Business School, Professor Andre Perold, make the following observation regarding the capital attribution process.

> *Full [attribution] of risk capital across the individual businesses of the firm . . . is generally not feasible. Attempts at such a full [attribution] can significantly distort the true profitability of individual businesses.*—Merton and Perold, p. 241

However, you should not take this to mean that attribution is impossible. Rather, we think Professors Merton and Perold's warning reinforces a two-part message about attributing capital to individual business activities: (1) there are different ways of measuring the capital consumed by a particular activity, and (2) these different measures have different uses. Perhaps a third message is that the user should be aware of the limitations of each measure, as *no one measure is suitable for every application.*

The problem in attributing capital is whether (and, if so, how) to assign a portfolio benefit—namely *diversification*—to the elements of the portfolio. Practitioners speak about three commonly employed measures of capital—*stand-alone, marginal,* and *diversified.* Different firms will calculate these capital numbers differently, but they tend to agree on the idea behind the measures.

Stand-Alone Capital

Stand-alone capital is the amount of capital that the business unit would require, if it were viewed in isolation. Consequently, stand-alone capital would be determined by the volatility of each unit's earnings.

Because it does not include diversification effects, stand-alone capital is most often used to evaluate the performance of the managers of the businesses. The business unit managers should not be given credit for portfolio effects, because they were not under the control of that manager. The weakness of that argument is that the unit is part of a group of businesses and the bank should be careful about encouraging its managers to ignore the interrelationships. It is possible to construct scenarios where businesses that are not profitable on a stand-alone basis add shareholder value within a diversified firm.

Marginal Capital

Marginal capital measures the amount of capital that the business unit adds to the entire firm's capital (or, conversely, the amount of capital that would be released if the business unit were sold).

It is generally agreed that marginal capital is most appropriate in evaluating acquisitions or divestitures. Marginal capital would not be an appropriate tool for performance evaluation, because it always underallocates total bank capital. And even if the marginal capital numbers were scaled up,[1] the signals sent about profitability are potentially very misleading.

Diversified Capital

Diversified capital (also referred to as *allocated capital*) measures the amount of the firm's total capital that would be associated with a particular business unit.

Diversified measures are sometimes referred to as *portfolio beta* measures because the apportionment of risk is based on the covariance of each business unit with the entire organization in the same way that stock's beta is calculated from its covariance with the market. Attributing business capital in this way has intuitive appeal and it is fairly widespread.

Obtaining the correlations required is a challenge. Estimates can be based on historical performance data within the institution and management's judgment. Conceptually it is possible to derive estimates for broad classes of activity (e.g., retail lending versus commercial lending) by modeling data on the stock prices of other banks (see Baud et al. for an example).

Simplified Example—Calculating Stand-Alone, Marginal, and Diversified Capital

To give you some insight into how these different capital measures relate to one another, we have constructed a stylized example. This example follows closely the example in Merton and Perold, although the volatility and correlations are different. Our example is summarized in Exhibit 8.4.

Our hypothetical bank is comprised of three business units. We have set up this illustration so that the "portfolio of businesses" provides the bank with significant diversification effects: The value of Business 1 is only moderately correlated with that of Business 2 ($\rho_{1,2}$ = 0.3) and less correlated with that of Business 3 ($\rho_{1,3}$ = 0.1); and the value of Business 2 is uncorrelated to that of Business 3 ($\rho_{2,3}$ = 0.0).

We first need to calculate total economic capital for the bank as a whole. If we were doing this for a real bank, we would most likely use a bottom-up approach. That is, we would use one of those models that we talked about in Chapter 4 to generate credit risk capital, a VaR model to generate market risk capital, and some kind of model to generate operational risk capital; then, we would sum the capital numbers. But for this simple example, we are going to think about capital in the top-down method and use a shortcut calculation method proposed by Robert Merton and Andre Perold.

EXHIBIT 8.4 Stylized Calculation of Stand-Alone, Marginal, and Diversified Capital

	Assets	Volatility	Capital		
Bank	3,000	19%	222		

	Assets	Volatility	Stand-Alone Capital	Marginal Capital	Diversified Capital
Business 1	1,000	20%	80	33	45
Business 2	1,000	25%	100	36	56
Business 3	1,000	40%	160	77	121
		Total	340	146	222
		Unattributed	–118	76	0

Merton–Perold Approximation

The Merton–Perold approximation is based on the Merton insight that debt looks like a put on the value of the firm's assets.

Since it looks like an option, I could value it as an option. To value a European-style option on an *equity*, I need to know the values of five variables: (1) current share price, (2) strike price, (3) volatility of the share price, (4) risk-free interest rate, and (5) time to maturity. To value a European-style option on *asset value*, the five variables I need to know are: (1) current asset value, (2) strike value, (3) volatility of the asset value, (4) risk-free interest rate, and (5) time to maturity. Suppose we have the following values for those five variables:

Current asset value	100
Strike value	110
Volatility of asset value	14%
Risk-free interest rate	10%
Time to maturity	1 year

If we used the Black–Scholes model to value this option, we would get a value for this put of 5.34.

Merton and Perold showed that, as long as the liabilities remain relatively constant, you can approximate the option value by the following simple formula*

$$0.4 \times (\text{Asset Value}) \times (\text{Volatility of Asset Value}) \times (\sqrt{T})$$

Plugging in the values for asset value, volatility of asset value, and time from above

$$0.4 \times 100 \times 0.14 \times 1 = 5.60$$

The actual value of the option is 5.34; the approximation gives me 5.60.

---

*This is done by approximating the Black–Scholes formula for a European-call option by a Taylor series expansion. See chapter by Merton and Perold, "Management of Risk Capital in Financial Firms," in *Financial Services: Perspectives and Challenges*, edited by S. Hayes, Harvard Business School Press, 1993, p. 242.

Using the Merton–Perold approximation, the economic capital for the bank as a whole would be

$$\text{Total Bank Capital} = 0.4 \times (\text{Asset Value}) \times (\text{Volatility of Asset Value}) \times (\sqrt{T})$$
$$= 0.4 \times 3,000 \times 0.19 \times 1$$
$$= 222$$

Stand-Alone Capital for the Three Business Units   We can again use the Merton–Perold approximation to obtain stand-alone economic capital measures for each of the three businesses:

Business 1 = 0.4 × 1,000 × 0.20 × 1 = 80
Business 2 = 0.4 × 1,000 × 0.25 × 1 = 100
Business 3 = 0.4 × 1,000 × 0.40 × 1 = 160

Note that the sum of the stand-alone capital for the three business units is 340. The difference between this sum and the capital of 222 for the entire bank is due to *diversification*. Stand-alone capital for the individual businesses does not take into account the diversification that the businesses provide to one another.

Marginal Capital for the Three Business Units   Marginal capital is obtained by calculating total bank capital including and excluding the business unit and then taking the difference between the two total bank capital numbers.

In addition to calculating the stand-alone capital for the three individual businesses, we also calculated some hypothetical stand-alone capital numbers:

- Pretending that the firm was comprised only of Businesses 2 and 3, assets would be 2,000 and asset volatility would be 24%. (Why is the volatility so low? It is because I assumed that the correlation between Businesses 2 and 3 is zero.) Using the Merton–Perold approximation, stand-alone capital for Businesses 2 and 3 together would be 189.
- Pretending that the firm was comprised only of Businesses 1 and 3, assets would be 2,000 and asset volatility would be 23%. Using the Merton–Perold approximation, stand-alone capital for Businesses 1 and 3 together would be 186.
- Pretending that the firm was comprised only of Businesses 1 and 2, assets would be 2,000 and asset volatility would be 18%. Stand-alone capital for Businesses 1 and 2 together would be 186.

Since total economic capital for the bank—including Business 1—is 222 and capital without Business 1 is 189, the marginal capital for Business 1 is 33. Likewise, marginal capital for Business 2 is 36; and marginal capital for Business 3 is 77.

	Stand-Alone			
	Assets	Volatility	Capital	Marginal Capital
Businesses 2 and 3	2,000	24%	189	Business 1 = 222 − 189 = 33
Businesses 1 and 3	2,000	23%	186	Business 1 = 222 − 186 = 36
Businesses 1 and 2	2,000	18%	146	Business 1 = 222 − 146 = 77

Diversified Capital for the Three Business Units   Diversified capital can be calculated by multiplying the business unit's stand-alone capital by the correlation between the unit and the entire bank (including the unit in question). That is, for Business unit i, diversified capital would be calculated as

$$(\text{Diversified Capital})_i = \rho_{i,B} \times (\text{Stand-Alone Capital})_i$$

where $\rho_{i,B}$ is the correlation between Business Unit i and the entire bank.[2] Units with low correlation obviously receive a greater reduction in their stand-alone capital than units that are highly correlated.

Stand-Alone, Marginal, and Diversified Capital—Summary

Exhibit 8.5 summarizes our discussion in this subsection. For business units, there are three capital numbers that are of interest—stand-alone capital, diversified capital, and marginal capital. The three measures are used for different applications within the firm. If the firm wants to evaluate the performance of a business unit manager, it will rely on stand-alone capital. (The firm will not want to compensate a business unit manager for diversification effects that the manager did not generate.) For pricing decisions and decisions regarding reallocation of the firm's capital among the various businesses, the firm will use diversified capital. Finally, for decisions about entering or exiting a business, the firm will use marginal capital.

ATTRIBUTING CAPITAL TO TRANSACTIONS

The issues surrounding attribution to transactions are similar to those discussed at the business level. One can allocate fully the equivalent of a diversified measure, or think about allocating at the margin—that is, the additional risk capital this transaction requires at, say, the 99.9th confidence level. The idea of stand-alone capital is not applied to transactions.

EXHIBIT 8.5 Stand-Alone, Marginal, and Diversified Capital—Summary

Capital Measure	Characteristics	Typical Application
Stand-Alone	Total bank capital is less than the sum of the stand-alone capital for the businesses (due to diversification).	Performance evaluation: *How did the manager of the business do when viewed as an independent entity?*
Diversified	Total bank capital is equal to the sum of the diversified capital for the businesses.	Pricing and capital allocation: *How much of the bank's capital is attributed to this business when diversification benefits are included?*
Marginal	Total bank capital is greater than the sum of the marginal capital for the businesses.	Entry/Exit decisions: *How much capital is released if this business is exited?*

In the jargon of credit portfolio management, the measure of the amount of capital attributed to a transaction is commonly expressed in the form of a "risk contribution" measure. In this section, we look at some of the risk measures that have been proposed and are available in the credit portfolio models. As Chris Finger of the RiskMetrics Group points out, the first step in selecting the best risk contribution measure is to decide which characteristics are desirable. Some desirable characteristics of an attribution scheme are summarized in Exhibit 8.6.

Standard Deviation-Based Risk Contribution Measures

The most common method of calculating risk contributions is to calculate the standard deviation of the entire portfolio and then allocate portfolio

EXHIBIT 8.6 Desirable Characteristics of an Attribution Scheme

- Additivity—Attributions sum to total capital.
- Practicality—Calculations are robust.
- Does not depend qualitatively on arbitrary parameters.
- Rewards high credit quality.
- Penalizes for size, even on a normalized basis (concentration effect).
- Penalizes for high correlations with the rest of the portfolio.

Source: Adapted from RiskMetrics Group presentation: Investigation of Economic Capital Allocation Schemes.

standard deviation to individual transactions. If the weights are scaled appropriately, all individual risk contributions will sum to total portfolio risk (see the Statistics Appendix for a proof):

$$\sigma_p = \sum_{i=1}^{N} RC_i$$

For example, RiskMetrics Group's CreditManager (described in Chapter 4) starts by recognizing that portfolio variance is the sum over all covariances of the positions; so the portfolio standard deviation can be allocated on the basis of the sums of columns in the covariance matrix. Consequently, in CreditManager, the standard deviation–based risk contribution measure is[3]

$$RC_i = \frac{1}{\sigma_p} \left(\sigma_i^2 + \sum_{i \neq j}^{N} \rho_{ij} \sigma_i \sigma_j \right)$$

Standard deviation–based risk contributions are common in credit portfolio models. They are very attractive, because the individual risk contributions sum to total economic capital for the firm. However, there are several things that a user should keep in mind about standard deviation–based risk contribution measures:

- A standard deviation–based risk contribution measure is implicitly looking at changes in portfolio standard deviation with respect to *small* change in position size. Mathematically, this is written as

$$RC_i = w_i \frac{\partial \sigma_p}{\partial w_i}$$

- There can be instances where the risk contribution can exceed the exposure. (If a transaction has a very high correlation with the rest of the portfolio, its risk contribution can be bigger than the exposure.)
- The relative risk of transactions may shift as one moves from standard deviation to a high percentile of the loss distribution.

Marginal Risk Contributions

The idea behind a marginal risk contribution is very simple: We want to calculate the riskiness of the portfolio, with and without the transaction, and marginal risk contribution would be the difference between the two:

> *Marginal Percentile Risk*
> = Xth *percentile with new exposure*
> − Xth *percentile without new exposure*

Clearly, because you are calculating the risk for the portfolio twice, this method for calculating the "marginal" may not be practical for portfolios that contain a large number of transactions.

Tail-Based Risk Contributions

So far we've been talking about the amount of risk an individual transaction contributes—*on average*—to the portfolio. Would you ever be interested in a different kind of question: *For those periods where the portfolio is under stress (meaning that losses are large enough that you may indeed need that economic capital) is this transaction one of the contributors to that?*

In contrast to the standard deviation–based risk measures and the marginal risk measures, which measure *on average* how much a transaction contributes to the riskiness of the portfolio, a tail-based risk contribution measure is asking how much risk this transaction contributes when the portfolio is under stress. A tail-based risk contribution is based on the credit's simulated contribution to large losses.

Such a measure could efficiently attribute economic capital without a scaling factor using a Monte Carlo model. We don't want to know in my simulations how many times this transaction defaults. What we want to know is how many times this transaction defaults at the same time that the portfolio is experiencing stress.

The way to think about a tail-based risk contribution measure is in terms of a *conditional* loss rate. We want to count the number of times in the simulation that this transaction defaults. The loss rate for Asset "A" conditional on portfolio loss exceeding a given threshold can be expressed as

$$
\text{Conditional Loss Rate of "A"} = \frac{(\text{Conditional Number of Defaults for "A"})}{(\text{Number of Portfolio Losses Above 98th Percentile})}
$$

And this conditional loss rate can be used to attribute capital to asset "A":

$$
\text{Conditional Attribution to "A"} = (\text{Conditional Loss Rate of "A"}) \times \text{LGD(A)}
$$

To implement this, we need to define that "threshold." Suppose that, for the determination of economic capital for this portfolio, we are using a confidence level of 99.97%. The threshold we will define will be lower than 99.97%; let's use 98%. In the simulations, we want to track those defaults that occur when aggregate losses are sufficient to push portfolio loss into the 98%–100% range. (See Exhibit 8.7.)

There is no question that we could calculate a tail-based risk contribution measure. The question is whether it really provides any additional information. To provide an "apples-to-apples" comparison of a tail-based risk measure with a standard deviation–based measure, we need to obtain both from the same credit portfolio model. So we used the Rutter Associates Macro Factor Demonstration Model that we described in Chapter 4 to generate both tail-based risk measures and standard deviation–based measures. The results of this comparison are graphed in Exhibit 8.8.

In this graph, the transactions are ranked from the ones with the least risk to those with the highest risk. Does this tail-based risk measure provide any additional information?

- Look first at the very low-risk transactions. The nine transactions with the lowest risk almost line up on a straight line. For that group of nine "best" transactions, the tail-based risk measure doesn't add any information.
- Next look at the highest-risk transactions. While not as dramatic as is the case for the lowest-risk transactions, the seven transactions with the highest risk also line up on almost a straight line. For that group of seven "worst" transactions, the tail-based risk measure doesn't add any information.

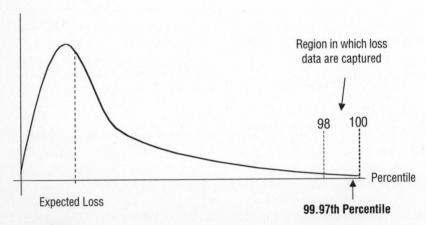

EXHIBIT 8.7 Logic Behind a Tail-Based Risk Contribution Measure

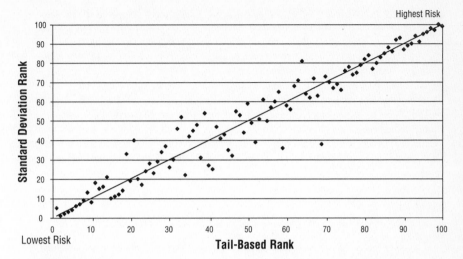

EXHIBIT 8.8 Comparison of Standard Deviation–Based and Tail-Based Risk Contribution Measure

■ However, in the middle of the graph, the transactions don't come close to lining up on a straight line. The tail-based risk measure adds information—information that is not contained in the standard deviation–based risk contribution measure.

To summarize, the tail-based risk measure clearly provides additional information, particularly for the bulk of the portfolio (i.e., other than the very best and very worst transactions).

The model vendors are starting to incorporate tail-based risk contribution measure. In Moody's–KMV Portfolio Manager, it is called "tail risk contribution." In the RiskMetrics Group's CreditManager, it is called "expected shortfall."

Evaluation and Adoption of the Risk Contribution Measures

Since we started with Chris Finger's list of the desirable characteristics for a risk contribution measure, it makes some sense to look at his conclusions (in Exhibit 8.9).

To provide some insight into what financial institutions are actually doing, we conclude this section with some results from the *2002 Survey of Credit Portfolio Management Practices* that we described in Chapter 1.

EXHIBIT 8.9   Evaluation of Risk Contribution Measures

- Most risk contribution measures are additive and sensitive to credit quality.
- Standard deviation-based risk measures are robust though not as sensitive to correlations as tail-based risk measures.
- Marginal risk measures can produce undesirable size behavior and are somewhat sensitive to confidence level choices.
- Tail-based risk measures appear to be the appropriate mix between sensitivity and robustness.

Source: This exhibit was adapted from a RiskMetrics Group presentation: Investigation of Economic Capital Allocation Schemes.

2002 SURVEY OF CREDIT PORTFOLIO MANAGEMENT PRACTICES

Do you attribute economic capital to individual units or individual transactions?

80% of the respondents to the survey answered this question. All of the following responses are expressed as percentages of the number of respondents answering this question.

Yes	91%
No	9%

If yes,

Standard-deviation-based risk contribution measures	48%
Marginal (incremental) risk contribution measures	24%
Tail-Risk risk contribution measures	14%
Other	14%

The survey respondents who indicated Other provided several alternative measures, including: Internal capital factors, Average portfolio effects, Capital is assigned to individual transactions and business units using an average capital measure based on the risk parameters of the transaction or unit (i.e., PD, LGD, EAD, loan size), Pragmatic, One factor model used.

PERFORMANCE MEASURES—THE NECESSARY PRECONDITION TO CAPITAL ALLOCATION

Before we can optimize the allocation of capital, we must measure the return being earned on the capital already employed in the bank.

The Goal: Move to the Efficient Frontier

Exhibit 8.10 is a diagram we talked about in Chapter 2. The dots represent different portfolios. The line—the efficient frontier—is where the portfolio manager wants to be, because every point on an efficient frontier is a point of (1) minimum risk for a given level of expected return and (2) maximum expected return for a given level of risk. We can almost guarantee that any financial institution will be at one of the interior points; and what the portfolio manger wants to do is go northwest (i.e., move toward the efficient frontier).

Drawing a picture of an efficient frontier is one thing; quantifying it is another. How would we know if we were on the efficient frontier? If we were on the efficient frontier, the return per unit of risk would be equal for all transactions.

$$\frac{R_i}{\sigma_i} = \frac{R_j}{\sigma_j} = \frac{R_k}{\sigma_k} = \cdots$$

The reason we know this relation identifies a point on the efficient frontier is that, if it were true, there would be no way to improve the return for this firm as a whole. To see why this must be true, let's suppose that it is not true.

Assume i, j, *and* k *are business units (but they could equally well be transactions). Suppose the return per unit of risk is higher for Business Unit* i *than for Business Unit* j. *To improve the overall risk-adjusted return for this company, I would want to reassign capital: I would take capital away from Business Unit* j *and give the capital to Business Unit* i.

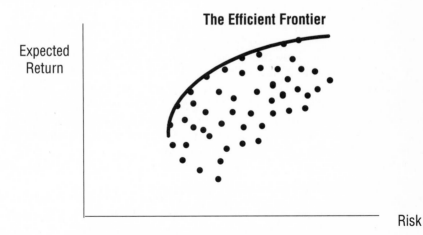

The Efficient Frontier

Expected Return

Risk

EXHIBIT 8.10 The Goal: Get to the Efficient Frontier

As I devote more capital to Business Unit i, the portfolio gets more concentrated in transactions from Business Unit i; so the risk associated with Business Unit i increases.

Conversely, as I take capital away from Business Unit j, the portfolio becomes less concentrated in Business Unit j transactions and Business Unit j becomes less risky. That means the return per unit of risk is falling for Business Unit i and is rising for Business Unit j. I would continue to move capital from Business Unit i to Business Unit j only until the point at which they are equal.

The preceding equation is a little bit more informative than the picture, but not very much more informative. We need to find some way to quantify this performance measure; and that is the topic of the remainder of this section.

Performance Measures Used by Equity Portfolio Managers

The first place to look for an effective performance measure might be in the equity markets, where portfolio managers have been working for a long time. The dominant performance measure in the equity market is the Sharpe Ratio. (The name comes from its inventor, William Sharpe, a Nobel laureate.)

The Sharpe Ratio is expressed as the excess return for the transaction (i.e., the difference between the expected return for the transaction and the risk-free return) divided by the risk of the transaction.

$$Sharpe\ Ratio_i = \frac{R_i - R_f}{\sigma_i}$$

Graphically, the Sharpe Ratio is the slope of the line from the risk-free rate to the portfolio in question. Exhibit 8.11 shows two portfolios. I know that the Sharpe Ratio for Portfolio 2 is higher than that for Portfolio 1, because the slope of the line to Portfolio 2 is higher than the slope of the line to Portfolio 1.

Finally, let's look at the relation between the Sharpe Ratio and the efficient frontier. In Exhibit 8.12, Portfolios 1 and 2 have the same level of risk. Note that the Sharpe Ratio is higher for Portfolio 2 than for Portfolio 1. Also note that there is no feasible portfolio with this risk level that has a higher expected return. What this means is that *points on the efficient frontier represent the highest Sharpe Ratio for that level of risk. Put another way, every point on an efficient frontier is a maximum Sharpe Ratio—the maximum Sharpe Ratio for that level of risk.* So it follows that if you have the maximum Sharpe Ratio, you will be on the efficient frontier.

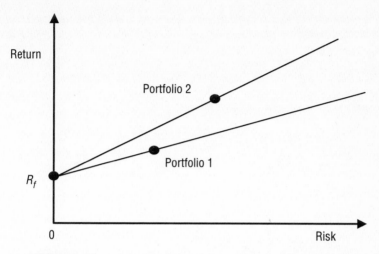

EXHIBIT 8.11   Sharpe Ratio = Slope of Ray from Risk-Free Rate

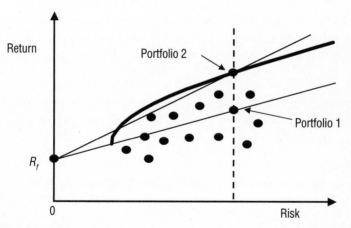

EXHIBIT 8.12   Efficient Frontier = Maximum Sharpe Ratio for Given Levels of Risk

Other Performance Measures for Equities

While the Sharpe Ratio is the most commonly discussed performance measure for equities, it is not the only one. There are two others that you will likely hear about.

Today, most equity portfolio managers are measured against some benchmark portfolio (e.g., the S&P 500). The *Information Ratio* (also attributed to Professor Sharpe) is the portfolio's excess return *relative to the benchmark portfolio* divided by the increase in risk for the portfolio in question *relative to the risk of the benchmark portfolio.*

The performance measure called M-squared was proposed by another Nobel laureate, Franco Modigliani, and his granddaughter, Leah. It compares portfolios by hypothetically leveraging them up or down so that they will have the same level of risk. (This is done by either borrowing and investing the borrowed funds in the portfolio being evaluated or selling some of the portfolio in question and investing those funds at the risk-free rate.)

Performance Measures Used in the Equity Market

Sharpe Ratio	$\dfrac{R_P - R_f}{\sigma_P}$
Information Ratio (*Sharpe*, 1981)	$\dfrac{R_P - R_B}{\sigma_{(P-B)}}$
M-Squared (*Modigliani & Modigliani*, 1997)	$\dfrac{R_{P'} - R_f}{\sigma_B} = \dfrac{\sigma_B(R_P - R_f)}{\sigma_P} + R_f$

RAROC

While all of us talk about RAROC, the calculation we are doing is actually something different. RAROC stands for "risk-adjusted return on capital"; but as we see, we are actually doing a calculation that would better be characterized as RORAC ("return on risk-adjusted capital") or RARORAC ("risk-adjusted return on risk-adjusted capital"). This being said, I expect us to continue to talk about RAROC, because RORAC and RARORAC are too hard to pronounce.

RAROC can be calculated at the institution level, at the business unit level, or at the individual transaction level. RAROC is a single period measure.

Gerhard Schroeck (2002) notes that, in a RAROC approach, in order to determine whether a transaction creates or destroys value, it is sufficient to compare the calculated RAROC with the hurdle rate. As long as the RAROC of the transaction exceeds the shareholders' minimum required rate of return—the hurdle rate—the transaction is judged to create value for the firm. Otherwise, it will destroy value.

Calculating RAROC   A stylized RAROC calculation is provided in Exhibit 8.13. The numerator represents the economic earnings of the unit. Note that credit risk enters the adjusted return calculation in the form of expected losses. However, since we noted (in Chapter 2) that expected losses are a cost of being in the credit business—rather than a risk—I would hesitate to call the numerator "risk-adjusted." The adjustments for the cost of funds, noninterest expenses, and taxes and adjustments are all predictable.

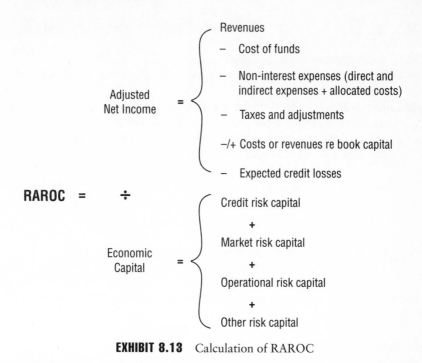

Revenues

   – Cost of funds

   – Non-interest expenses (direct and indirect expenses + allocated costs)

   – Taxes and adjustments

   –/+ Costs or revenues re book capital

   – Expected credit losses

Credit risk capital

+

Market risk capital

+

Operational risk capital

+

Other risk capital

EXHIBIT 8.13 Calculation of RAROC

Less clear is the adjustment for costs or revenues associated with book capital; and financial institutions differ in the way they treat book capital. The more common approach is to give each unit credit for the book capital deployed (i.e., to reflect earnings on the risk capital as if it were invested in a risk-free asset). However, some practitioners keep the return on book capital for a central "treasury" function.

The denominator in the RAROC calculation is *economic capital*. Furthermore, economic capital is a risk-adjusted capital measure. While it is at least theoretically possible to calculate economic capital via a top-down approach, our view is that most financial institutions will employ a bottom-up approach. In Exhibit 8.13, we presume that economic capital is simply the sum of the capital calculated for credit risk, market risk, operational risk, and possibly other risks. However, as we noted earlier, some financial institutions are moving to the next step and adjusting this calculation to reflect the fact that these risks will not be perfectly positively correlated.

Advantages and Disadvantages of RAROC[4] RAROC has a number of advantages:

- It reflects a bank's concern with total risk. (It does so by using economic capital as the risk measure.)
- It is straightforward to implement and to communicate.
- It divides the risks faced by a business unit into those it can influence and those it cannot.
- Through its use of economic capital, it adjusts the risk of an individual transaction to that of the bank's equity by effectively changing the leverage of the transaction. (This means that RAROC avoids the need to estimate the external beta of the transaction.)

However, the single hurdle rate can also lead to problems. Managers are likely to reject those transactions that will lower the average RAROC for the unit—even if the net present value of the transaction is positive. Consequently, a RAROC-based capital allocation system can lead to the firm's accepting high-risk projects with negative net present values and rejecting low-risk projects with positive net present values.

Relation of RAROC to the Efficient Frontier and Sharpe Ratio   How does RAROC relate to the efficient frontier and the Sharpe Ratio? We have already seen that, if you are maximizing the Sharpe Ratio, you will be on the efficient frontier. If RAROC is calculated properly, maximizing RAROC generally implies maximization of the Sharpe Ratio. For the interested reader, I provide the following demonstration.

Rationalizing RAROC with the Sharpe Ratio*

The Capital Asset Pricing Model (CAPM) implies that

$$R_j - R_f = \beta \times (R_m - R_f)$$

where

$$\beta = \rho_{jm} \frac{\sigma_j}{\sigma_m}$$

If we substitute the definition of β into the first equation, we get

$$R_j - R_f = \rho_{jm} \frac{\sigma_j (R_m - R_f)}{\sigma_m}$$

and after rearranging

$$\frac{R_j - R_f}{\rho_{jm}\sigma_j} = \frac{R_m - R_f}{\sigma_m}$$

*This demonstration was initially shown to me by Lee Wakeman.

Note that, in the preceding equation, the right-hand term is the Sharpe Ratio for the market portfolio. We can see that the left-hand term is close to RAROC by calculating a crude RAROC using the Merton–Perold approximation for the economic capital that we introduced earlier (with T=1) and comparing it to the left-hand term in the preceding equation:

Left-hand Term in Preceding Equation	Crude RAROC using the Merton–Perold Approximation
$\dfrac{R_j - R_f}{\rho_{jm}\sigma_j}$	$\dfrac{R_j - R_f}{(0.4)A_j\sigma_j}$

It should be clear that if you maximize the RAROC, you would be maximizing the "left-hand term" and if you maximize the "left-hand term" you would be maximizing the Sharpe Ratio.

The preceding also suggests that RAROC should include a correlation term—the correlation of the portfolio being considered with "the market." The question is how to define "the market" but this is an issue we do not delve into at this point.

Economic Profit (aka EVA or SVA or NIACC)

Because of the problem with RAROC noted previously (i.e., the possibility of accepting high-risk projects with negative net present values and rejecting low-risk projects with positive net present values) RAROC is often transposed into "economic profit." Economic profit is a more direct measure of whether a firm (or a business unit within that firm) is creating value for its shareholders (and is a proxy for the basic rule that the firm should accept all positive net present value projects and reject all negative net present value projects). It is expressed simply as adjusted net income (as previously defined) minus the cost of capital deployed.

$$\text{Economic Profit} = \begin{array}{l}\text{Adjusted Net Income}\\ - [\text{Economic Capital} \times\\ \text{Required Return on Capital}]\end{array}$$

Up to this point we have alluded to shareholders' required rate of return without formalizing the notion. Practitioners generally apply a single cost of capital, estimated at the bank level, to all business units. This could be debated on theoretical grounds, but practical considerations lead most institutions to adjust the amount of capital assigned to units based on risk and then apply a bank-wide required return. This return might be estimated using the Capital Asset Pricing Model, the bank's stock beta, and the equity risk premium, but more likely it is a blended rate reflecting the bank's actual costs of permanent financing, and input from outside sources on equity financing costs.

The advantage of using economic profit over RAROC measures is the direct relationship between economic profit and value creation. While it is true that any division with a RAROC above the cost of capital will also have a positive economic profit, the signals sent by the two measures may conflict with incentive compensation schemes.

How Are Financial Institutions Measuring Performance?

To provide some insight into what financial institutions are actually doing, we provide some results from the 2002 *Survey of Credit Portfolio Management Practices* that we described in Chapter 1.

2002 SURVEY OF CREDIT PORTFOLIO MANAGEMENT PRACTICES

Do you explicitly evaluate the performance of your portfolio(s) of credit assets?

Yes	90%
No	10%

If yes,

Return on Assets or Return on Equity	17%	*These responses*
		sum to greater
Return on Regulatory Capital	17%	*than 100%,*
RAROC (Risk Adjusted Return on Economic Capital)	78%	*because many*
		respondents
NIACC (Net Income After Capital Charge)	31%	*checked more*
		than one answer.
Sharpe Ratio (or Information Ratio)	14%	
Other	8%	

The survey respondents who indicated Other provided several alternative measures, including: Net Income After Provisions, Plan to incorporate regulatory/economic capital into performance measures, RAROA, Subsections of portfolio analyzed on RAROC.

OPTIMIZING THE ALLOCATION OF CAPITAL

The majority of banks employ an informal optimization process, in which decisions about the deployment of capital are made in the light of the performance measures we introduced in the preceding section. With sufficient information it is possible to formally model the optimization, but this is still asking a lot of the data—the quality of the output will be no better than the input—and bank managers (see Baud for a discussion of a formal optimization model).

A commonly asked question is how to treat regulatory capital in an optimization process that theoretically should look only at economic capital. If this always exceeded regulatory capital then we could ignore it—the "constraint" of regulatory capital would be nonbinding. When this is not the case, firms use a variety of ad hoc approaches.

- One approach is to impose an explicit charge for regulatory capital in the calculation of economic profit. This explicitly penalizes businesses that require high amounts of regulatory capital in the creation of their economic profit. The higher the "cost" assigned to regulatory capital the greater the penalty. Unfortunately, this also masks real economic value. For example, if one unit is very regulatory capital intensive, but highly profitable on an economic basis, its return will be knocked down in comparison to other lines. But this may be the wrong signal, since the bank may want to figure out how to reduce the regulatory capital requirement, or obtain additional capital to grow the otherwise highly profitable business.
- Another approach is to work with whatever capital number is larger, that is, calculate economic profit relative to regulatory capital if that exceeds economic capital. This method has some appeal since it charges each business for the larger of the two capital numbers, but it suffers from a "summing up" problem. By taking the larger of the two capitals for each business, the bank will appear to have deployed more capital than it actually has, and the profit calculations will not make sense when aggregated bank-wide.
- Short of a mathematical model to tie regulatory capital and economic capital together, bankers can combine elements of both approaches by looking at business units in terms of the benefits, at the margin, of another unit of regulatory capital. Formally, this is known as evaluating shadow prices, but intuitively it simply involves calculating the benefit achieved if a constraint, that is, regulatory capital, could be loosened slightly. It applies equally well to other constraints, such as computing capacity or human resources. Shadow prices send the correct signal

about where the most value can be created for an additional unit of capital or any other resource.

To provide some insight into what financial institutions are actually doing, we provide some results from the 2002 *Survey of Credit Portfolio Management Practices* that we described in Chapter 1.

In an optimal portfolio the marginal return per unit of risk within the bank will be equal across businesses. That is, taking a unit of capital away from one business and giving it to another will not add additional value to

---

2002 SURVEY OF CREDIT PORTFOLIO MANAGEMENT PRACTICES

83% of the survey respondents answered the following questions; and the response percentages are based on the number who answered this question.

If you explicitly evaluate the performance of individual business units or transactions, what do you do in those instances in which the regulatory capital attributed to the business unit (transaction) exceeds the economic capital that would be attributed to that business unit (transaction)?

Replace economic capital with regulatory capital in the return calculation	7%
Adjust the return calculation to include a charge for "excess" regulatory capital (e.g., the amount by which regulatory capital exceeds economic capital)	11%
Other	82%

The survey respondents who indicated Other provided several alternative measures, including: Ignore regulatory capital, Situation currently being reviewed, Units not measured on regulatory capital, Business decision not based on regulatory capital, We try to securitize the assets???, Decisions based on economic capital, ROC is not basis of performance movement, We ignore regulatory capital, Economic capital as is, Not applicable, Nothing, No action, Excess reg. cap. managed on group level, We are not subject to regulatory capital, No adjustment yet, Performance evaluated on economic capital, Report both for decision maker to review, Neither, Just focus on economic capital, We use both measures for internal estimates.

shareholders because the return lost equals the return gained. Bankers can use this concept, along with basic measures of economic profitability, to keep moving the institution in the right direction without resorting to mathematical models.

NOTES

1. In the stylized example to follow, marginal capital could be scaled up by multiplying each business unit's capital by 1.518%, the ratio of total bank capital to the sum of the marginal capitals.

2. Using this relation between diversified capital and stand-alone capital, we show that the sum of the diversified capital over all the businesses in the bank is equal to total bank economic capital. First, we need an expression for the correlation of business i to the bank. We assume that the ith business has an asset value A_i and hence a weight w_i (between 0 and 1) in the total assets of the bank (so that $A_i = w_i A_{Bank}$). The risk of a bank's portfolio of businesses can be viewed as a variance–covariance matrix (see the Statistics Appendix for a detailed explanation), so the variance of the portfolio of N businesses can be expressed as

$$\sigma_B^2 = \sum_{i=1}^{N} w_i \sum_{j=1}^{N} w_j \sigma_{i,j} = \sum_{i=1}^{N} \sigma_{i,B}$$

where

$$\sigma_{i,B} = w_i \sum_{j=1}^{N} w_j \sigma_{i,j}$$

is the covariance of business i with the portfolio of businesses. The correlation between business i and the bank $(\rho_{i,B})$ is thus given by

$$\rho_{i,B} = \frac{1}{\sigma_i \sigma_B} \sum_{j=1}^{N} w_j \sigma_{i,j}$$

Using this and the Merton–Perold approximation for stand-alone capital ($= 0.4 \times \sigma_i A_i = 0.4 \times \sigma_i w_i A_{Bank}$), it follows that:

$$\sum_{i=1}^{N} (\text{Diversified Capital})_i = \sum_{i=1}^{N} \rho_{i,p} (\text{Stand-Alone Capital})_i$$

$$= \sum_{i=1}^{N} \frac{w_i \sum_{j=1}^{N} w_j \sigma_{i,j}}{w_i \sigma_i \sigma_B} (0.4)\sigma_i w_i A_{Bank}$$

$$= \frac{(0.4)A_{Bank}}{\sigma_B} \sum_{i=1}^{N} \sum_{j=1}^{N} w_i w_j \sigma_{i,j}$$

$$= \frac{(0.4)A_{Bank}}{\sigma_B} \sigma_B^2$$

$$= (0.4)A_{Bank}\sigma_B$$

$$\equiv \text{Total Bank Economic Capital}$$

3. This expression for risk contribution is equivalent to the one in equation A.32 in the Statistics Appendix.
4. This section draws heavily on Schroeck (2002).

APPENDIX TO CHAPTER 8:
Quantifying Operational Risk[1]

Financial institutions recognize the importance of quantifying (and managing) operational risk. While losses like the $1.6 billion loss suffered by Barings in 1995 capture most of the attention, operational losses are widespread. PricewaterhouseCoopers compiled press reports indicating that financial institutions lost in excess of $7 billion in 1998 due to operational problems and that the largest financial institutions lose as much as $100 million annually.[2] Operational Risk, Inc. indicates that, since 1980, financial institutions have lost more than $200 billion due to operational risk.

Supervisors also recognize the importance of quantifying operational risk. In its June 1999 Consultative Document, the Basle Committee on Banking Supervision expressed its belief that operational risks (including reputational and legal risks) "are sufficiently important for banks to devote the necessary resources to quantify the level of such risks and to incorporate them into their assessment of their overall capital adequacy." Indeed, the Committee indicated its intention to require regulatory capital for operational risk.

The problem is how to accomplish the quantification. The Basle

Committee mentioned that the options ranged from a simple benchmark to modeling techniques. The objective of this column is to provide an overview of the techniques being employed.

The Basle Committee conjectured that a simple benchmark measure of operational risk could be based on an aggregate measure of the size of the institution,

$$(\text{Operational Risk})_i = \Psi(\text{Size})_i$$

where Ψ is a parameter relating operational risk to institution size. The Committee suggested gross revenue, fee income, operating costs, managed assets, or total assets adjusted for off-balance-sheet exposures as possible measures of the size of the institution. While such a relation has some intuitive appeal and is easy to calculate, it does not capture the relation of operational risk to the nature of the institution's business. Indeed, a recent empirical examination by Shih, Samad-Khan, and Medapa (2000) suggests that little of the variability in the *size* of operational losses is explained by the size of a firm—revenue, assets, or number of employees.[3] Moreover, such an approach runs the risk of setting up perverse incentives—a financial institution that dramatically improves the management and control of its operational risk could actually be penalized by being required to hold more capital, if the improvements lead to an increase in the volume of the institution's business.

Most of the published descriptions of operational risk modeling subdivide the models into two *groups*: Top-down models estimate operational risk for the entire institution. Bottom-up models estimate operational risk at the individual business unit or process level. Moreover, the models could appropriately be subdivided on another dimension—within the two groups, three *approaches* to modeling operational risk can be identified:

1. The approach I refer to as the *Process Approach* focuses on the individual processes that make up the financial institution's operational activities. (Because of this focus, all the process approaches are bottom-up approaches.) In the same way that an industrial engineer examines a manufacturing process, individual operational processes in the financial institution are mapped (decomposed) to highlight the components that make up the process. For example, Exhibit 8A.1 provides a process map for a transaction settlement.

   Each of the components of the process is examined to identify the operational risk associated with the component (e.g., in the case of Exhibit 8A.1, the number of days necessary to complete the process). By aggregating the operational risk inherent in the individ-

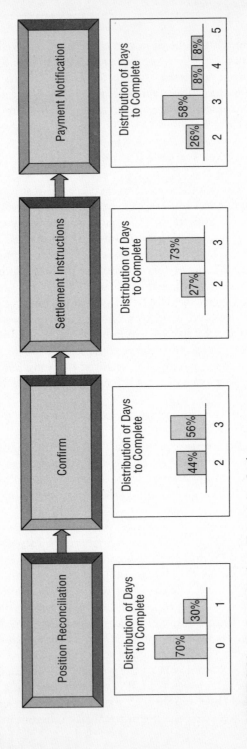

EXHIBIT 8.A1 Process Map for a Transaction Settlement

Source: Algorithmics.

ual components, the analyst can obtain a measure of operational risk in the process.

2. In the approach I refer to as the *Factor Approach*, the analyst is attempting to identify the significant *determinants* of operational risk—either at the institution level or at the level of an individual business or individual process. The objective is to obtain an equation that relates the level of operational risk for institution *i* (or Business *i* or process *i*) to a set of factors:

$$(\text{Operational Risk})_i = \alpha + \beta(\text{Factor 1}) + \gamma(\text{Factor 2}) + \ldots$$

If she or he is able to identify the appropriate factors and obtain measures of the parameters $(\alpha, \beta, \gamma, \ldots)$, the analyst can estimate the level of operational risk that will exist in future periods.

3. The focus of the *Actuarial Approach* is on the identification of the loss distribution associated with operational risk—either at the level of the institution or at the level of a business or process. (This contrasts to the first two approaches, both of which focus on identifying the sources of operational risk.) Exhibit 8A.2 illustrates a stylized loss distribution, which combines both the frequency of the loss events and their severity.

Exhibit 8A.3 categorizes the various operational risk models that have been publicly discussed.[4]

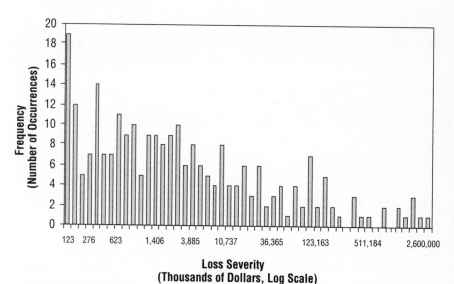

EXHIBIT 8.A2   Stylized Loss Distribution
Source: NetRisk.

EXHIBIT 8A.3   Modeling Approaches

	Process	Factor	Actuarial
Top-Down Models		Risk Indicators "CAPM-Like" Models	Empirical loss distributions
Bottom-Up Models	Causal Networks Statistical quality control and reliability analysis Connectivity	Predictive Models	Empirical loss distributions Explicit distributions parameterized using historical data Extreme value theory

PROCESS APPROACHES

Causal Networks   The process illustrated in Exhibit 8A.1 is a causal network. The analysis begins with a graphical map of the components in the process, with linkages between the components visible. Historical data are used to produce statistics for the behavior of the components and the process in the past. (This permits the analyst to identify problem areas.) Scenarios or simulations can be employed to predict how the process will behave in the future.

Statistical Quality Control and Reliability Analysis   Similar to causal networks, this technique is widely used in manufacturing processes.

Connectivity   The focus is on the connections between the components in a process. The analyst creates a "connectivity matrix" that is used to estimate potential losses for that process. If the processes are aggregated, a "failure" in one component will propagate across the process and through the institution.

FACTOR APPROACHES

Risk Indicators   The analyst identifies the significant factors using regression techniques. (In addition to volume, factors can include audit ratings, employee turnover, employee training, age of the system, and investment in new technology.) The analyst can use the resulting equation to estimate expected losses.

"CAPM-Like" Models   In contrast to focusing on the frequency and/or severity of operational losses, this approach would relate the volatility in share returns (and earnings and other components of the institution's valuation) to operational risk factors.

Predictive Models   Extending the risk indicator techniques described previously, the analyst uses discriminant analysis and similar techniques to identify factors that "lead" operational losses. The objective is to estimate the probability and severity of future losses. (Such techniques have been used successfully for predicting the probability of credit losses in credit card businesses.)

ACTUARIAL APPROACHES

Empirical Loss Distributions   The objective of the actuarial approach is to provide an estimate of the loss distribution associated with operational risk. The simplest way to accomplish that task is to collect data on losses and arrange the data in a histogram like the one illustrated in Exhibit 8A.2. Since individual financial institutions have data on "high-frequency, low-severity" losses (e.g., interest lost as a result of delayed settlements) but do not have many observations of their own on the "low-frequency, high-severity" losses (e.g., losses due to rogue traders), the histogram will likely be constructed using both internal data and (properly scaled) external data. In this process, individual institutions could benefit by pooling their individual observations to increase the size of the data set. Several industry initiatives are under way to facilitate such a data pooling exercise—the Multinational Operational Risk Exchange (MORE) project of the Global Association of Risk Professionals (GARP) managed by NetRisk, a project at PricewaterhouseCoopers, and a BBA project.

Explicit Distributions Parameterized Using Historical Data   Even after making efforts to pool data, an empirical histogram will likely suffer from limited data points, especially in the tail of the distribution. A way of smoothing the histogram is to specify an explicit distributional form. However, a number of analysts have concluded that, rather than specifying a distributional form for the loss distribution itself, better results are obtained by specifying a distribution for the frequency of occurrence of losses and a different distribution for the severity of the losses.[5] In the case of frequency, it appears that most analysts are using the Poisson distribution. In the case of severity, analysts are using a range of distributions, including a lognormal distribution and the Weibull distribution. Once the two distributions have been parameterized using the historical data, the analyst can combine the two distributions (using a process called "convolution") to obtain a loss distribution.

Extreme Value Theory   Because large operational losses are rare, an empirical loss distribution will be sparsely populated (i.e., will have few data points) in the high severity region. Extreme value theory—an area of statistics concerned with modeling the limiting behavior of sample extremes—can help the analyst to obtain a smooth distribution for this important segment of the loss distribution. Specifically, extreme value theory indicates that, for a large class of distributions, losses in excess of a high enough threshold all follow the same distribution (a generalized Pareto distribution).

NOTES

1. This originally appeared as a "Class Notes" column in the March 2000 issue of *RISK*. Thanks are due to Dan Mudge and José V. Hernández (NetRisk), Michael Haubenstock (PricewaterhouseCoopers), and Jack King (Algorithmics) for their help with this column.
2. *American Banker*, November 18, 1999.
3. Note that this study did not deal with the frequency of operational losses.
4. Much of the discussion that follows is adapted from Ceske/Hernández (1999) and O'Brien (1999).
5. The proponents of this approach point to two advantages: (1) it provides more flexibility and more control; (2) it increases the number of useable data points.

Statistics for Credit Portfolio Management

Mattia Filiaci

These notes have been prepared to serve as a companion to the material presented in this book. At the outset we should admit that the material is a little schizophrenic. For example, we spend quite a bit of time on the definition of a random variable and how to calculate expected values and standard deviations (topics from first-year college statistics books); then, we jump over material that is not relevant to credit portfolio management and deal with more advanced applications of the material presented at the beginning.

At this point, you should ask: "What has been skipped over and does it matter?" Most of the omitted material is related to hypothesis testing, which is important generally in statistics, but not essential to understanding credit portfolio models or credit risk management.

Though there are some complex-looking expressions in this document and even an integral or two, those of you not mathematically inclined should not worry—it is unlikely that you will ever need to know the formula for the gamma distribution or to actually calculate some of the probabilities we discuss. What you need is some common sense and familiarity with the concepts so that you can get past the technical details and into questions about the reasonableness of an approach, the implications of a given type of model, things to look out for, and so on.

These notes are divided into three sections. The first covers basic material, the second covers more advanced applications of the basic material, and the last section describes probability distributions used in credit risk modeling and can be used as a handy reference.

BASIC STATISTICS

Random Variables

A "random variable" is a quantity that can take on different values, or realizations, but that is fundamentally uncertain. Some important random
variables in credit portfolio modeling include

- The amount lost when a borrower defaults.
- The number of defaults in a portfolio.
- The value of a portfolio in one year.
- The return on a stock market index.
- The probability of default.

An example of a random variable is X, defined as follows.

X = Number of BB-rated corporations defaulting in 2003

X is random because we can't know for sure today what the number of BB
defaults will be next year. We use the capital letter X to stand for the unknown quantity because it is a lot more convenient to write "X" than to
write "Number of BB-rated corporations defaulting in 2003" every time
we need to reference that quantity.

At the end of 2003 we will have a specific value for the unknown
quantity X because we can actually count the number of BB-rated companies that defaulted. Often the lowercase letter x stands for a specific realization of the random variable X. Thus, if five BB-rated firms default in
2003 we would write $x = 5$. You might also ask, "What is the probability
that the number of BB-rated firms defaulting in 2003 is five?" In statistics
notation, this would be written $P(X = 5)$, where $P(\ldots)$ stands for the
probability of something.

More generally, we want to know the probability that X takes on any
of the possible values for X. Suppose there are 1,000 BB-rated firms. Then
X could take any integer value from 0 to 1,000, and the probability of any
specific value would be written as $P(X = x)$ for $x = 0 \ldots 1,000$. A *probability distribution* is the formula that lets us calculate $P(X = x)$ for all the
possible realizations of X.

Discrete Random Variables   In the preceding example, X is a *discrete* random variable because there are a finite number of values (actually 1,001
possible values given our assumption of 1,000 BB-rated firms). The probability that X takes on a specific value, $P(X = x)$, or that X takes on a

specified range of values (e.g., $P(X < 10)$), is calculated from its probability distribution.

Continuous Random Variables   In addition to discrete random variables there are *continuous random* variables. An example of a continuous random variable is the overnight return on IBM stock. A variable is continuous when it is not possible to enumerate (list) the individual values it might take.[1] The return on IBM shares can take any value between –100% (price goes to zero) and some undefined upper bound (we say "infinity" while recognizing that the probability of a return greater than 100% overnight is virtually zero).[2]

A continuous random variable can also be defined over a bounded interval, as opposed to unbounded or semi-infinitely bounded, such as returns. An example of a bounded interval is the amount of fuel in the tank of a randomly chosen car on the street (there is an upper limit to the amount of fuel in a car). Of course, if a continuous random variable is defined as a fraction, it will be bounded by zero and one (e.g., dividing the fuel in the tank by the maximum it can hold). Another example can be probabilities themselves, which by definition are defined between zero and one (inclusive of the endpoints). It might be difficult to think of probability itself as being a random variable, but one might envision that probability for some process may be constant or static in certain dimensions but stochastic in others. For example, probabilities governing default change over the dimension of time, but are constant at any given instant (so that default probabilities across firms or industries may be compared).

Probability

A probability expresses the likelihood of a given random variable taking on a specified value, or range of values. By definition probabilities must fall between zero and one (inclusive of the endpoints). We also define probabilities such that the sum of the probabilities for all mutually exclusive realizations (e.g., the roll of a die can only take one value for each outcome) of the random variable equals unity.

In Chapter 3, we talked about using Standard & Poor's CreditPro to look at the historical probability of a BB-rated company experiencing a rating change, or a default, over the next year. Exhibit A.1 shows these data for a period of 11 years.

As you can see, the default rate (percentage) varies quite a bit from year to year. The average default rate over the whole period is 1.001%. The variation about this mean is quite big, though, as one can see: The highest rate listed is 3.497%, the lowest is 0. In fact the standard deviation is 1.017% (we will cover standard deviation in detail).

EXHIBIT A.1 CreditPro Output for Defaults of BB-Rated Firms from 1990 to 2000

Year	1990	1991	1992	1993	1994	1995	1996	1997	1998	1999	2000
# of BB-rated firms	286	241	243	286	374	428	471	551	663	794	888
# of BB-rated firms defaulted	10	6	0	1	1	3	3	1	5	8	10
Default rate	3.497%	2.490%	0.000%	0.350%	0.267%	0.701%	0.637%	0.181%	0.754%	1.008%	1.126%

Probability Distributions

A "probability distribution" is a table, graph, or mathematical function characterizing all the possible realizations of a random variable and the probability of each one's occurring.

The probability distribution describing the roll of a fair die is graphed in Exhibit A.2. Of course, this is the *uniform* probability distribution because each outcome has the same likelihood of occurring.

Real-World Measurements versus Probability Distributions In general, when we toss a fair die, one expects that the distribution of each value will be uniform—that is, each value on the die should have equal probability of coming up. Of course, in the real world we won't see that for two reasons. The first is that we can make only a finite number of measurements. The second is that the die may not be *perfectly* fair. But setting aside for the moment that the die may not be *perfectly* fair, it is a fundamental concept to understand that if we make many, many tosses, the distribution we see will become what we *expect*. What do we mean by this? Well, let's take an example. In the following table we have a series of 12 measurements of the roll of an eight-sided die, numbered 1 through 8.

Toss	Result	Toss	Result	Toss	Result
1	7	5	3	9	8
2	2	6	5	10	2
3	6	7	6	11	4
4	1	8	3	12	6

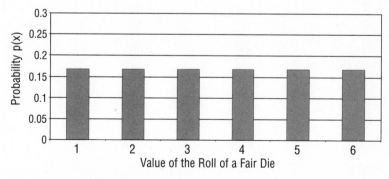

EXHIBIT A.2 Uniform Probability Distribution

Let's plot the results on a frequency graph, or distribution, shown in Exhibit A.3. On the vertical (y-) axis we have the number of occurrences and on the x-axis all the possible results (1–8).

As you can see, this graph is not perfectly flat like the uniform distribution shown in Exhibit A.1. We see that for example, the number 6 comes up 3 times, while the numbers 1, 4, 5, 7, and 8 come up only once. Theoretically, the average occurrence for each possible outcome for 12 tosses is $^{12}/_8 = 1.5$. Of course, we can't count 1.5 times for each toss, but the average over all the tosses is 1.5. If one were to take many more tosses, then each possible outcome should converge to the theoretical value of $^1/_8$ the total number of tosses.

The Average or Mean   Is there a way to *summarize* the information shown in the occurrences on the frequency graph shown in Exhibit A.2? This is the purpose of statistics—to distill a few useful numbers out of a large data set of numbers. One of the first things that come to mind is the word "average." What is the average? For our die-tossing example, we first add up all the outcomes:

$$7 + 2 + 6 + 1 + 3 + 5 + 6 + 3 + 8 + 2 + 4 + 6 = 53$$

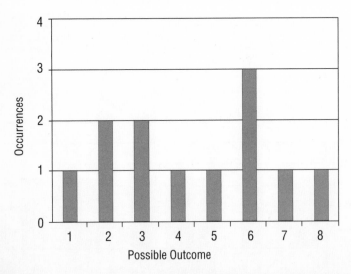

EXHIBIT A.3   Frequency Plot of the Results from Tossing an Eight-Sided Die 12 Times

To get the average we must divide the sum of the results by the number of measurements (12):

$$\frac{53}{12} = 4.4167$$

Now we can ask ourselves a different question: "What do we *expect* the average to be, knowing that we are tossing a (supposedly) fair die with 8 sides?" If you know that a 1 has the same probability of showing up as an 8 or 2 or 4, and so on, then we know that the average *should* be

$$1*\left(\frac{1}{8}\right) + 2*\left(\frac{1}{8}\right) + \cdots + 8*\left(\frac{1}{8}\right) = \left(\frac{1+2+3+4+5+6+7+8}{8}\right) = 4.5.$$

Notice that we take the average of all the possibilities. What this amounts to is multiplying each outcome by its probability ($1/8$) and adding up all of these products. All we just did in the arithmetic was to take the common factor (probability) out and multiply the sum (of the possible outcomes) by this probability. We could do this only because the probability is the same for each outcome. If we had a different probability for each possible outcome, we would have to do the multiplication first. This is important when we discuss nonuniform probability distributions next.

Using a more formal notation for average, we usually denote it by the Greek letter *mu* ("μ," pronounced "mee-u"). Now we introduce the "summation" symbol, denoted by the uppercase Greek letter capital *sigma* ("Σ"). Usually there is a subscript to denote the index and a superscript to show the range or maximum value. From our example, we can rewrite the average above as:

$$\mu_x = \frac{1}{8}\sum_{i=1}^{8} i$$

$$= \frac{1}{8}\left(1+2+3+4+5+6+7+8\right) = 4.5$$

In general, we write the average of N measurements as:

$$\mu_x = \frac{1}{N}\sum_{i=1}^{N} x_i \tag{A.1}$$

Now remember that if we know the underlying probability distribution for some group of measurements, then we can calculate the expected value of the average. To get the average we multiply each possible outcome by the probability of its occurring. In the language we've just introduced, that means we write:

$$\mu_x = \sum_{i=1}^{N} p_i x_i$$

where each p_i is the probability that the value x_i occurs. Note that when we make a measurement in the real world, we give equal importance to all of our measurements by adding them all up (the x_i's) and dividing by the total number of measurements. In a manner of speaking, each measurement is given an equal probability or "weight" of $1/N$. When we know the underlying distribution, we know that each probability p_i is a function of the possible outcome value, so we have $p_i = f(x_i)$, where $f(x_i)$ is the functional form of the probability distribution (you will see many more of these in just a bit). If all the p_i's are equal, then you have a uniform distribution and you can take out the common factor. If not, we have to do the multiplication first (as we mentioned earlier).

Expected Value and Expectation   As already discussed, taking an expected value of some variable (let's just call it "x") which has a known distribution [let's say $f(x)$] is equivalent to multiplying each possible value of x by the corresponding probability it will occur [i.e., the probability distribution function $f(x)$] and summing up all the products. We took the example of rolling a fair die. But we can also think of an example of a measurement that does not take on only discrete values. Let's say we want to model the heights of people off the street. We may have a *theory* that the distribution of heights is not *uniform* (as in the case of the roll of a fair die), but has some specific functional shape given by the probability *density* $f(x)$ (we see many shapes of distributions in this appendix). Then we can calculate the *expected value* of the heights of people. Using the language we've just introduced, the expected value (or expectation) of a random variable x is written in shorthand as "$E[x]$," and is equal to the mean μ:

$$Mean \equiv \mu_x \equiv E[x] = \sum_i x_i f(x_i), \text{ if } x \text{ is discrete} \qquad (A.2a)$$

$$Mean \equiv \mu_x \equiv E[x] = \int_x x f(x) dx, \text{ if } x \text{ is continuous} \qquad (A.2b)$$

If you are not used to the integral sign just think of it as a sum, like Σ, but where the thing you are summing is a *continuous* value. Also, the subscripts *i* and *x* under the summation and integral signs indicate that the sums are taken over all possible outcomes of the random variable (e.g., the intervals discussed at the beginning). One may also generalize the concept so that you can take the expectation of a function of *x* [e.g., $g(x)$], so its expectation is given by

$$E[g(x)] = \int_x g(x)f(x)dx$$

(A.3)

For symmetric distributions like the "bell curve," the expectation of the (normally distributed) random variable is the same value as the position of the peak. This is not the case for asymmetric distributions like the lognormal distribution, for example. This property is called *skew* (more on that later). The expectation of the random variable, $E[x]$, is also called the 1st moment of the distribution.

Standard Deviation and Variance   What if we did not know that the data of our example ultimately come from the toss of a die, as is often the case in the real world? Then we wouldn't know that the limiting distribution is uniform. The only statistics we could go by is the average, *so far*. But is there some other statistic we could look at? The answer is that there are in theory many more, but the most utilized second statistic is called *standard deviation*. It is directly related to *variance*, which is just the square of the standard deviation.

What we'd like to have is some measure of how much our measurements *vary* from the mean. After all, whether they are all close to the mean or far from it will change our view on the probability of obtaining a particular measurement in the *future*. Let's say we want to measure merely the differences from the mean. Then, we could construct the following table.

Toss	Difference from Mean	Toss	Difference from Mean	Toss	Difference from Mean
1	2.583	5	−1.417	9	3.583
2	−2.417	6	0.583	10	−2.417
3	1.583	7	1.583	11	−0.417
4	−3.417	8	−1.417	12	1.583

Now, how can we represent these numbers as a single average? Well, suppose we take the average of these deviations:

$$\text{Average(differences from mean)} = \frac{(2.583 + \cdots + 1.583)}{12} = 0$$

You probably saw that coming, but this means that the average of the differences is not a useful statistic. That's because the negative ones will cancel out the positive ones, since they are differences from the average to start with. One idea to get around this problem is to use the squares of the differences—that way all the numbers will be positive and there will be no cancellations, as we see in the following table.

Toss	Square of Difference from Mean	Toss	Square of Difference from Mean	Toss	Square of Difference from Mean
1	6.674	5	2.007	9	12.840
2	5.840	6	0.340	10	5.840
3	2.507	7	2.507	11	0.1736
4	11.674	8	2.007	12	2.507

Now, what if we take the average of all of these numbers? It turns out that

$$\text{Average(squares of differences from mean)} = \frac{(6.674 + \cdots + 2.507)}{12} \qquad \text{(A.4)}$$
$$= 4.576$$

The value we calculated in equation A.4 is called the *variance* of the data. But we have to remember that this is the average of a bunch of squares, so to get back to our original "units," we must take a square root. This is the definition of *standard deviation*. By convention, standard deviation is denoted by the lowercase Greek letter sigma ("σ") and variance by the notation "Var[...]," or equivalently, "σ^2." One may use a subscript on the sigma to refer to the random variable whose standard deviation we are measuring. The definition using the same notation we used for the average is:[3]

$$\text{var}[x] \equiv \sigma_x^2 = \frac{1}{N-1} \sum_{i=1}^{N} (x_i - \mu_x)^2 \qquad \text{(A.5)}$$

Equation A.5 gives us a formula for the *best estimate* of the standard deviation. This formula is also called a *best estimator* for the variance (or standard deviation). To continue with our example, we have for the 12 tosses

$$\text{var}[x] = (6.674 + \ldots + 2.507)/11 = 4.992 \qquad (A.6)$$

and so the standard deviation is

$$\sigma_x = \sqrt{4.992} = 2.234$$

Variance Calculated from a Probability Distribution   Now let us go back to the idea of a "model" distribution. How do we calculate what we expect to see for the variance if we assume some functional form for the probability distribution? We have seen how the variance or standard deviation of a group of measurements tells you how much they vary from the mean. When we use a probability distribution, the variance tells us how "wide" or "narrow" it is (relatively speaking). Using our "expectation" notation ($E[\ldots]$), it is defined to be:

$$\text{var}[x] = E[(x - \mu_x)^2] = \sigma^2 \qquad (A.7)$$

where "σ" (sigma) again is the standard deviation. Remember that standard deviation has the same units as x, not variance. You can rewrite equation A.7 by writing out the square in the brackets:

$$\begin{aligned}
\text{var}[x] &= E[(x - \mu_x)(x - \mu_x)] \\
&= E[x^2 - 2x\mu_x + \mu_x^2] \\
&= E[x^2] - 2\mu_x E[x] + \mu_x^2 \\
&= E[x^2] - 2\mu_x^2 + \mu_x^2
\end{aligned}$$

so

$$\text{var}[x] = E[x^2] - \mu_x^2 \qquad (A.8)$$

Note that in making this calculation we assumed that the expectation of a constant (such as the predefined average or mean μ) is the constant itself, and the same goes for its square (i.e., $E[\mu^2] = \mu^2$), and that $E[x\mu] = \mu E[x]$. What equation A.8 is telling us is that if we know the mean of the distribution, we can calculate the variance (and thus standard deviation) by calculating the expectation of x^2:

$$E[x^2] = \sum_i x_i^2 f(x_i), \text{ if } x \text{ is discrete} \qquad\qquad (A.9a)$$

$$E[x^2] = \int_x x^2 f(x)dx, \text{ if } x \text{ is continuous} \qquad\qquad (A.9b)$$

Using equation A.8 with equation A.9.a or A.9.b often simplifies the math for calculating $Var[x]$. Variance is also called the 2nd moment of the distribution.

Finally, let's use equation A.8 and equation A.9.a. to calculate what we expect the variance and standard deviation to be (given we make many measurements) for our eight-sided die example. We already calculated the expected value (average) to be 4.5. So now all that is left is:

$$
\begin{aligned}
E[x^2] &= \frac{(1^2 + 2^2 + 3^2 + 4^2 + 5^2 + 6^2 + 7^2 + 8^2)}{8} \\
&= \frac{(1 + 4 + 9 + 16 + 25 + 36 + 49 + 64)}{8} \\
&= \frac{204}{8} = 25.5
\end{aligned}
$$

So the variance is

$$var[x] = E[x^2] - \mu_x^2 = 25.5 - (4.5)^2 = 25.5 - 20.25 = 4.25$$

Note that the variance we obtained from the 12-toss example (see equation A.6) is slightly different (4.992). The standard deviation for our uniformly distributed variable is:

$$\sigma = \sqrt{4.25} = 2.062$$

to three significant digits. Notice that this result differs from the real-world result of 2.234 by about 7.7 percent. However, with increasing numbers of tosses the real-world result should converge to the theoretical value 2.062.

Binomial Distributions   A frequently encountered distribution is the binomial distribution. The textbook application of the binomial distribution is the probability of obtaining, say, 5 heads in the toss of a fair coin 30 times. A better application for our purposes is describing the number of defaults one would expect to encounter in a portfolio of loans (each loan having equal default probability).

Exhibit A.4 shows the distribution of X where X is the number of defaults experienced in a portfolio of 100 loans to 100 different firms. It is assumed that each firm has the same probability of defaulting (i.e., $p = 8\%$), and that defaults are *independent*. If defaults are independent, the default of one firm has no bearing on the probability of any other firm's defaulting. Independence and correlation are described in more detail further on.

To calculate the probabilities in the chart, we required the formula for the binomial distribution, which is available in textbooks or Excel.

$$P(X = x), \text{ for } x = 1...100 = \frac{100!}{x!(100 - x)!} p^x (1 - p)^{100 - x} \qquad (A.10)$$

The outcome of rolling a die or flipping a coin is an example of a discrete distribution because it is possible to list all the possible outcomes. Looking at the binomial distribution in Exhibit A.4 you might think it looks a lot like the normal distribution—the classic bell-shaped curve. In fact, the binomial distribution converges to the normal distribution when the number of events becomes very large.

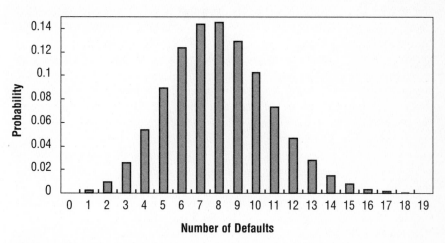

EXHIBIT A.4 Binomial Distribution: Probability of Experiencing $X = n$ Defaults with 100 Loans, Each with a Default Rate of 8%. (We assume independence among obligors.)

Before discussing continuous probability distributions, such as the normal, we need to introduce additional terminology.

Probability Density Functions

Exhibits A.2 and A.4 are plots of *relative frequency*, while Exhibit A.3 shows absolute frequency. The sum of the relative frequencies (read off the *y*-axis) equals one. A *probability density* plot is a rescaled plot of the relative frequency. Specifically, a probability density graph has been rescaled so that the total *area* sums to one. An event that is four times more likely than another event will have four times the area associated with it as opposed to four times the height.

This might seem like an arbitrary definition, but it is essential for working with continuous distributions. By transforming the probability into an area, we can apply the mathematics of integrals (sums) in order to work with continuous random variables.

Cumulative Distribution Function Suppose we are making some kind of measurements, let's say the heights of a large group of randomly selected people. Once we've made many measurements, we can plot a probability distribution, as described previously. Let's say you want to build a relatively short door in a small house. What you'd like to know is how many people in general will fit through the door. Another way to ask this question is: "What is the probability that the next random person will hit their head, walking normally?" The cumulative distribution function is what gives you the answer to that question directly. You just have to take the probability distribution you have, and for every point, you plot the fraction of total measurements that fall below the current point (e.g., height). Formally speaking, for any random variable X, the probability that X is less than or equal to a is denoted by $F(a)$. $F(x)$ is then called the cumulative distribution function (CDF). The CDF for the binomial distribution shown in Exhibit A.4 is plotted in Exhibit A.5. Recall that this is the distribution of the number of defaults in 100 loans, each with an 8% probability of defaulting.

Next, notice in Exhibit A.5 that the median (the value for which the cumulative probability equals one-half) is not equal to 8, as one might expect, given an 8% default rate, but is approximately 7.2, indicating the distribution is not symmetric about the mean and thus is *skewed* (to the left). Also notice that by the time one gets to 16 defaults we have accumulated nearly 100% of the probability, or to put it differently, we would say there is almost 100% probability of experiencing 16 or fewer defaults.

Percentiles A percentile is directly related to the cumulative distribution function. For example, if one refers to the 95th percentile, then this means

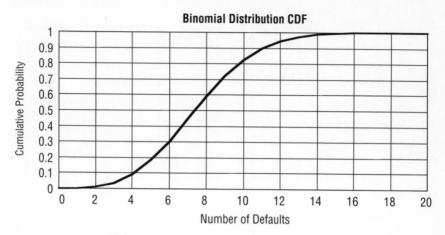

EXHIBIT A.5 Cumulative Distribution Function

that one is interested in the value the variable will take on when the CDF is equal to 95%. The value of the 50th percentile is called the *median* of the distribution. The median is equal to the mean only if the skewness (defined next) is zero. To illustrate this, we have plotted the CDF for three different probability distribution functions in Exhibit A.6: the normal, Poisson, and lognormal distributions.[4] Note that the 50th percentile (the value corresponding to 0.5 on the vertical axis) is well below the mean (equal to 8 for all of them) for all except the normal distribution (see Exhibit A.6).

Note how the normal distribution CDF passes through the value 0.5 (50%) at the value of the average (=8). This is the median of the distribution, and is lower for the other two functions.

Skew   The skew of a distribution tells you how much the center "leans" to the left or right. It is also called the 3rd moment of the distribution and is written mathematically

$$\text{Skewness} = E[(x - \mu_x)^3] \tag{A.11}$$

where μ_x is the mean. Because this number is not relative, usually one looks at a skewness *coefficient*, defined as skewness/σ^3. Exhibit A.7 shows plots of four different probability distributions and provides the skewness coefficients.

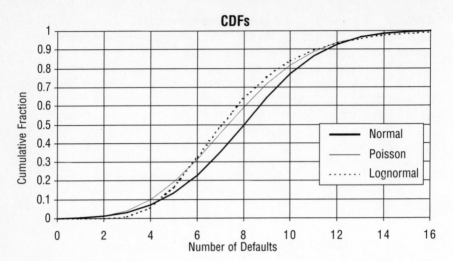

EXHIBIT A.6 Plots of the Cumulative Distribution Function for Three Different Probability Distributions

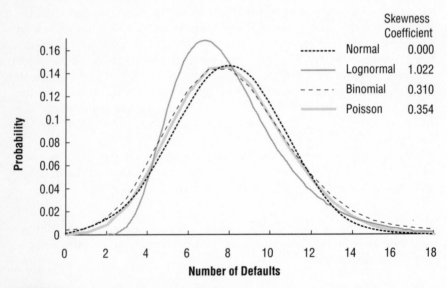

EXHIBIT A.7 Four Distributions with the Same Mean and Standard Deviation but Different Skewness Coefficients

Kurtosis   Kurtosis tells you how flat or sharp the peak of a distribution is, or equivalently, how fat or slim the tails are, relative to the normal distribution (see Exhibit A.8). Any area taken away from near the center of the distribution (as compared to the normal distribution) is symmetrically redistributed away from the center, adding the area equally to both of the tails. A distribution with this property has leptokurtosis. Distributions of credit returns (and equity returns as well, but to a lesser degree) are thought to exhibit leptokurtosis. Going the other way, any area taken away from under the tails is redistributed to the center, making the peak sharper. Kurtosis is also called the 4th moment of the distribution and is formally written

$$\text{Kurtosis} = E[(x - \mu_x)^4] \tag{A.12}$$

Again, to give a relative number (to compare different distributions), one defines another measure, called degree of excess, equal to Kurtosis/σ^3 – 3. The normal distribution has excess of zero. To get a sense of kurtosis, compare the tails of the normal and lognormal distributions (even though the lognormal one has a higher peak as shown in Exhibit A.8, it

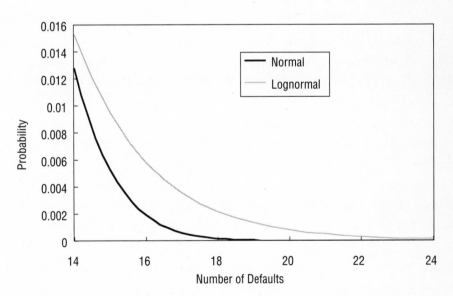

EXHIBIT A.8   Closeup of the Tails of Two Distributions with the Same Mean and Variance. (The fatter tail of the lognormal is reflected in its skewness coefficient and excess kurtosis.)

still has greater kurtosis than the normal distribution for the same mean and variance).

Examples of Uses of Probability Distributions in Finance

Suppose you want to know: "What is the probability of Microsoft's moving up by more than 2% tomorrow?" If we suppose that future behavior (specifically, the basic statistics) is similar to past behavior, this is like asking the question: "What is the fraction of the total number of daily returns of the stock price[5] in some prior recent time period for which the returns are greater than 0.02?" We looked at daily returns for Microsoft for a period of three years, from September 8, 1998 to September 4, 2001. From the data one can calculate the average and standard deviation of the daily returns, which were 0.00013 and 0.02976, respectively. (This standard deviation of the daily returns corresponds to an annual volatility of 2.976% * $\sqrt{252}$ = 47.24%.) We entered these values into the CDF function for the normal distribution (in Excel) and used the value 0.02 for the cutoff, which yielded 74.78%. This means that, assuming a normal distribution for the returns, 74.78% of the returns should be *less* than 0.02 for the given three-year period. To get the probability that Microsoft moves up by more than 2% in one day, we subtracted this value from 100%, and we got 25.22%.

It is interesting to compare this to the actual fraction of the total number of returns greater than 0.02 for the three-year period. We found this to be 22.4%. Since this number is close to the expected one assuming the normal distribution of the returns, this probability distribution may be a good one for modeling stock returns.[6] In fact, we can construct a histogram based on the data and compare it to the normal distribution we obtain using the historically calculated average and standard deviation of the returns. These are shown in Exhibit A.9. To obtain the historical data histogram, we count the number of returns observed in a given interval of one standard deviation (see the x-axis) centered about the mean, and divide by the total number of observations. To get the equivalent normal distribution histogram, we first get the CDF values at each interval boundary using the mean and standard deviation we just calculated from the historical data, then calculate the difference between each boundary. This gives us the area of the normal distribution for each CDF.

Exhibit A.9 shows that though similar overall, the historical and theoretical distributions differ quite a bit in some regions (see for example the region between –1 and 0 standard deviations from the mean—there are many more MSFT returns in this region than the normal distribution would anticipate).

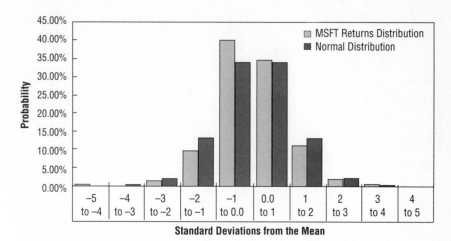

EXHIBIT A.9 Histogram of Distribution of Returns for MSFT and the Equivalent Normal Distribution for Each CDF

Tail Risk: Lognormal Distribution The tail of the lognormal distribution shown in Exhibit A.8 shows how different it is from the normal distribution for this region. In credit value at risk modeling, this is the most critical part of the distribution. Consider the following question: "What is the probability that we have greater than $\mu + 2\sigma$ defaults occurring in a portfolio of N different names when we assume a binomial distribution and when we assume a lognormal distribution?" For the example we gave, we had $\mu = 8$ and $\sigma = 2.71$, so $\mu + 2\sigma = 13.43$. Of course we can't have fractional defaults, so we can round up to 14 and put this value into our CDF equations for the binomial and lognormal distributions. We find that $P(x \geq 14) = 1.33\%$ for the binomial distribution, and $P(x \geq 14) = 2.99\%$ for the lognormal distribution. Modeling default events using a lognormal distribution rather than a binomial distribution results in more frequent scenarios with a large number of total defaults (e.g., greater than $\mu + \sigma$) even though the mean and standard deviation are the same. Though the choice of lognormal distribution may seem arbitrary, in fact, one credit portfolio model, called Credit Risk+ (see Chapter 4 for a more detailed discussion), uses the gamma distribution, which is much more similar to the lognormal distribution than the binomial distribution.

Beta Distribution: Modeling the Distribution of Loss Given Default One specific application for the beta distribution has been in credit portfolio risk management, where in two popular commercial applications it is used to model the distribution of loss given default (LGD—also called *severity*), on an individual facility basis or for an obligor or sector. Exhibit A.10 shows

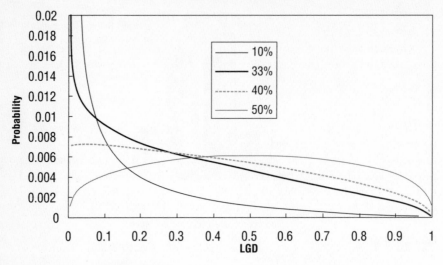

EXHIBIT A.10   Beta Distribution Models for LGD

the beta distributions for four different average LGDs. The recovery rate (sometimes called RGD, recovery given default) is defined to be 1 – LGD. Notice that the distribution with the lowest average LGD (10%) is highly skewed. The one with the 50% mean LGD is symmetric. For more details about the beta distribution (or any others just mentioned) and its parameters, see the last section of this Appendix.

The mean LGD (*severity*) for the corresponding distribution is given in the legend box.

Covariance and Correlation

Covariance   Covariance is a statistical measure relating two data series (e.g., x and y), describing their comovement. The mathematical definition is

$$\mathrm{cov}[x,y] \equiv \sigma_{x,y} = \frac{1}{N-1} \sum_{i=1}^{N} (x_i - \mu_x)(y_i - \mu_y) \qquad (A.13)$$

where μ_x and μ_y are the average (expectation) of x and y, respectively. Note that covariance has the same units as x. As discussed before regarding standard deviation and variance, equation A.13 is the *best estimator* of the covariance. If one is working directly with the underlying probability distribution, the covariance is defined as:

$$\text{cov}[x, y] \equiv \sigma_{x,y} = E[(x - \mu_x)(y - \mu_y)]$$

One can rewrite the formula in a more convenient way consistent with the earlier definition of expectation and variance (see equation A.8):

$$\text{cov}[x,y] \equiv \sigma_{x,y} = E[xy] - \mu_x\mu \qquad \text{(A.14)}$$

Covariance between two data series will increase in two ways: first, when more points for the two data series lie on the same side of the mean, and the second, when the *absolute value* of these points increases (i.e., they *vary* more, or have greater variance). One can eliminate the second undesirable effect regarding absolute values by using *correlation* instead of covariance.

Correlation The correlation *coefficient* (meaning it has no units, by definition) is a statistical measure, usually denoted by the Greek letter ρ (pronounced "rho") describing the comovement of two data series (e.g., x and y) in *relative* terms. The mathematical definition is

$$\rho_{xy} = \frac{\text{cov}[x,y]}{\sigma_x \sigma_y} = \frac{\displaystyle\sum_{i=1}^{N}(x_i - \mu_x)(y_i - \mu_y)}{\sqrt{\displaystyle\sum_{i=1}^{N}(x_i - \mu_x)^2}\sqrt{\displaystyle\sum_{i=1}^{N}(y_i - \mu_y)^2}} \qquad \text{(A.15)}$$

where μ_x and μ_y are the average (expectation) of x and y, respectively, σ_x and σ_y are the standard deviation of x and y, respectively, and cov[x,y] is the covariance of x with y. Defined this way, correlation will always lie between −1 and +1: +1 meaning x and y move perfectly together and −1 meaning x and y move perfectly opposite each other.

Example from the Equity Market We took one year of daily S&P 500 data and for the share price of MSFT and CAT, starting from September 7, 2000. Using equation A.15, we calculated the correlations between all three daily quoted data and obtained the "correlation matrix" below. Note that correlation can be positive or negative. These numbers suggest that Caterpillar often moved opposite from the S&P 500 (which might be surprising to some) and somewhat followed Microsoft during this period. The movements of Microsoft and the S&P 500 though seem to have been almost independent (correlation close to 0).

The correlations between the S&P 500 index, Microsoft, and Caterpillar for a one-year period are as follows:

	S&P 500	MSFT
MSFT	0.0314	
CAT	−0.6953	0.3423

We can see how correlation works better with a graph. Exhibit A.11 shows the daily prices for MSFT and CAT and the S&P 500. One can see that there are regions where MSFT and the S&P 500 follow each other more than others. This is an important thing to remember—correlations change with time. For example if we divide the one-year period in two, we get the following correlations.

1st Half	S&P 500	MSFT	2nd Half	S&P 500	MSFT
MSFT	0.5279		MSFT	0.8062	
CAT	−0.5987	−0.4390	CAT	0.6064	0.7637

We note two things: First, the correlations are much larger in the 2nd half of the period than the first, and second, that correlations are not "additive." The correlation between the S&P 500 and MSFT is quite positive in both periods, but over the entire period they correlate weakly. Also, one would think that the opposite correlations between the S&P 500 and CAT

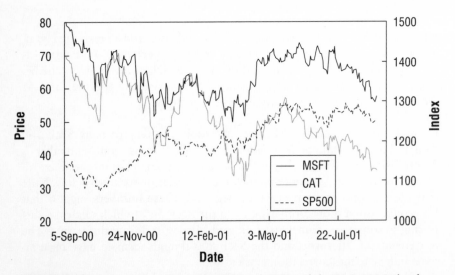

EXHIBIT A.11   Plot of Share Price of MSFT and CAT and the S&P 500 Index for a One-Year Period

would cancel each other over the entire period, but they do not—they end up being quite negative. The only correlations that make some intuitive sense are the ones between MSFT and CAT.

Linear Regression

Often one is interested in determining how well some observable (e.g., consumption) is dependent on some other observable (e.g., income). A linear regression is performed if one believes there is a linear relationship between two variables. Formally, a linear regression equation has the form:

$$y_i = \alpha + \beta x_i + \varepsilon_i \qquad (A.16)$$

where

y is the dependent variable
x is the independent variable
α is a constant
β is the slope coefficient and
ε is the error or *residual* term.

One of the main results of the linear regression calculation is the estimation (in a statistical sense) of the slope, β. It turns out that the regression coefficients α and β are given by:

$$\beta = \frac{\text{cov}[x,y]}{\text{var}[x]}, \text{ and } \alpha = \mu_y - \beta\mu_x \qquad (A.17)$$

These are the results for what is called ordinary least-squares (OLS) regression. The technique is based on minimization of the squares of the differences of the errors (i.e., minimizing ε^2) by varying the constant coefficient, α, and the slope, β. Note that it is not necessary that the two variables of interest be directly linearly related. It is often possible to perform a transformation on one of the variables in order to produce a linear relationship for which a linear regression may be calculated. An example is

$$y = Ax^\beta e^\varepsilon$$

Taking the (natural) logarithm of the equation yields a new parameter $z = \ln(y)$ so we get:

$$z = \alpha + \beta \ln(x) + \varepsilon$$

where $\alpha = \ln(A)$, so one may (linearly) regress the variable z on the variable $\ln(x)$. This cannot be done for example with the relationship

$$y = \alpha + \frac{1}{\beta + x} + \varepsilon$$

Again, the best way to understand the intuition behind linear regression is through an example and a picture. Exhibit A.12 shows a plot of the average (regional) EDF (expected default frequency) for North America and Europe. One can see that though they have very different absolute values, their movement is similar. This is made even clearer in Exhibit A.13, which shows the data sets plotted against each other. The straight line is the result of the linear regression of the two, with the resulting equation for the *correlation coefficient* (written like this, it is also often called R-squared or R^2).

The goodness of fit parameter is given by the linear correlation coefficient, ρ (see Exhibit A.12). It is defined mathematically in exactly the same way as the correlation coefficient defined above in equation A.15. In terms of the *slope* coefficient β, it is written

$$\rho_{xy}^2 = \beta \frac{\text{cov}[x,y]}{\text{var}[y]} \tag{A.18}$$

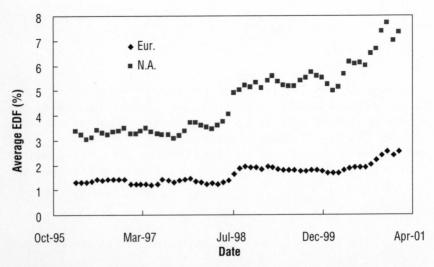

EXHIBIT A.12 Average Expected Default Frequency (EDF) for Europe and North America

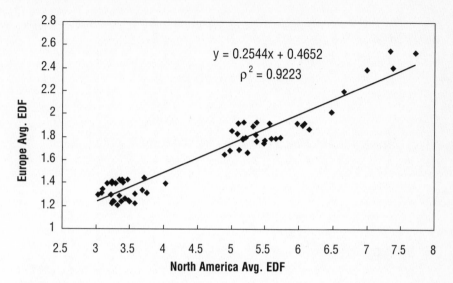

EXHIBIT A.13 Relative Plot of the Same Data as in Exhibit A.12 Along with the Regression Line. (The regression equation and goodness of fit parameter are also shown.)

Significance of the Slope Coefficient The slope coefficient (β) tells us how strongly a given random variable depends on another one. It does not tell us how confident we can be that we will obtain a certain measurement of the dependent variable given a value of the independent one—that is, what the goodness of fit or correlation coefficient tells us.

Probability Theory

In this section, we discuss some general concepts from probability theory that are relevant to some of the analytical techniques that a credit portfolio manager might encounter.

Joint Probability A joint probability is just the likelihood that two (or more) random variables take on particular values. Said another way, it is the probability of the joint occurrence of two events E_1 and E_2. It is formally written $P(E_1 \cap E_2)$ or $P(E_1 E_2)$.[7] The sum of all the possible joint probabilities is always equal to one. For a discrete random variable, this is like saying

$$1 = \sum_i \sum_j f(x_i, y_j)$$

where $f(x,y)$ is the joint probability distribution, and for a continuous random variable,

$$1 = \int_x \int_y f(x,y)dxdy$$

EXAMPLE: THE PROBABILITY OF TWO FAIR COINS BOTH LANDING HEADS

Suppose we toss two fair coins. What is the probability that both of them will land heads? For any pair of tosses, there is $.5 \times .5 = 0.25$ or 25% chance that both of them will be heads. Note that the two measurements are independent (one coin has no way of knowing what the other coin is doing), but there is still a non-zero joint probability. The formal way of writing independence of two events is $P(E_1 E_2) = P(E_1)P(E_2)$.

Default Correlation and Joint Default Probability   When a random variable can take on only two values (e.g., 0 or 1, miss or hit, default or no-default), it is called a *binomial* variable. Given the probability of one of the states occurring (e.g., default) for each of two different variables (e.g., call them p_x and p_y), and the probability that both will result in the same state (e.g., "0"

EXAMPLE: THE PROBABILITY OF GM AND HP BOTH DEFAULTING NEXT YEAR

Consider the chance that two firms both default over a year time period. Based on the results from a well-known commercial application (Moody's–KMV Credit Monitor, discussed in Chapter 3), we found that the probabilities of default for GM and HP are 0.13% and 0.11%, respectively. However, when one calculates the joint probability of default, if the process of default for the two companies were independent, then we would get a probability of $0.0013 * 0.0011 = 0.00000143$, or 0.0143 bp (basis points: a basis point is equal to 0.0001). However, when one takes into account default *correlation*, we actually get a joint probability of default of 0.00611% or 0.611 bp, nearly 43 times higher than the probability would be if we considered the two companies to behave completely independently. (It turns out that the default correlation of the two companies is 0.05, which is small but not negligible.)

---

or "default")—call this probability J, then there exists a precise relationship between the (default) correlation ρ_{xy} and the joint probability (of default) J:

$$\rho_{xy} = \frac{J - p_x p_y}{\sqrt{p_x(1-p_x)}\sqrt{p_y(1-p_y)}} \qquad (A.19)$$

This formula is derived later on in this Appendix.

Conditional Probability   Sometimes, people confuse conditional probabilities with joint probabilities. Suppose we rigged our coin tossing experiment so that an electromagnet is turned on (with 100% probability) if coin A lands tails (call this event A_T), which influences coin B to have a greater likelihood of landing heads (say it is now 75% instead of 50%). For the sake of argument let's say coin B always lands right after coin A. In this case the probability of coin B's landing tails (call this event B_T) conditional on coin A's landing heads (call this event (A_H) is 50%. Formally, this is written $P(B_T | A_H) = 50\%$, where "|" denotes "conditional on." The probability of coin B's landing heads conditional on A's landing heads is also the same: $P(B_H | A_H) = 50\%$. However, if A lands tails, we have the following conditional probabilities: $P(B_H | A_T) = 75\%$ and $P(B_T | A_T) = 25\%$. Now what are the joint probabilities? The conditional probabilities can be summarized as

$P(B_x|A_y)$	A_H	A_T
B_H	0.5	.75
B_T	0.5	.25

The joint probabilities can be summarized as

$P(B_x \cap A_y)$	A_H	A_T
B_H	0.25	.375
B_T	0.25	.125

Notice that because of the correlation of A's landing tails with coin B, the probability $P(A_T B_H) = .375$ is greater than the "normal" one (=.25), while $P(A_T B_T)$ is lower.

It turns out that if the conditional probability is equal to the unconditional one, then the two events are independent: $P(B_H | A_H) = 50\% = P(B_H)$. There is actually a general relationship (called Bayes' Law) between joint probabilities and conditional probabilities, and is written:

$$P(E_1 | E_2) = \frac{P(E_1 E_2)}{P(E_2)} \qquad (A.20)$$

where E_1 and E_2 are two events. For continuous random variables, if there exists a functional form for the joint probability distribution, [let's call it $f(x,y)$] then the *conditional* distribution is written

$$f(x \mid y = Y) = \frac{f(x,y)}{f(Y)} \tag{A.21}$$

where

$$f(Y) = \int_x f(x,Y)dx \tag{A.22}$$

is called the *marginal* (i.e., unconditional) distribution.

Joint Normality   Often two variables have some correlation ρ and are normally distributed. In this case the distributions will have the *bivariate* normal joint probability density:

$$f(x,y) = \frac{1}{2\pi\sigma_x\sigma_y\sqrt{1-\rho^2}} \exp\left(-\frac{\varepsilon_x^2 + \varepsilon_y^2 - 2\rho\varepsilon_x\varepsilon_y}{2(1-\rho^2)}\right) \tag{A.23}$$

$$\varepsilon_x = \frac{x-\mu_x}{\sigma_x}$$

$$\varepsilon_y = \frac{y-\mu_y}{\sigma_y}$$

EXAMPLE: IBM RETURNS

We looked at 12 months of returns and trading volume on IBM stock from June 1, 2000 to May 31, 2001, and found that the average daily return was −0.023%, with a standard deviation of 3.20% (corresponding to an annual volatility of 50.9%). From the data, we can also calculate, for example, the average return and standard deviation conditional on a trading volume that is 2s or greater than the mean volume. There were eight such events (out of 252), and the average return for these was −0.770% (more than 30 times the unconditional average), while the standard deviation was 3.508%. These numbers are very different from those of the unconditional distribution.

Exhibit A.14 shows three plots of the joint normal distribution function equation A.23 for three different correlations: 0, –0.95 and 0.95. Notice that for the negative (positive) correlation in Panel C (Panel B), the value of x for the maximum probability decreases (increases) when y increases. The two variables in question could be any random processes, like the number of people enrolling in college and the number of people graduating high school in a given year, for example. This is an example where the joint distribution would have high correlation. Another example could be the joint distribution of returns for Microsoft and Caterpillar.

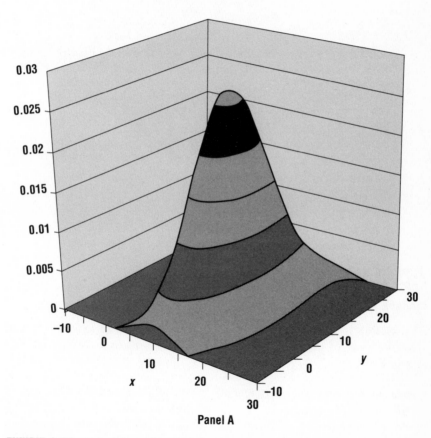

Panel A

EXHIBIT A.14 Joint Normal Probability Distributions for Two Variables with $\mu_x = \mu_y = 10$, $\sigma_x = 2$ and $\sigma_y = 3$. (Panel A: $\rho = 0.0$, Panel B: $\rho = 0.95$, Panel C: $\rho = -0.95$.)

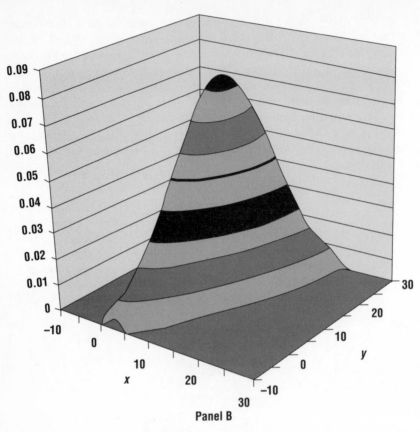

Panel B

EXHIBIT A.14 *(Continued)*

APPLICATIONS OF BASIC STATISTICS

Modern Portfolio Theory

This section is an introduction to the statistics needed for a basic, sound understanding of the analytical calculations required in modern portfolio theory (MPT).

Combining Two (Normally Distributed) Assets into a Portfolio   Consider a portfolio of only two assets. We can denote the value of these assets at horizon by V_1 and V_2 and we can assume to start off with their means as μ_1 and μ_2 and their standard deviations as σ_1 and σ_2. What we want to know is the expectation and standard deviation of the portfolio of two assets: $V_p = V_1 + V_2$. Using the definition of expectation, we have

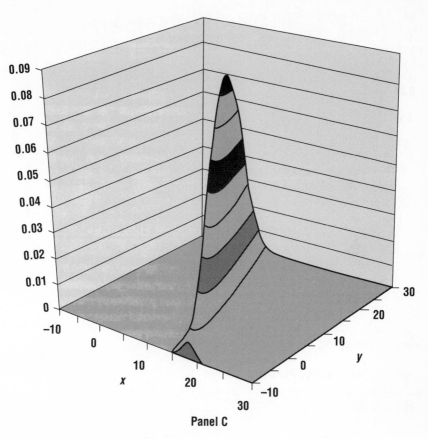

Panel C

EXHIBIT A.14   *(Continued)*

$$\mu_p = E[V_p] = E[V_1 + V_2] = E[V_1] + E[V_2] = \mu_1 + \mu_2$$

So we see that the calculation for the mean of the portfolio of two assets is straightforward. But for the variance, we have, using equation A.8,

$$\begin{aligned}
\text{var}[V_p] = \sigma_p^2 &= E[V_p^2] - \mu_p^2 = E[(V_1 + V_2)^2] - \mu_p^2 \\
&= E[V_1^2 + 2V_1V_2 + V_2^2] - \mu_p^2 \\
&= E[V_1^2] + 2E[V_1V_2] + E[V_2^2] - \mu_p^2 \\
&= E[V_1^2] + 2E[V_1V_2] + E[V_2^2] - \mu_1^2 - \mu_2^2 - 2\mu_1\mu_2
\end{aligned}$$

So now what to do? Recalling again the definition of variance equation A.8 for each individual asset, we have

$$\text{var}[V_p] = \text{var}[V_1] + \text{var}[V_2] + 2E[V_1V_2] - 2\mu_1\mu_2$$
$$= \text{var}[V_1] + \text{var}[V_2] + 2[E(V_1V_2) - \mu_1\mu_2]$$

Now recalling the formula for covariance equation A.14, we have

$$\sigma_p^2 = \text{var}[V_1] + \text{var}[V_2] + 2\,\text{cov}[V_1, V_2] \tag{A.24}$$

This is a very important result and we use it for a portfolio of arbitrary size. Using the definition for correlation equation A.15, the variance may also be written

$$\sigma_p^2 = \sigma_1^2 + \sigma_2^2 + 2\sigma_1\sigma_2\rho_{12} \tag{A.25}$$

Combining Many Assets into a Portfolio   Now we consider a portfolio of N assets. We can denote the value of these assets at horizon by $V_1, V_2, \ldots, V_N$, and assume that their means are $\mu_1, \mu_2, \ldots, \mu_N$ and their standard deviations are $\sigma_1, \sigma_2, \ldots, \sigma_N$.

Expected Value of the Portfolio   From the derivation for the portfolio of two assets, it is straightforward to see that the expected value of the portfolio will be

$$\mu_p = E[V_p] = E[V_1 + V_2 + \cdots + V_N] = E[V_1] + E[V_2] = \mu_1 + \mu_2 + \cdots + \mu_N$$

so using the notation introduced at the beginning,

$$\mu_p = \sum_{i=1}^{N} \mu_i \tag{A.26}$$

Variance of the Portfolio   The standard deviation of the portfolio is a bit trickier, but easy once you see how it works for three assets:

$$\text{var}[V_p] = E[V_p^2] - \mu_p^2 = E[(V_1 + V_2 + V_3)^2] - \mu_p^2$$
$$= E[V_1^2 + V_2^2 + V_3^2 + 2V_1V_2 + 2V_1V_3 + 2V_2V_3] - \mu_p^2$$
$$= E[V_1^2] + E[V_2^2] + E[V_3^2] + 2E[V_1V_2] + 2E[V_1V_3] + 2E[V_2V_3] - \mu_p^2$$

so

$$var[V_p] = E[V_1^2] + E[V_2^2] + E[V_3^2] + 2E[V_1V_2] + 2E[V_1V_3] + 2E[V_2V_3]$$
$$-\mu_1^2 - \mu_2^2 - \mu_3^2 - 2\mu_1\mu_2 - 2\mu_1\mu_3 - 2\mu_2\mu_3$$

Collecting the individual variances we have

$$var[V_p] = var[V_1] + var[V_2] + var[V_3] + 2E[V_1V_2] + 2E[V_1V_3] + 2E[V_2V_3]$$
$$-2\mu_1\mu_2 - 2\mu_1\mu_3 - 2\mu_2\mu_3$$

and again using the definition of covariance,

$$\begin{aligned}var[V_p] &= var[V_1] + var[V_2] + var[V_3] + 2\,cov[V_1,V_2] + 2\,cov[V_1,V_3]\\ &\quad + 2\,cov[V_2,V_3]\\ &= var[V_1] + var[V_2] + var[V_3] + 2\,cov[V_1,V_2] + 2\,cov[V_1,V_3]\\ &\quad + 2\,cov[V_2,V_3]\end{aligned}$$

If we write this as a sum, we see that for three assets

$$\sigma_p^2 = \sum_{i=1}^{3}\sigma_i^2 + 2\sum_{i=1}^{3}\sum_{j=i+1}^{3} cov[V_i,V_j] \tag{A.27}$$

We can get a better understanding of this formula by looking at what we call the *covariance matrix*—a table that lists all the values of the covariances. The covariance matrix for a three-asset portfolio is as follows.

$cov[V_1,V_1] = \sigma_1^2$	$cov[V_2,V_1] = \sigma_1\sigma_2\rho_{12}$	$cov[V_3,V_1] = \sigma_1\sigma_2\rho_{13}$
$cov[V_1,V_2] = \sigma_1\sigma_2\rho_{12}$	$cov[V_2,V_2] = \sigma_2^2$	$cov[V_3,V_2] = \sigma_2\sigma_3\rho_{23}$
$cov[V_1,V_3] = \sigma_1\sigma_3\rho_{13}$	$cov[V_2,V_3] = \sigma_2\sigma_3\rho_{23}$	$cov[V_3,V_3] = \sigma_3^2$

Note that $\sigma_{ij} = \sigma_{ji}$ so the matrix is symmetric about the diagonal. Comparing the entries to equation A.27, we see that *the portfolio variance is simply the sum of all the entries in the covariance matrix.*

Noting this, we can easily generalize equation A.27 for N assets, so we have

$$\sigma_p^2 = \sum_{i=1}^{N}\sigma_i^2 + 2\sum_{i=1}^{N}\sum_{j=i+1}^{N} cov[V_i,V_j] \tag{A.28}$$

Using the fact that by definition (see equations A.5 and A.13),

$$\sigma_i^2 = \text{var}[V_i] = \text{cov}[V_i, V_i]$$

we can rewrite equation A.28 in the simpler notation:

$$\sigma_p^2 = \sum_{i=1}^{N} \sum_{j=1}^{N} \text{cov}[V_i, V_j]$$

emphasizing the fact that the portfolio variance is the sum of all the entries in the covariance matrix.

Generalized Portfolio with Different Weights on the Assets   So far we have considered only a portfolio of equally weighted assets. What if we have different weights (e.g., shares or numbers) for each asset? How do we calculate the variance of the portfolio? This is straightforward if one looks again at the definition of variance and covariance. It turns out that (I leave this as an exercise):

$$\sigma_p^2 = \sum_{i=1}^{N} \sum_{j=1}^{N} w_i w_j \, \text{cov}[V_i, V_j] \tag{A.29}$$

where w_i is the weight or number of shares of the ith asset. Again, we can represent this with a matrix that looks something like that in Exhibit A.15. The total portfolio variance will be the sum of all the elements of this matrix. We use the shorter notation "$\sigma_{i,j}$" to indicate $\text{cov}[V_i, V_j]$.

EXHIBIT A.15   Stylized Matrix for Calculating the Total Portfolio Variance (equation A.29)

$w_1^2 \sigma_1^2$	$w_1 w_2 \sigma_{12}$	$w_1 w_3 \sigma_{13}$	$\cdots$	$w_1 w_{N-1} \sigma_{1,N-1}$	$w_1 w_N \sigma_{1N}$
$w_1 w_2 \sigma_{12}$	$w_2^2 \sigma_2^2$	$w_2 w_3 \sigma_{23}$	$\cdots$	$w_2 w_{N-1} \sigma_{2,N-1}$	$w_2 w_N \sigma_{2,N}$
$w_1 w_3 \sigma_{13}$	$w_2 w_3 \sigma_{23}$	$w_3^2 \sigma_3^2$	$\cdots$	$w_3 w_{N-1} \sigma_{3,N-1}$	$w_3 w_N \sigma_{3,N}$
$\cdots$	$\cdots$	$\cdots$	$\cdots$	$\cdots$	$\cdots$
$w_1 w_{N-1} \sigma_{1,N-1}$	$w_2 w_{N-1} \sigma_{2,N-1}$	$w_3 w_{N-1} \sigma_{3,N-1}$	$\cdots$	$w_{N-1}^2 \sigma_{N-1}^2$	$w_N w_{N-1} \sigma_{N,N-1}$
$w_1 w_N \sigma_{1N}$	$w_2 w_N \sigma_{2,N}$	$w_3 w_N \sigma_{3,N}$	$\cdots$	$w_N w_{N-1} \sigma_{N,N-1}$	$w_N^2 \sigma_N^2$

Risk Contribution

Another important concept in modern portfolio theory is the idea of the risk contribution of an asset to a portfolio. It is important to remember that it can be defined in more than one way, but the most common definition is what we call marginal standard deviation—the amount of variation that a particular asset (call it "A") adds to the portfolio. If the asset has a weight or number of shares of w_A, then its risk contribution is defined by:

$$RC_A = w_A \frac{\partial \sigma_p}{\partial w_A} \tag{A.30}$$

The fraction on the right-hand side after "w_A" contains the "partial derivative" symbol ("∂"). All this means is that (in the fraction) we are calculating the *change* in the portfolio standard deviation with respect to *a very small* change in the weight (i.e., dollar amount or number of shares) of the particular asset. Another way of saying this is that this derivative tells us the *sensitivity* of the portfolio standard deviation with respect to asset A. Calculating RC_A in this way is equivalent to adding up all the elements of the row (or column, since it is symmetric) corresponding to asset "A" of the covariance matrix we introduced earlier and dividing this sum by the portfolio standard deviation. This confirms that the sum of all the risk contributions (RC_i) is equal to the portfolio standard deviation—that is,

$$\sigma_p = \sum_{i=1}^{N} RC_i \tag{A.31}$$

To derive equation A.31, we need to apply equation A.30 to equation A.29. First, we note that

$$\frac{\partial \sigma_p^2}{\partial w_A} = 2\sigma_p \frac{\partial \sigma_p}{\partial w_A}$$

so that

$$\frac{\partial \sigma_p}{\partial w_A} = \frac{1}{2\sigma_p} \frac{\partial \sigma_p^2}{\partial w_A}$$

Now we can use the expression for the portfolio variance equation A.29 to calculate

$$\frac{\partial \sigma_p^2}{\partial w_A} = \sum_{j=1}^{N} w_j \operatorname{cov}[V_A, V_j] + \sum_{i=1}^{N} w_i \operatorname{cov}[V_i, V_A]$$

and so we have that

$$RC_A = \frac{w_A}{2\sigma_p} \left(\sum_{j=1}^{N} w_j \operatorname{cov}[V_A, V_j] + \sum_{i=1}^{N} w_i \operatorname{cov}[V_i, V_A] \right) \qquad (A.32)$$

To show that equation A.32 obeys equation A.31, simply sum over all the assets in the portfolio:

$$\sum_{A=1}^{N} RC_A = \sum_{j=1}^{N} \frac{w_A}{2\sigma_p} \left(\sum_{j=1}^{N} w_j \operatorname{cov}[V_A, V_j] + \sum_{i=1}^{N} w_i \operatorname{cov}[V_i, V_A] \right)$$

$$= \frac{1}{2\sigma_p} \left(\sum_{A=1}^{N} \sum_{j=1}^{N} w_A w_j \operatorname{cov}[V_A, V_j] + \sum_{A=1}^{N} \sum_{i=1}^{N} w_A w_i \operatorname{cov}[V_i, V_A] \right)$$

$$= \frac{1}{2\sigma_p} \left(\sigma_p^2 + \sigma_p^2 \right)$$

$$= \sigma_p$$

Derivation of the Default Event Correlation Formula

We now turn to the derivation of the equation for default event correlation as a function of a joint probability equation A.19.

Assume two binomial random variables X and Y (that can have values of 0 or 1) have a joint probability distribution $p(x,y)$. Assume a joint probability $p(1,1) = J$.

Start with definition of correlation (see equation A.15):

$$\rho_{xy} = \frac{\operatorname{cov}[X, Y]}{\sigma_x \sigma_y} \qquad (A.33)$$

We now try to calculate $\operatorname{cov}[X, Y]$ using its definition calculated using the joint probability density for discrete random variables:

$$\text{cov}[X,Y] \equiv E[(X-\mu_x)(Y-\mu_y)] = \Sigma_{i,j}(x_i-\mu_x)(y_j-\mu_y)p(x_i,y_j)$$

where $p(x_i,y_j) = P(X = x_i \text{ and } Y = y_j)$.

Let the marginal probabilities be μ_x and μ_y:

$$\mu_x = p(1,0) + p(1,1)$$
$$\mu_y = p(0,1) + p(1,1)$$

Using the above definition for covariance,

$$\text{cov}[X,Y] = p(0,0)(0-\mu_x)(0-\mu_y) + p(0,1)(0-\mu_x)(1-\mu_y)$$
$$+ p(1,0)(1-\mu_x)(0-\mu_y) + p(1,1)(1-\mu_x)(1-\mu_y)$$

Now recall that:

$$p(1,1) = J$$
$$p(1,0) = \mu_x - J$$
$$p(0,1) = \mu_y - J$$

so

$$p(0,0) = 1 - \mu_x - \mu_y + J$$

Inserting these into the preceding yields:

$$\text{cov}[X,Y] = (1-\mu_x-\mu_y+J)(-\mu_x)(-\mu_y) + (\mu_y-J)(-\mu_x)(1-\mu_y)$$
$$+ (\mu_x-J)(1-\mu_x)(-\mu_y) + J(1-\mu_x)(1-\mu_y)$$

and just doing the algebra,

$$\text{cov}[X,Y] = (-\mu_x+\mu_x^2+\mu_x\mu_y-J\mu_x)(-\mu_y)+(\mu_y-J)(-\mu_x+\mu_x\mu_y)$$
$$+(\mu_x-J)(-\mu_x+\mu_x\mu_y)+J(1-\mu_x-\mu_y+\mu_x\mu_y)$$
$$\text{cov}[X,Y] = \mu_x\mu_y-\mu_y\mu_x^2-\mu_x\mu_y^2+J\mu_x\mu_y-\mu_x\mu_y+\mu_x\mu_y^2+J\mu_x-J\mu_x\mu_y$$
$$-\mu_x\mu_y+\mu_x^2\mu_y+J\mu_y-J\mu_x\mu_y+J-J\mu_x-J\mu_y+J\mu_x\mu_y$$

and after canceling terms, we get

$$\text{cov}[X,Y] = J - \mu_x\mu_y$$

Inserting this into equation A.33 yields equation A.19 for the default event correlation (ρ_{xy}).

IMPORTANT PROBABILITY DISTRIBUTIONS

We now turn our attention to the specifics of the probability distributions that we have encountered in this book and that are useful to understand in credit portfolio management.

Normal

By far the most common of any distribution, the normal distribution is also called the *bell curve* or the Gauss distribution, after the prominent mathematician and physicist, Carl Friedrich Gauss, of the early eighteenth century. Many distributions converge to the normal one when certain limits are taken. For example, the normal distribution is the limiting distribution of the binomial one when the number of trials tends to infinity (more on that later).

The normal distribution is given by the density function

$$f(x) = \frac{1}{\sqrt{2\pi}\sigma} e^{\frac{-(x-\mu)^2}{2\sigma^2}} \tag{A.34}$$

A plot of this function is shown in Exhibit A.16.

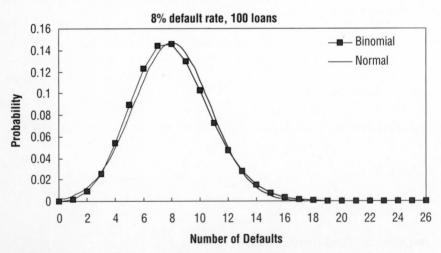

EXHIBIT A.16 Comparison of the Normal Distribution to the Binomial Distribution for the Same Parameters as in Exhibit A.4

Note that the normal distribution extends out to negative values and is perfectly symmetric about the mean (=8%). The binomial and normal are close approximations to each other, but there are times when one is not appropriate and the other will be, for example, in the modeling of probabilities. The fact that the normal permits negative values means that it will not be used (typically) to describe the probability of default.

Upper/Lower Bounds The normal distribution has no lower or upper bounds. It has a non-zero value all the way up (down) to infinity (minus infinity).

Parameters The bell curve has two parameters that describe it completely—the mean (μ) and the standard deviation (σ) or variance (=σ^2).

Principal Applications The normal distribution has applications everywhere—in every science, social science (e.g., economics and finance), engineering, and so on. It is the most basic (nontrivial) distribution, and many other distributions are compared to it.

Lognormal

The lognormal distribution is a variation on the normal distribution, in which the natural logarithm of a random variable is normally distributed. When plotted against the random variable itself, the distribution is asymmetric and allows only positive (or zero) values.

The lognormal distribution is given by the following density function:

$$f(x) = \frac{1}{\sqrt{2\pi}\sigma x} e^{\frac{-(\ln(x)-\mu)^2}{2\sigma^2}} \tag{A.35}$$

Note the similarity to the normal distribution. Here the parameters μ and σ *do not* refer to the mean and standard deviation of the distribution (see Parameters, below), but are the parameters of the corresponding normal distribution. Exhibit A.17 shows a plot of the lognormal distribution compared to the normal distribution.

Upper/Lower Bounds The lower bound is zero, and the upper is infinity.

Parameters The lognormal distribution has two parameters directly related to the corresponding normal distribution. Suppose y is a normally distributed random variable with mean μ and variance σ^2 (that is, $y \sim$

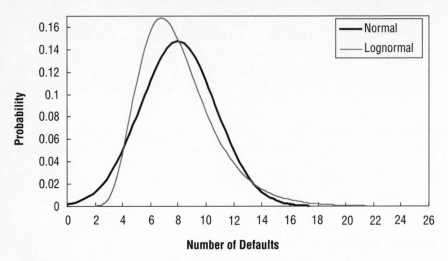

EXHIBIT A.17 Comparison of the Lognormal Distribution with the Normal Distribution with the Same Mean (= 8) and Standard Deviation (= 2.713)

$N(\mu, \sigma^2)$). Then the variable $x = e^y$ is log-normally distributed with a mean equal to $\exp(\mu + \sigma^2/2)$ and a variance equal to $\exp(2\mu + \sigma^2)[\exp(\sigma^2) - 1]$.[8]

Principal Applications In econometrics, the lognormal distribution has been particularly useful in modeling size distributions, such as the distribution of firm sizes in an industry or the distribution of income in a country. In financial applications it is widely used in modeling the behavior of stock prices, which are always positive (greater than zero). This implies that the logarithm of the stock price is normally distributed. This assumption is used in the Black–Scholes option pricing formula and theory.

Binomial

The binomial distribution comes out of the answer to the question: "What is the probability that I will get v number of aces after tossing a die n times?

The binomial distribution gives the probability that v events will occur in n trials, given an event has a probability p of occurring, and is explicitly written as:

$$f_{n,p}(v) = \frac{n!}{v!(n-v)!} p^v (1-p)^{n-v}$$

(A.36)

where the exclamation mark "!" denotes the factorial symbol (e.g., 5! = 5·4·3·2·1 = 120, and by definition, 0! = 1). This distribution converges to the normal distribution when n tends to infinity. It converges more rapidly if p is close to $1/2$. Note that default probabilities are much smaller than $1/2$, reflecting the fact that default probability distributions (and loss distributions, for that matter) are far from normally distributed.

Upper/Lower Bounds   The lower bound is zero and the upper is n, the total number of "trials" (e.g., rolls of the die, spins of the wheel, names in the loan portfolio, and so on). See Exhibit A.18. Note the different vertical scales.

Parameters   The binomial distribution has two parameters: the total number of "trials," n (e.g., the number of loans in a portfolio), and the probability of an event to occur, p (e.g., the probability of default). The expected value of the distribution is given by np, and the variance is given by $np(1 - p)$.

Principal Applications   In credit risk modeling, the binomial distribution is used sometimes as a starting point for more complex models (which require the incorporation of correlation effects between obligors). For example, the normal (Gauss) distribution can be derived from the binomial when taking the limit that n goes to infinity.

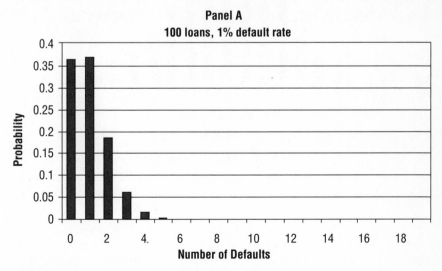

Panel A
100 loans, 1% default rate

EXHIBIT A.18   Binomial Distribution with Three Different Probabilities of Default. (Panel A: 1%, Panel B: 3%, Panel C: 8%.)

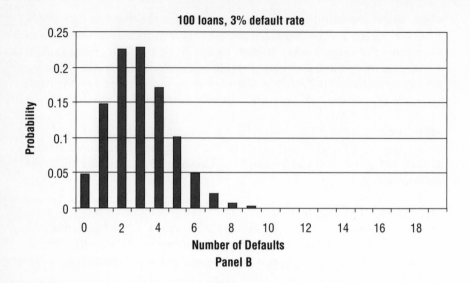

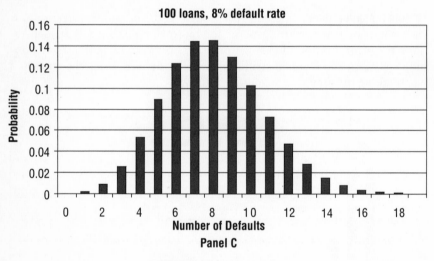

EXHIBIT A.18 *(Continued)*

Poisson

The Poisson distribution is the mathematical distribution governing a random variable in which one counts "rare" events, but at a definite average rate. This is called a "Poisson process"—a process in which discrete events are observable in an area of opportunity—a continuous interval (of time, length, surface area, etc.)—in such a manner that if we shorten the area of opportunity enough, we obtain three conditions: (1) the probability of observing that exactly one success in the interval is stable; (2) the probability of observing that more than one success in the interval is 0; (3) the occurrence that a success in any one interval is statistically independent of that in any other interval. Examples include finding the probability of the number of:

Radioactive decays per second

Deaths per month due to a
disease

Imperfections per square meter
in rolls of metals

Telephone calls per hour
received by an office

Cashews per can of mixed nuts

Bacteria in a given culture
per liter

Typing errors per page

Cases of a rare disease per year

Stoppages on a production line
per week

Flaws in a bolt of fabric

Customers arriving at a service
station per minute

Requests arriving at a server
computer per second

Accidents at a particular
intersection per month

Firms defaulting in a portfolio
of loans per year

The distribution was invented by the French mathematician Simeon-Denise Poisson (1781–1840) and was first applied to describe the probability of a particular number of Prussian soldiers being killed by being kicked by horses. Actuaries use a Poisson distribution to model events like a hurricane's striking a specific location on the eastern seaboard of the United States.

The Poisson distribution is related to a "rare" event (though rare is a relative term) in which the time of arrival is exponentially distributed—that is, the probability of arrival time decreases exponentially (i.e., as e^{-rt}, where r is some average arrival rate and t is time) with increasing time. The Poisson distribution describes the probability of having v "arrivals" (e.g., defaults) in a fixed time interval, as already discussed. Later on, the *gamma* distribution is discussed, and it is also part of the same family. The gamma distribution describes the probability distribution of the time of the kth "arrival" (if $k = 1$ then the gamma distribution becomes the exponential distribution).

The Poisson distribution is a limiting form of the binomial distribution, that being when the probability of an event is very small (e.g., default events), and the number of "trials" n (e.g., the number of names in a portfolio) is large.

It turns out that this distribution, $p_\mu(n)$, that is, the probability of n events occurring in some time interval, is equal to:

$$p_\mu(n) = e^{-\mu}\frac{\mu^n}{n!}$$

(A.37)

where μ is the expected mean number of events per unit of time and the exclamation mark ("!") is the factorial symbol or operation (e.g., $5! = 5\cdot4\cdot3\cdot2\cdot1 = 120$, and by definition, $0! = 1$).

Upper/Lower Bounds   The lower bound is zero and the upper is infinity.

Exhibit A.19 shows the Poisson distribution for the same parameters as in Exhibit A.16. Notice how close the Poisson distribution is to the binomial. It is a little flatter near the peak and a little more fat-tailed than the binomial distribution.

Parameters   The Poisson distribution takes only *one* parameter: the average of the distribution, μ. It turns out that the variance is equal to the mean, so the standard deviation is $\sqrt{\mu}$.

Principal Applications   There is an incredibly large array of applications for the Poisson distribution. In physics it is well-known for being the distribution governing radioactive decay. In credit portfolio management, it is used as the starting point to model default event probability distributions in the Credit Risk+ model, described in Chapter 3.

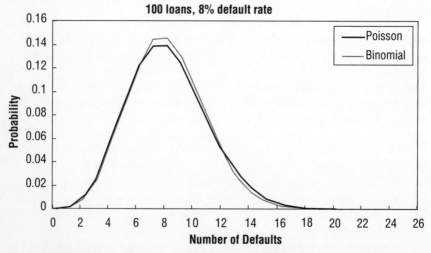

EXHIBIT A.19   Comparison of the Poisson Distribution to the Binomial

Beta

The beta distribution is described by two parameters (α and β) and applies to a random variable constrained between 0 and $c > 0$.

The beta distribution density is given by

$$f(x) = \frac{\Gamma(\alpha+\beta)}{\Gamma(\alpha)\Gamma(\beta)}\left(\frac{x}{c}\right)^{\alpha-1}\left(1-\frac{x}{c}\right)^{\beta-1}\left(\frac{1}{c}\right) \tag{A.38}$$

where $\Gamma(\,\ldots\,)$ is the gamma *function*, not to be confused with the gamma distribution. The mean and variance of this distribution are given by

$$\mu = \frac{\alpha}{\alpha+\beta}$$

and

$$\sigma^2 = \frac{\alpha\beta}{(\alpha+\beta)^2(\alpha+\beta+1)}$$

This functional form is extremely flexible in the shapes it will accommodate. It is symmetric if $\alpha = \beta$, asymmetric otherwise, and can be hump-shaped or U-shaped. In credit risk analysis, these properties make it ideal for modeling the distribution of losses for a credit, given that default has occurred for that credit (called loss given default, or LGD). Exhibit A.20 shows four examples of the beta distribution.

Upper/Lower Bounds   The lower bound is zero, while the upper can be set to any constant (c), but usually 1.

Parameters   The beta distribution is described by two parameters (α and β). The mean is equal to $\alpha/(\alpha+\beta)$ and the variance is $\alpha\beta/[(\alpha+\beta)^2(\alpha+\beta+1)]$.

Gamma

As mentioned earlier, the gamma distribution derives from the same family as the *exponential* and the *Poisson* distributions. The general form of the Gamma distribution is given by

$$f(x) = \frac{\lambda^P}{\Gamma(P)}e^{-\lambda x}x^{P-1}, \quad x \geq 0 \tag{A.39}$$

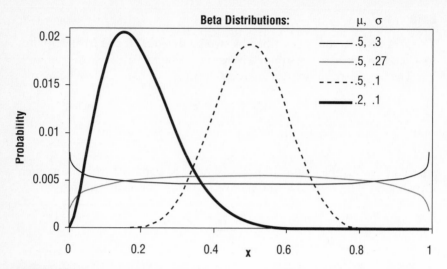

EXHIBIT A.20 Four Examples of the Beta Distribution, Showing the Mean (μ) and Standard Deviation (σ) of Each

where $\Gamma(\,.\,.\,.\,)$ is the gamma *function* (see next section).[9] The mean is P/λ and the variance is P/λ^2. The gamma distribution has been used in a variety of settings, including the study of income distribution and production functions.

Exhibit A.21 shows the gamma distribution as compared to the lognormal one for the same mean (8) and standard deviation (2.71). The two distributions are quite similar, though the gamma distribution has a bit more leptokurtosis.

Upper/Lower Bounds The lower bound is zero and the upper is infinity.

Parameters The gamma distribution has two parameters, P and λ, both determining the mean ($= P/\lambda$) and the variance ($= P/\lambda^2$).

Principal Applications In econometrics, this function has been used in a variety of settings, including the study of income distribution and production functions (W. H. Greene, *Econometric Analysis*, Macmillan Publishing Company, 1980).

Gamma Function The gamma *function* is not a probability distribution but is an important mathematical function used in the gamma and beta distrib-

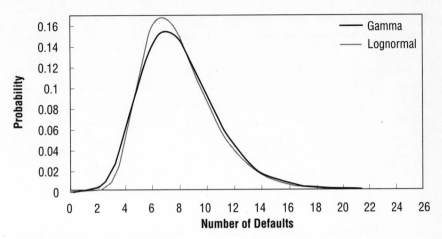

EXHIBIT A.21   Comparison of Gamma Distribution with the Lognormal
Distribution

utions. It comes up in many areas of science and engineering, as well as
economics and finance. The function is generally written as an integral:

$$\Gamma(p) = \int_0^\infty t^{p-1} e^{-t} dt$$

For an integer p,

$$\Gamma(p) = (p-1)!, \quad p = 1, 2, \dots$$

which follows the recursion

$$\Gamma(p) = (p-1)\Gamma(p-1)$$

For p greater than 1, the gamma function may be regarded as a gener-
alization of the *factorial* operation for non-integer values of p. In addition,

$$\Gamma\left(\frac{1}{2}\right) = \sqrt{\pi}$$

For integer values of p,

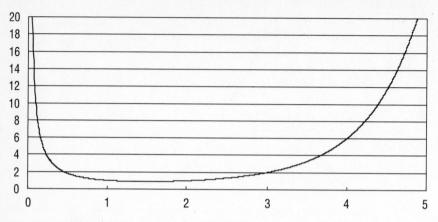

EXHIBIT A.22   Gamma Function Plotted from $x = 0$ to $x = 5$

$$\Gamma\left(p+\frac{1}{2}\right)=\left(p-\frac{1}{2}\right)\Gamma\left(p-\frac{1}{2}\right)$$

For values of p that are not multiples of $^1/_2$, the gamma function must be numerically approximated. Exhibit A.22 shows a plot of the gamma function up to $p = 5$.

NOTES

1. Note that a discrete random variable may take an infinite number of values, but only because the interval considered is infinite, while a continuous variable has an infinite number of values in a finite interval (e.g., 0 to 1) as well.
2. This is written in mathematical shorthand as "[–1, ∞)"—the bracket means inclusive, and the parenthesis means exclusive.
3. Notice that we have $N - 1$, not N, in the denominator of the right-hand side of equation A.5. The reason for this is due to the fact that for a small number of measurements the best estimate for the standard deviation is not clear (or rather it will take more space than is allowed by this book to explain). It makes little difference when N is large (e.g., greater than 20).
4. Refer to pp. 314–324 for details concerning each distribution function.
5. We define the continuously compounded return as $\ln(S_i/S_{i-1})$, where "$\ln(\ldots)$" means "natural logarithm of," and S_i is today's share price.

6. Anyone familiar with stock price modeling or option pricing knows that this statement should be taken with a grain of salt. It is well known that stock returns are not exactly normally distributed and exhibit leptokurtosis over the normal distribution. That is, real data exhibit returns that should occur much less frequently than are predicted by a normal distribution with the same mean and standard deviation.

7. The symbol "∩" denotes "intersection of," and may be remembered as being similar to the letter capital "A," standing for "and."

8. To calculate the mean (i.e., $E[x]$) use equation A.2.b with equation A.34 for $f(x)$ and make the substitutions $x = e^y$ and $dx = e^y dy$. Complete the square in the exponential to simplify the integral. For the variance, use the result for the mean along with equations A.8 and A.34 and make the same substitutions just mentioned for x and dx.

9. If one thinks of x as being time and λ as being an average "arrival" rate (per unit time), then equation A.39 describes the probability distribution in time of the Pth event's arrival. Note that if $P = 1$ one obtains the exponential distribution.

References

CHAPTER 1   The Revolution in Credit—
Capital Is the Key

Federal Reserve System Task Force on Internal Credit Risk Models. "Credit Risk Models at Major U.S./ Banking Institutions: Current State of the Art and Implications for Assessment of Capital Adequacy." Board of Governors of the Federal Reserve System, May 1998.

OCC. "Loan Portfolio Management." *Comptroller's Handbook*, Washington, D.C., April 1998.

Smithson, Charles. "Managing Loans: The State of Play." *Credit*, December/January 2001, pp. 26–31.

Vasicek, Oldrich. "The Loan Loss Distribution." KMV Technical Document, December 1997.

CHAPTER 3   Data Requirements and Sources for
Credit Portfolio Management

Altman, Edward I. "Financial Ratios Discriminant Analysis and the Prediction of Corporate Bankruptcy." *Journal of Finance*, September 1968.

———. "Measuring Corporate Bond Mortality and Performance." *Journal of Finance*, September 1989.

———. "Measuring Corporate Bond Mortality and Performance." *Journal of Finance*, 1998, pp. 909–922.

———. "Predicting Financial Distress of Companies: Revisiting the Z-Score and ZETA® Models." Altman, Edward I. Zeta Services Paper, July 2000.

Altman, Edward I. and Vellore M. Kishore. "Almost Everything You Wanted to Know about Recoveries on Defaulted Bonds." *Financial Analysts Journal*, November/December 1996, pp. 57–64

Araten, Michel and Michael Jacobs Jr. "Loan Equivalents for Revolving Credits and Advised Lines." *RMA Journal*, May 2001.

Asarnow, Elliot and James Marker. "Historical Performance of the U.S. Corporate Loan Market: 1988–1993." *Journal of Commercial Lending*, Spring 1995, pp. 13–32.

Bangia, Anil, Francis Diebold, and Til Schuermann. "Ratings Migration and the Business Cycle, With Applications to Credit Portfolio Stress Testing." *Journal of Banking & Finance*, 2002 (26: 2/3), pp. 235–264.

Bahar, Reza and Krishan Nagpal (1999). "Dynamics of Rating Transition." Standard & Poor's working paper.

Black, Fischer and Myron Scholes. "The Pricing of Options and Corporate Liabilities." *Journal of Political Economy*, 1973.

Falkenstein, Eric, Andrew Boral, and Lea V. Carty. "RiskCalc™ for Private Companies: Moody's Default Model." Moody's Investors Service, Global Credit Research, May 2000.

Fung, Glenn and O. L. Mangasarian. "Proximal Support Vector Machine Classifiers." Data Mining Institute Technical Report 01-02, February 2001. KDD 2001, San Francisco, August 26–29, 2001.

Jarrow, R.A. and S.M. Turnbull. "Pricing Derivatives on Financial Securities Subject to Credit Risk." *Journal of Finance*, 50(1), 1995.

KMV Corporation. "Private Firm Model®: Introduction to the Modeling Methodology." October 2001.

Longstaff, Francis and Eduardo Schwartz. "A Simple Approach to Valuing Risky Fixed and Floating Rate Debt." *Journal of Finance*, July 1995.

Merton, Robert. "On the Pricing of Corporate Debt." *Journal of Finance*, 1974.

Nickell, Pamela, William Perraudin, and Simone Varotto (2000). "Stability of Rating Transitions." *Journal of Banking & Finance*, 24, 203–227.

Sobehart, Jorge R. and Roger M. Stein. "Moody's Public Firm Risk Model: A Hybrid Approach to Modeling Short Term Default Risk." Moody's Investors Service, Global Credit Research, March 2000.

VandeCastle, Karen. "Suddenly Structure Mattered: Insights into Recoveries of Defaulted Debt." *RatingsDirect*, May 24, 2000.

CHAPTER 4   Credit Portfolio Models

Altman, Edward I. and Vellore M. Kishore. "Almost Everything You Wanted to Know about Recoveries on Defaulted Bonds." *Financial Analysts Journal*, November/December 1996, pp. 57–64.

Basle Committee on Banking Supervision. Credit Risk Modeling: Current Practices and Applications. April 1999 (available through www.bis.org).

Carty, Lea V. and Dana Lieberman. "Corporate Bond Defaults and Default Rates 1938–1995." Moody's Investors Service, Global Credit Research, January 1996.

Carty, Lea V. and Dana Lieberman. "Defaulted Bank Loan Recoveries." Moody's Investors Service, Global Credit Research, Special Report, November 1996.

Frye, John. "Depressing Recoveries." *Risk*, November 2000.

Gordy, Michael. "A Comparative Anatomy of Credit Risk Models." *Journal of Banking & Finance*, 24 (2000), pp. 119–149.

Institute of International Finance (IIF) and International Swaps and Derivatives Association (ISDA). "Modeling Credit Risk: Joint IIF/ISDA Testing Program. February 2000.

Koyluoglu, H. Ugar and Andrew Hickman. "A Generalized Framework for Credit Risk Portfolio Models." New York: Oliver, Wyman and Co., September 14, 1998.

KMV Corporation. "Technical Note: Valuation and Spreads." November 1998.

KMV Corporation. "Technical Note: The Portfolio Loss Distribution." November 1998.

KMV Corporation. "Global Correlation Factor Structure." December 1999.

Lopez, Jose A. and Marc R. Saidenberg. "Evaluating Credit Risk Models." Paper presented at the Bank of England Conference on Credit Risk Modeling and Regulatory Implications, September 21–22, 1998.

Merton, Robert. "On the Pricing of Corporate Debt." *Journal of Finance*, 29 (1974).

Morgan, JP. *CreditMetrics*. New York: Technical document, April 2, 1997.

Saunders, Anthony. *Credit Risk Measurement*. New York: Wiley, 1999.

Xiao, Jerry Yi. "Importance Sampling for Credit Portfolio Simulation." *RiskMetrics Journal*, 2(2), Winter 2001–2002.

CHAPTER 5 Loan Sales and Trading

Barnish, Keith, Steve Miller, and Michael Rushmore. "The New Leveraged Loan Syndication Market." *Journal of Applied Corporate Finance*, Spring 1997, p. 79.

Cilia, Joseph. "Syndicated Loans." *Capital Market News*, Federal Reserve Bank of Chicago, March 2000, pp. 7–8.

Smith, Roy and Ingo Walter. Chapter on "International Commercial Lending." *Global Banking*, Oxford University Press, 1997, pp. 22–41.

White, James and Kathleen Lenarcic. "A New Institutional Fixed Income Security: Are Bank Loans for You?" *Journal of Fixed Income*, September 1999, p. 81.

CHAPTER 6   Credit Derivatives

General

British Bankers Association. *1997/1998 Credit Derivatives Survey*, July 1998.

JP Morgan. *Guide to Credit Derivatives*, 1999.

Prebon Yamane and Derivatives Week Survey, September 1998.

Derivatives Strategy. "What's a Default," January 2001.

Smithson, Charles and Gregory Hayt. "Credit Derivatives: The Basics." *RMA Journal*, February 2000.

Smithson, Charles and Gregory Hayt. "How the Market Values Credit Derivatives." *RMA Journal*, March 2000.

Smithson, Charles and Gregory Hayt. "Credit Derivatives: Implications for Bank Portfolio Management." *RMA Journal*, April 2000.

Smithson, Charles and Hal Holappa. "Credit Derivatives: What Are These Youthful Instruments and Why Are They Used?" *Risk*, December 1995.

Smithson, Charles, Hal Holappa, and Shaun Rai. "Credit Derivatives: A Look at the Market, Its Evolution and Current Size." *Risk*, June 1996.

Pricing

Black, Fischer and Myron Scholes. "The Pricing of Options and Corporate Liabilities." *Journal of Political Economy*, 81 (1973), pp. 637–659.

Merton, Robert C. "Theory of Rational Option Pricing." *Bell Journal of Economics and Management Science*, Spring 1973.

Structural Models

Merton, Robert C. "On the Pricing of Corporate Debt." *Journal of Finance*, 29 (1974), pp. 6–22.

Longstaff, Francis and Eduardo Schwartz. "A Simple Approach to Valuing Risky Fixed and Floating Rate Debt." *Journal of Finance*, March 1995.

Reduced Form Models

Das, Sanjiv and Peter Tufano. "Pricing Credit-Sensitive Debt When Interest Rates, Credit Ratings and Credit Spreads Are Stochastic." *Journal of Financial Engineering*, June 1996.

Duffie, Donald and Kenneth Singleton. "Econometric Modeling of Term Structures of Defaultable Bonds." Working Paper, Graduate School of Business, Stanford University, 1994.

Jarrow, Robert A. and Stuart M. Turnbull. "Pricing Derivatives on Financial Securities Subject to Credit Risk." *Journal of Finance*, 50(1), March (1995).

Madan, D.B. and H. Unal. "Pricing the Risks of Default." (1996).

CHAPTER 7   Securitization

Batchvarov, Alexander, Ganesh Rajendra, and Brian McManus (Merrill Lynch). "Synthetic Structures Drive Innovation." *Risk*, June 2000.

Culp, Christopher L. and Andrea M.P. Neves. "Financial Innovations in Leveraged Commercial Loan Markets." *Journal of Applied Corporate Finance*, Summer 1998.

Merritt, Roger, Michael Gerity, Alyssa Irving, and Mitchell Lench. "Synthetic CDOs: A Growing Market for Credit Derivatives." Fitch IBCA, Duff & Phelps Special Report, February 6, 2001.

Ratner, Brian (Asset Backed Finance, UBS Warburg). "Successfully Structuring and Applying Balance Sheet CDOs." Credit Risk Summit 2000.

Toft, Klaus (Goldman Sachs & Co.). "Ratings and Risk Modeling of Synthetic CBOs and CLOS." Credit Risk Summit 2000.

CHAPTER 8   Capital Attribution and Allocation

Baud, Nicolas et al. "An Analysis Framework for Bank Capital Allocation." Credit Lyonnais, February 2000.

James, C. "RAROC Based Capital Budgeting and Performance Evaluation: A Case Study of Bank Capital Allocation." Unpublished Working Paper, University of Florida, 1996.

Matten, Chris. *Managing Bank Capital*, 2d ed. New York: Wiley, 2000.

Merton, Robert and Andre Perold. "Management of Risk Capital in Financial Firms." In *Financial Services: Perspectives and Challenges*, S.L. Hayes ed., Harvard Business School Press, 1993, pp. 215–245.

Nishiguchi, Kenji, Hiroshi Kawai, and Takanori Szaki. "Capital Allocation and Bank Management Based on the Quantification of Credit Risk." FRBNY Economic Policy Review, October 1998.

Schroeck, Gerhard. *Risk Management and Value Creation in Financial Institutions*. New York: Wiley, 2002.

Zaik, Edward, John Walter, and Gabriela Kelling, with Chris James. "RAROC at Bank of America." *Journal of Applied Corporate Finance*, 9(2), Summer 1996.

Appendix to Chapter 8

Basle Committee on Banking Supervision, 1999. Consultative Paper: "A New Capital Adequacy Framework." Basle: Bank for International Settlements, June.

Ceske, Robert and José V. Hernández, 1999. "Measuring Operational Risk—Where Theory Meets Practice." NetRisk, October. An abridged version of this paper appeared in *Operational Risk*, a Risk Special Report, November 1999.

O'Brien, Niall, 1999. "The Case for Quantification." *Operational Risk*, a Risk Special Report, July.

Shih, Jimmy, Ali Samad-Khan, and Pat Medapa, 2000. "Is the Size of an Operational Loss Related to Firm Size?" *Operational Risk*, January.

Index

Acquisitions, 185
Active management, 39, 225
Actuarial models, 109, 141, 150
Agent bank, 184
Altman, Ed, 47, 49, 51, 95, 122
Amortization, 171–172, 238
Analysis of variance (ANOVA), 50
Araten, Michel, 99
Arbitrage CDOs, 234–236
Arbitrage-free securities, 212–213
Asarnow, Elliot, 98–100
Asian financial crisis, 198
Asset classes, 202
Asset correlation, measurement of, 113–114
Asset value, 69–70
Asset volatility models, 110
Auditor, collateralized trust obligations, 228–229
Auto loans, 225
Autoregressive integrated moving average (ARIMA) model, 136–137
Autoregressive moving average (ARMA) model, 137

Balance sheet CDOs, 233–234
Bank for International Settlements (BIS), 14
Banking Book, 16
Banking industry, *see* Banks
  portfolio approach, 3–5
  returns and, 2–3
  risks, 1–2
Bank of America, 191, 198, 236
Bankruptcy, 53, 63, 92, 189, 197, 238
Banks:
  balance sheet CDOs, 234
  commercial, 10, 191
  credit derivatives and, 203
  European, 34
  foreign, 189
  investment, 191
  securitization regulation, 238–240
  as syndicators, 189–191
Basis risk, 205
Basket credit default swaps, 200–201
Basle Committee on Banking Supervision:
  Basle Accord (1998), 239
  Consultative Document (2001), 238, 270

functions of, generally, 12–14, 16–19
  operational risk quantification, 270–271
  securitization, 237–239
Basle I, 205, 234
$BENCH_1$, 88–89, 214
Best-efforts syndication, 184
Beta:
  coefficient, 170
  distribution, 152, 295–296, 321
  implications of, 266
Binomial distribution, 288–290, 316–318
Bistro, 232
Black-Scholes-Merton option pricing, 209
Black-Scholes option pricing, 79–80, 250
Boeing, 112–113
Bond investments, 199–200, 202
Bond recovery, 95–97
Bond Score (CreditSights), 83–84
Bootstrapping, 217
Bottom-up measurement, 245–247, 271, 274
Bristol-Myers Squibb, 30–31
Buyer, credit default swap, 196–197

Call Reports, 203
Capital, *see specific types of capital*
  allocation, *see* Capital allocation
  attribution, *see* Capital attribution
  economic, 8–11
  importance of, 6
  measures of, 6–8
  regulatory, 11–21
Capital Accord (1988):
  components of, 12–13
  Consultative Document (1999), 16–17
  Consultative Document (2001), 17, 20
  credit derivatives, 15–16
  defined, 12
  flaws in, 13
  Market Risk Amendment (1996), 13–14
  proposed new Accord (2001), 17–21
Capital allocation:
  economic profit, 265
  efficient frontier, 258–260
  equity portfolio management, performance measures, 260–262
  optimization strategies, 267–269